THE GEOGRAPHY
OF FREEDOM

THE ODYSSEY OF ELISÉE RECLUS

the Geography of Freedom

MARIE FLEMING

Introduction by George Woodcock

BLACK
ROSE
BOOKS

Montréal - New York

Black Rose Books No. Q 122

Canadian Cataloguing in Publication Data

Fleming, Marie
 The geography of freedom
Includes index.
Bibliography: p
ISBN 0-921689-17-9 (bound)—ISBN 0-921689-16-0 (pbk.).

1. Reclus, Elisée, 1830-1905.
2. Anarchists—France—Biography.
I. Title.

HX894.R43F58 1988   335.8′3′0924   C88-090103-9

Cover design: Richard Parent; cover photograph of Elisée Reclus by Félix Nadar

The photographs are copies from Joseph Ishill, ed., *Elisée and Elie Reclus: In Memoriam*
(Berkeley Heights, NJ: Oriole Press, 1927). The book is in the Labadie Collection
of the Dept. of Rare Books and Special Collections, University of Michigan Library,
Ann Arbor.

1006462754
3981 boul. St-Laurent   **Black Rose Books**
Montréal, Qué. H2W 1Y5   340 Nagel Dr.
Canada   Cheektowaga, NY 14225
                                                          USA

Printed and bound in Québec, Canada

Table of Contents

Acknowledgements   9

Elisée Reclus: An Introduction
by George Woodcock   11

Introduction
On Re-reading Radical History   19

One
Rejecting the Father   27

Two
Beyond Earthly Paradise   39

Three
Affirming Differences   54

Four
Republican Battles   71

Five
Communard's Wrath   86

Six
Anarchy and Theory   95

Seven
Science and Rebellion   112

Eight
Education, Violence, Solidarity   126

Nine
Property and Theft   142

Ten
Party of Rebels   156

Eleven
Changing Times   170

Twelve
The Battle for Truth   180

Endnotes   199

Bibliography   227

Index   241

Acknowledgements

I express my thanks to Robert Gellately who read through the entire manuscript of this book and whose many contributions remain unacknowledged, to Black Rose editor Jane Broderick who made numerous suggestions for improving the text, and to Vincent Wright who first put me on the trail of Elisée Reclus when I was a student at the London School of Economics and Political Science.

Elisée Reclus:An Introduction
by George Woodcock

We have long needed a biography of Elisée Reclus in English, if only to dispel the lunar myth of him that has long been fostered, even among anarchist writers. He has been seen all too often as a satellite figure, as a kind of intellectual moon who floated first in Bakunin's orbit and then was drawn into that of Kropotkin.

In fact, as Marie Fleming's biography abundantly shows, Reclus was a man of remarkable independence of nature and mind, and though he shared the basic standpoints of both the great Russians, he played as great a part as either of them in developing the main ideas that were current among anarchists in that period—anarchist communism, and propaganda by the deed—while he also helped enlarge the ideas of centralism and federalism that Proudhon had adumbrated in an earlier generation.

What distinguishes Reclus most strongly from the better-known anarchists of his time is the fact that he never became a full-time militant, and just as assiduously he avoided becoming a figurehead of anarchism in the manner that Proudhon, Bakunin, and Kropotkin

11

had successively been. He kept a low personal profile, a comrade among comrades, and he clearly felt it important for an anarchist to allow his convictions and his actions to grow from his role in society. In that he was rather like the peripatetic electrician Malatesta, except that his chosen calling, the trade at which he was best, was that of geographer.

Here there is a striking comparison to be made between Reclus and Kropotkin, also a geographer of considerable insight, expertise, and repute. Reared in Russia and steeped in the populist mystique of the "going to the people" movement, Kropotkin found himself morally bound to devote his time and energy to the cause of the masses, to the detriment of his scientific interests, which he felt it would be a selfish indulgence to pursue. So he set out on a course that was bound to destroy his geographical career, and though in later years he made use of his training to write important books, like *Mutual Aid*, which gave a scientific support to anarchist arguments, he never again returned professionally to geography, even though he was treated with great respect by English geographers for his brilliant work, many years ago, on the geography of East Asia.

Reclus had no such scruples, and geography, irradiated by his anarchist beliefs, remained at the centre of his life to the end, resulting, among many other works, in his monumental *Nouvelle Géographie universelle*, which appeared in nineteen volumes over the years between 1856 and 1894. He may have been fortunate in having been brought up in a strict Calvinist household, for his family were among the Protestant minority in France; it seems to have served as a kind of inoculation against the kind of revolutionary puritanism that often seemed to afflict Kropotkin, and also to an extent Proudhon and Bakunin, at crucial points in their lives. One has the impression of Reclus as a freer man in his personal ways, responding to situations according to his immediate feelings and reluctant to lock himself into narrow theoretical positions.

Though Reclus talked of anarchism when he was still in his twenties, having almost certainly picked up the word and the idea from reading Proudhon, and though he was somewhat intermittently associated with Bakunin's clandestine brotherhoods in the 1860s, it was not until after the Paris Commune that his sense of being nothing more than an anarchist really began to emerge. He had adopted a pragmatic attitude towards political action and parliamentary representation, and during the Franco-Prussian war he became a devoted republican and a temporary militarist, advocating a war *à l'outrance*. He was captured by the Versailles forces in the very early days of the Commune, when the National Guard made an incompetently organised rally out of Paris. He spent a period in prison, and then was banished and spent some years in Swiss exile.

This experience, as much as anything else, turned him into a revolutionary, but, like many of the people who later thought of themselves as anarchists—including Kropotkin, he considered himself at this time a socialist, even though he disagreed with the authoritarian tactics of Marx and his followers and aligned himself on the anti-political wing with Bakunin and with the libertarian faction that in 1872 set up the St-Imier International. Proudhon had called himself an anarchist in 1840, but it was not until the late 1870s that the French, Spanish, Italian, and Swiss internationalists who had remained close to Bakunin eventually adopted the name for themselves.

Even then they endeavoured—Reclus among them—to sustain their links with the general socialist movement that had grown up in the early days of the First International. It was only at the London Congress of the Second International in 1896 that the divisions between anarchism and socialism were made definite, and then the break was made by the Marxists who voted to exclude the anarchist minority among the delegates. The division has remained to this day; no modern anarchist would ever think of himself as a socialist. And from the final break with the organisation-minded socialists arose the simplification of organisation among the anarchists, and the breaking up of the old structures of the International into small, loosely linked affinity groups, a trend broken only in certain areas by the emergence of revolutionary syndicalism, with its mass groupings of the workers for militant action. Significantly, Reclus has very little to say about syndicalism and one can imagine—though Fleming leaves this question virtually unexplored—that while he clearly welcomed the loose freedom of the affinity groups as fitting his own inclinations and temperament, he must have been as distrustful as Malatesta showed himself to be at the 1907 Amsterdam anarchist congress of the authoritarian potentialities of a syndicate-dominated society.

One of the reasons why Reclus flourished so happily in a movement that had become radically decentralised into small groups depending on personal affinities was the power he had of empathising with individuals. The gentleness of manner, the lack of pride or pretension, that he combined with an almost ferocious integrity exemplified the emphasis on "love and brotherhood" that was the most positive and important legacy of his Christian upbringing. It allowed him to mingle without affectation among workers whose manners and whose education were very different from his own, and to understand the feeling they expressed in their special ways. Marie Fleming describes his "eager" attendance—even before he was a committed anarchist—at meetings

13

of workers after the French imperial government in 1868 had passed a law allowing freedom of meeting.

> In "coarse words pronounced by men without education, incorrect language, foolish remarks, passionate cries," he found the confirmation of his youthful belief in the elemental power of the masses. "Pressed one against the other, breathing an atmosphere of sweat and dust, they are there for hours in the hope of hearing a word of justice or liberty, small compensation for the miseries of each day."

Reclus's powers of empathy with the unfortunate led him into what the observer often perceives as contradictions between the gentleness of his nature and the violence of the deeds which he would justify, even if he himself did not think of committing them. He was one of the earliest defenders of the concept of propaganda by the deed, declaring: "The deed grows out of the idea, and the idea out of the deed." During the 1890s, some anarchists practised terrorist acts that brought the movement a good deal of equivocal publicity and police attention, and many of their comrades dissociated themselves from this kind of violence. Others, like Kropotkin, hedged uncomfortably, refusing to condemn the terrorists but declining to support them. Reclus, however, always sought the motive of desperation or idealism or moral indignation that lay behind the act, and tended to praise the intent without always examining the result very thoroughly. In a similar way, although he was in his personal life a man of almost conventional honesty, who would never think of appropriating for himself anything he had not worked for, he defended the thief who set out to adjust by direct action the system by which the rich legally robbed the poor.

In the cases of assassins and thieves alike one can detect a double strain in Reclus's attitude. As Marie Fleming remarks, over the years he had come to lament the "circuitous" route by which the achievement of social justice was conventionally obtained, and so "he would appreciate the boldness and directness of the individual recovery of property 'stolen' from the people." But there was also at work a kind of inspiring individualism that in Reclus balanced and modified his awareness—as an anarchist-communist—of the community's importance. As Fleming reminds us, he believed that "every person possessed the right to interpret the dictates of the voice within and to act accordingly." Which, once again, is not far from the views of certain kinds of radical Christian dissenters like the Quakers and the Doukhobors.

If the Christianity Reclus absorbed as a child and as a theological student was subsumed in certain ways into his developing anarchist beliefs, the link between those beliefs and his geographical vocation was there from the beginning. Geography was his chosen science and, as Fleming remarks, "for Reclus, anarchism was not merely belief; it was the truth as revealed through science." Science and faith, in fact, became significantly intermingled in his thought, and towards the end of this book and of his life we find him by implication admitting the religious strain in anarchism which Herbert Read and others detected, when he says:

> We profess a new faith, and as soon as this faith, which is also a science, becomes the faith of all those who seek the truth, it will take its place in the world of reality, for the first law of history is that society models itself after its ideals.

Geography and anarchism became the poles between which the faith of Elisée Reclus was suspended, and it is significant that he should have been a pioneer of "human geography" and that his greatest work should have been subtitled *La Terre et les Hommes*. Just as, like Kropotkin, he saw revolution as a variation in the rhythm of evolution, a kind of mutation in social relations, so in his studies of the earth and the species that populate it he saw a kind of paradigm of the anarchist vision. And in doing so he anticipated—as Kropotkin and Aldous Huxley did in their various ways—the ecological awareness that inspires so much contemporary anarchist thinking. Modern environmental concerns are eloquently anticipated in his remark that:

> A secret harmony exists between the earth and the people whom it nourishes, and when imprudent societies let themselves violate this harmony, they always end up regretting it.

And no contemporary ecologist could find fault with his declaration that:

> The truly civilised man understands that his interest is bound up with the interest of all and with that of nature. He repairs the damage caused by his predecessors and works to improve his domain.

Reclus did not see a simple equation between man and nature. He was a long-time vegetarian, and this stance came not merely from an aesthetic horror at the eating of meat, but from a respect for animals as deeply founded as his respect for human beings. Talking of domestic animals, and especially of cats, whom he seems to have seen as natural anarchists, he remarked: "There is not a human sentiment which on occasion they do not understand or share, not an idea which they may not devine, not a desire but what they forestall it." Fleming remarks that these are "touching

15

sentiments," and seems to imply that they may be a little far-fetched, but adds that they are also "an argument for increased sensitivity to animals and to nature." This was precisely the conclusion Reclus himself drew and expressed in other words.

> The study of primitive man has contributed to our understanding of the "law and order" man of our own day. Animal behaviour will help us penetrate deeper into the science of life, to increase both our knowledge of the world and our capacity to love.

Reclus was not alone among the anarchists of his own day. In another way, Kropotkin's *Mutual Aid*, by showing cooperation as developing before the evolution of humanity, posed a continuity between animal and human societies, and therefore a basic identity between them. Many late-nineteenth-century anarchists became vegetarians and protested against cruelty to animals and their treatment as subordinate beings. But few had such a complete sense of the unity of the whole natural world as Reclus, or of the interdependence between man and the other species in terms of their eventual welfare. He would have been entirely at home among the anarchist-ecologists of today, and it is especially appropriate that his life and his ideas should be brought to light again almost a century after he lived and that they should strike one with their remarkable timeliness.

From an Autographed Photograph to PROF. PAUL GHIO

ELISÉE RECLUS

ELISÉE RECLUS

Photograph by PAUL RECLUS

Introduction
On Re-reading Radical History

Elisée Reclus was a prominent geographer and anarchist in late-nineteenth-century Europe. Even before his death in 1905, however, there were signs that the once influential Reclus was becoming a marginal figure in radical history. A biography by the anarchist Max Nettlau, which appeared in German in 1928,[1] was not enough, on its own, to avert the slide into obscurity. It was somewhat of a surprise, therefore, when, in 1978, the geographer Gary Dunbar published a book, *Elisée Reclus: Historian of Nature*.[2] A year later, in 1979, my study of Reclus appeared as *The Anarchist Way to Socialism* (the earlier edition of the present book).[3]

It is strange that, after so many years, two studies of a forgotten nineteenth-century geographer and anarchist should appear within the space of a few months. I do not want to dismiss this as simply coincidence. I think that we should see it as possible that the reasons for the neglect of Reclus and the reasons for the sudden interest in his life and work might be connected. This problem is too complex to explore here, but it might be possible to suggest some questions that need to be raised.

For example, what are we to make of the fact that one of these studies approached Reclus as a geographer and the other tried to deal with his anarchism? We know that Reclus saw his geography and anarchism as closely related, even inseparable. He is reported to have said to the Dutch socialist Ferdinand Domela Nieuwenhuis: "Yes, I am a geographer, but above all I am an anarchist."[4] Why is it that, as we moved into the fourth quarter of the twentieth century, the "geographer" Dunbar and the "political theorist" Fleming took an interest in a forgotten nineteenth-century geographer-anarchist? This interest may be an expression of wider social-political changes. In the context of the academy, this interest may indicate a weakening of the disciplinary boundaries that for a time seemed so permanent.

This point seems easier to make in 1988 in the wake of the debates following the reception of Michel Foucault's work on the disciplinary society. However, as a student, in the early 1970s, working her way through piles of library and archival materials in Paris, and totally unaware of Foucault and his work, I did not have the faintest idea of my complicity in challenges to the hegemony of the disciplines.

Some readers, accustomed as we are to narrow specialisations, might feel uncomfortable with such generalisations. Let us examine the question of Reclus's neglect in terms of anarchism, more narrowly defined. A commonsense explanation points to the neglect of all European anarchists following the victory of Marxism. Without denying that there is something to this, we would have to provide some explanation for the attention paid to other individuals traditionally identified as anarchists. What student of European history has not heard of Proudhon, Bakunin, or Kropotkin?

Nor has Reclus's commitment to anarchism been open to question. Certainly, among his contemporaries he was thought to be virtuous to a fault. Kropotkin was not alone when he stated that the man was an anarchist "to the deepest recesses of his mind, to the smallest fibre of his being."[5] "For me," wrote Nettlau, "he represented a true realisation of anarchy."[6] "Elisée Reclus," said Johann Most, "I count as one of the greatest inspirers since I became an anarchist."[7]

I would suggest that the neglect of Reclus was somehow connected to his failure to win a place among the "official" anarchist representatives determined late in the nineteenth century. I also think that this "absence" from the list of major figures, by way of a strange kind of logic, transformed Reclus into an enigmatic figure. As the "ideal" anarchist, despite his obscurity, he had to be recognised, and, since it became standard practice in the history of European anarchism to make references to his life and importance, he became assured of a "presence" in the pantheon.

In an effort to know more about the shadowy figure that Elisée Reclus had become, I followed the traces he had left in archives and libraries throughout Western Europe. Tracking him down was an adventure, and I turned up what was for me one surprise after another. The picture that emerged contrasted dramatically with conventional wisdom.

Reclus called himself an anarchist at the age of twenty-one (in 1851), and there is no evidence that he ever retreated from this self-description. However, there is little doubt that, for the next twenty years, he was prepared for some accommodation to the existing order and in time might have supported the parliamentary institutions of the day. It is not difficult to show that he was beginning to see that the "battle for democracy" might be won through outwitting the liberals in their own arena. These options were abruptly and emphatically rejected with his emotional-intellectual revulsion following the savage repression of the Paris Commune in 1871. His bitterness toward the capitalist state and his rejection of all party-political activity developed thereafter.

When I began my research, I had expected to find some socialistic tendencies in Reclus, but I was unprepared for the depth of the anarchists' commitment to an alternative vision of socialism. At several crucial points, anarchism and socialism were thought of as virtually identical in all important respects. In 1873 Peter Kropotkin insisted that socialists of "the most varied shades" shared a "rather complete agreement in their ideals."[8] Reclus commented on the close relationship among all socialists in 1882, years after the anarchists had become a distinct group within the socialist movement.[9] Many anarchists sought public recognition of this position by attempting to infiltrate the Second International from its founding in 1889 until the London Congress of 1896.

It is frequently suggested that European anarchists were convinced of the possibility of an apocalyptic transformation of society, that they put their faith in an imminent revolution that would establish a veritable heaven on earth. But Reclus (as well as Kropotkin) came to believe in precisely the opposite. As the century progressed, he became remarkably insistent on the necessity of a gradual or evolutionary process as the key to movement in the direction of revolution. The struggle for socialism, he maintained, involved attacking the prejudices, fears, and illusions that were the psychological supports of the existing social-economic order. Only insofar as the hold of these supports could be loosened would revolution succeed.

The results of my research also led me to conclude that any explanation of the historic split between anarchists and socialists would have to go well beyond a discussion of the quarrel between

Bakunin and Marx, however much traditional interpretations insisted on its importance. I have been criticised for not paying enough attention to this famous dispute, but this is one point on which I have not modified my opinion. On the contrary, in the years since I began my study of Reclus, historians have in general become even more wary of explaining the past in terms of powerful personalities.

In the context of radical history, there were further consequences of attributing too much importance to the dispute between Bakunin and Marx. In particular, such interpretations have tended to conceal the shift resulting from the "scientific" direction introduced into anarchist theory by Reclus and Kropotkin. This point was striking to me from the outset, and I stressed it in the earlier edition of this book. Over the years, however, I have been able to grasp dimensions of this "scientising" of anarchism that were not clear to me at that time.

It never occurred to Reclus, no less than it did to Marx—nor, for that matter, to their "progressive" contemporaries—to question the authority of science. Thus, on the one hand, Reclus the anarchist was more scrupulous than Marx in renouncing any route to socialism which might prove supportive of the capitalist state; on the other hand, however, he joined Marx in acknowledging the "bourgeois" claim that science was the impartial arbiter of right and wrong. The question of Reclus's religious origins takes on added significance once we see him readily professing a "new faith... which is also a science."[10]

The linking of religion and socialism, which seems especially obvious in Reclus's case, is an old insight, and it has recently been shown to have been much more complex than formerly believed. In the context of the present study, we can now raise the question of what it meant that socialists like Reclus and Marx espoused the faith in science proclaimed by the very order they set out to destroy. From this perspective, one can share something of the disbelief felt by Bakunin when Reclus suggested that, rather than brood over the loss of revolutionary instinct in the masses, he should be comforted by the "great scientific movement of the epoch."[11]

In his generous appraisal of my earlier study of Reclus, Frank Harrison was right to point out that it is my view that an emphasis on Bakunin has directed us away from discussing the importance of the "scientific" direction introduced into anarchism by Reclus and Kropotkin in the fourth quarter of the nineteenth century. I would want to add that Marxist rhetoric also contributed to the relegation of anarchists, as a group, to the realm of the non-scientific or utopian. However, Harrison seems to see it as unproblematic that the anarchists flocked to express their allegiance to science, and he seems to be pleading for the admission of Bakunin as well to this circle when he writes: "My argument here... is that scientists like Reclus and Kropotkin gave body to the argument elaborated by Bakunin."[12] My point several years ago was that the scientific move was a significant shift in European anarchism and that we should examine the consequences and implications. Today I would advise caution in assessing the steps taken by Reclus and Kropotkin as an "advance" and in assimilating Bakunin to perspectives which he rejected.

In an attempt to distinguish his position on anarchism from mine, Harrison writes: "There is consistency [among the anarchists] rather than contrast, continuity rather than conflict."[13] I can only respond that I did not set out to find conflicts, but then again I was not overly concerned with continuities. In the course of my research, I became aware that, unlike most of the accounts of anarchism with which I was familiar, my own work was resisting the emphasis on continuities and common denominators, and seeking a much more differentiated analysis.

In drawing these conclusions I understand now that I was abandoning the assumption that Reclus was contributing to the hammering out of an anarchist way of viewing the world whose truth could be affirmed in less successful efforts, perhaps from as long ago as the time of the ancient Greeks. I also sensed problems with seeing the modern representatives as some variation on the "Seven Sages of Anarchism"[14]—William Godwin, Pierre-Joseph Proudhon, Max Stirner, Michael Bakunin, Peter Kropotkin, Benjamin Tucker, and Leo Tolstoy.[15] I saw Godwin's statements as containing little more than verbal resemblances to those of the late-nineteenth-century anarchists. The individualism of Tucker, no less than that of Stirner, seemed to me to be a far cry from Reclus's anarchist communism, and I knew that Reclus himself found Tolstoy's pacifism utterly unacceptable.

I then tried to sort out how it had come about that these theorists had all been grouped together as representing some sort of truth about anarchism. It seems that the anarchism of late-nineteenth-century Europe, which was initially perceived by contemporaries as a new phenomenon, almost immediately was regarded as the embodiment of a peculiar way of looking at the world, rather than as a movement that had developed in response to specific social-economic grievances in given historical circumstances. The search which had begun for precursors and continuities was an effort to link the "new" with something familiar from the past.

This approach was adopted by defenders of the existing order—who were anxious to assure themselves that there was no real threat. One study claimed that "these [anarchist] doctrines are not new; they have existed for all time, and not only does one find the same ideas, but even the same ideas expressed in the same terms." The author was comforted by the "banality" of the theories, which in themselves, he believed, were perfectly harmless and even "natural" intellectual diversions for philosophers. [16] It is more disturbing that the search for precursors was also practised by supporters of the anarchist movement—who were keen to demonstrate that they were custodians of a truth that had been germinating for centuries, if not from time immemorial.

Paul Eltzbacher's "scientific" attempt, in 1900, to grasp the "essence" of anarchist thought "proved" the assumption unwittingly built into his analysis that "negation of the State" was the only common element in anarchist thought. [17] His status as a German judge, and quintessential representative of the status quo, nowhere seems to have led to a questioning of his "impartial" treatment—even by Kropotkin who recommended it to the readers of the *Encyclopaedia Britannica* as "the best work on Anarchism." But it was a mystery to Eltzbacher what to do with the discovery, made through his own careful analysis, that the anarchist negation of the state had "totally different meanings" in the various exponents of anarchism. I came to suspect that there was something wrong with gathering such diverse meanings into the unity of a putative anarchist tradition. My suspicion had nothing to do with a denigration of the contributions of Proudhon or Bakunin, though in my eagerness to distinguish their various positions from that of Reclus I may have given this impression. I hope that in this revised edition I have been more careful.

Like all students of nineteenth-century anarchism I have had the good fortune to follow in the steps of George Woodcock. In his introduction to this present book he has kindly declined to comment on our differences, but I sense an uneasiness on his part that anarchism will lose its identity if it is too closely associated with socialism and if we do not emphasise the place of the state in anarchist theories. I can only say that this identity is an abstraction that has to be examined. As a construct of the late nineteenth century, it may conceal interests which still "legislate" for us how we are to view the past.

In an exchange of views which we had after the publication of the earlier edition of this book, Woodcock claimed that my "rereading" of radical history—which he then insisted was a "misreading"—"detaches late 19th-century anarchism from its true roots." [18] I had not set out to do so, and when it was first pointed out I was uncertain as to how I should understand what I had done. I see now, some years later, that this notion of "true roots" is also an authority that we should question.

Woodcock is right to suggest how timely many of Reclus's views appear almost a century after his death and to point to similarities between Reclus's concerns about the environment and questions being raised by contemporary ecologists. A reader of this book will get a sense, I believe, of other ways in which Reclus would

24

not be out of place in the late twentieth century. There is, however, a large sense in which he would be a curiosity. I refer here to the notion of "brotherhood" which was such a powerful image in the construction of his theories and in his personal relations. It is obvious that the inspiration is Christian, and yet more could be said. For the present I shall content myself to tracing the notion of brotherhood to Reclus's Christian background and to charting its appearances throughout his writings.

I have not tried to find a neutral or de-gendered term as a substitute for "brotherhood." For obvious reasons, this would not have worked. And I did not want to work around the term by paraphrasing, another device often employed in an effort to avoid the sexism embodied in language. The Elisée Reclus that I have tracked down would be unrecognisable if we were to disallow the term "brotherhood."

I like Reclus's comments on cats! I disagree only with his characterising them as "moral." I see cats as happily beyond morality.

Elisée Reclus

Drawing by MAURICE DUVALET

One

Rejecting the Father

Jean-Jacques Elisée Reclus was born 15 March 1830 at Sainte-Foy-la-Grande, a small village in the department of the Gironde in southwest France.[1] Jacques Reclus, his father, was pastor in neighbouring Montcaret and teacher at the Protestant college of Sainte-Foy. At the age of eighteen, Elisée was bent on following in his father's footsteps and took up the study of theology. Three years later, however, he declared himself an anarchist, and soon after gave up all connection with organised religion.

In spite of this break with Christianity, what the young man rejected, in a sense, was the hypocrisy and other-worldliness of religion; he very much retained a faith in some sort of progress and a determination to put into practice the central messages of Christianity. The notion of universal brotherhood kindled in his father's house was a guiding light of Elisée's anarchism. Even in his pioneering geographical studies, in which he was a professional of international renown, there is the theme of the earth as "the 'beneficent mother' waiting for her sons to embrace as brothers."[2]

As the reference to the earth mother suggests, the brotherhood of which Elisée dreamed had no place for traditional father figures, and he became an anarchist in good part by rejecting that authority. His childhood and youth, in fact his whole life, consisted in a struggle to distance himself from almost everything represented by his father, and more generally by religion. In this negative sense, his father played an important role in shaping the kind of person Elisée was to become.

Pastor Reclus embodied a rigorous, Christian-inspired individuality and made much of announcing that he lived by the dictates of his conscience, so much so that his family was subjected to material hardship. As a young man in Sainte-Foy, Jacques's theological training, as well as the social connections of his own and his wife's family, placed him in a favourable position for advancement. In 1831, at the age of thirty-five, he was offered the presidency of the Consistoire. In an act of self-deprecation, he spurned those who encouraged him to get ahead and chose a life of old-style Calvinism. He left Sainte-Foy to tend to the humbler peasantry at Castétarbes and Orthez in the poorer department of the Lower Pyrenees, and although donations were his only source of income, he garnered enough to maintain his independence from the state. Pastor Reclus believed he must follow the biblical message literally.

The inflexibility of character which led him to live in accordance with deeply-held religious principles also rendered the pastor stern, colourless, authoritarian, and to his children utterly domineering. Elisée would remember:

> [H]is powerful personality dominated absolutely every one of his friends, his congregation, and all those who gravitated to him. It was impossible not to see him as a being apart, as the natural intermediary between each of his charges and that formidable world of the beyond where the Lord reigns surrounded by his angels. He represented the divinity; this was the first impression one had of him, an impression which was gradually transformed as it rendered him more human, but it left him, at least in the eyes of his son, as the Ideal of the inflexible Conscience.[3]

Elisée had anything but a happy relationship with his father; clearly, in fact, he found his father oppressive and his authoritarianism loathsome. His sister Louise, with whom he remained on good terms throughout his life, remembered that her brother's stay at Castétarbes had been a "life of sadness and dread, of which he never spoke without bitterness."[4]

The experience was all the more painful because Elisée's earliest years had been spent not in his father's house, but with his maternal grandparents in Laroche. In 1831, when the pastor went off to the Lower Pyrenees, Elisée stayed behind, presumably because of his young age, but for some reason he remained there until late 1838 when he rejoined the family at Castétarbes. The young Elisée, a friendly and active child with a vivid imagination, had been reasonably happy until the age of eight; his good-natured grandparents were not overly concerned with formal education and were light on discipline.[5]

Life as only one of many siblings was therefore an unpleasant return to reality. In 1838, when Elisée was reunited with his family, his mother, Marguerite Zéline Trigant, gave birth to her eighth child; five more would follow. The situation was exacerbated by the pastor's austere character. Shortly after the family reunion, for example, Elisée was reprimanded by his father for having "corrupted" Elie, an elder brother by three years; apparently the two boys had simply rambled about the countryside. Elisée was astonished at this show of paternal authority, and dared ask "how he had done wrong."[6] The father took the whole affair as a slight on the head of the household by a spoiled, undisciplined child; the young boy saw his father as a force to be endured in silence and defiance.

The early tensions in this relationship were partially mitigated by Elisée's mother, whom he described as "admirably zealous, but of another manner than her husband."[7] Madame Reclus shared her husband's religious fervour and abided by his decisions without complaint. Her submission had its limits, however, and at times she showed courage and independence of spirit. As a fairly well educated woman among poor peasants, Madame Reclus founded a school in Orthez; devotion to learning was, one suspects, mixed with the need to supplement the family income which suffered through the pastor's doctrinaire approach to life. She was also Elisée's teacher, and it is tempting to see her influence in the emphasis he later placed on the role of education in the struggle for a socialist society.

Life could not have been easy for Madame Reclus, wife of a poor pastor, mother of a large family, and local schoolteacher. Elisée said that she devoted every minute of her life to her children, although she had little time to give them.[8] While he felt deprived, however, Elisée was emotionally drawn to his mother, and in his many letters to her poured out deep affection and enduring respect.

Although Elisée's relationship with his father was unhappy, the pastor certainly succeeded in instilling in the boy the Calvinist scruples which would emerge in new forms years later. In fact, the father was far more successful than he could have imagined, for Elisée exhibited a certain scrupulousness early on and was especially disturbed that Christianity, which preached brotherhood and equality, was too complacent in the face of the reality of greed and social inequality. As a mature man he would recall how, as

29

a boy, he had attributed great significance to the idea of the heavenly father providing the "daily bread."

> It seemed to me that by a mysterious act a meal would descend from on high on all the tables of the world. I imagined that these words, repeated millions and millions of times, were a cry of human brotherhood, and that each, in uttering them, thought of all.[9]

Elisée sensed contradictions between the real message of the bible and his father's rejection of organised religion for a literal adherence to its words.[10] The young man's subsequent categorical approach to human salvation on earth may be viewed as an attempt to see the realisation of Christian ideals.

Elisée's concern with the meaning of Christian brotherhood was intensified as a result of experiences with the Moravian brothers in the German Rhineland. Pastor Reclus felt that the Moravians, who ran a school for German and foreign children in Neuwied, would inculcate a true Christian spirit in his children. So despite the family's poverty, Elisée's older brother and sister, Elie and Susi, went to study there in 1840. Elie stayed until 1843, a year after he was joined by Elisée, who then remained for two years.

The Moravians, Elisée would later write, were "docile subjects, with their lives regulated in advance by a disgusting ritual of childish practices and conventional lies."[11] He described the school director as cowardly and contemptible, a man who flattered the rich and ridiculed the poor. Not only did he suffer discrimination because of his poverty, said Reclus, but he was also victimised because of his nationality. Years later, he would recall Elie's and his own experiences at the hands of school comrades. Elie was beaten and called names like "French frog" and "froggie," each occasion being termed a little "Waterloo"; worse, the Moravian brothers encouraged such treatment.[12] Though devoted to Christ, the Moravian brothers had become totally un-Christian in their relations with the students. It is not surprising that Elisée, already sensitive to the religious "failings" of his scrupulous father, reacted so negatively to the brothers, who now gave new meaning to the word "hypocrisy."

Elisée's disillusionment with religion was accompanied by a growing interest in the "social question." In 1844, when he joined Elie at the Protestant college of Sainte-Foy, both their lives had reached a turning point.

The lifelong friendship between the Reclus brothers begun in late 1838 when Elisée arrived at Castétarbes was strengthened in the period 1844-47 when they were students at Sainte-Foy (where Elisée studied for a baccalauréat).[13] The pair presented a striking contrast in appearance and manner. The excitable Elisée was short and slender, with blue eyes and blond hair; while Elie, tall, broad, and dark, tended to be withdrawn and melancholic. Elisée was impressed by his older brother, who resembled their father in looks and personality. At Sainte-Foy, Elisée would remember, Elie showed "literary fervour," as did most of his friends. Attention was increasingly given to the "social question," especially as discussed in the works of Saint-Simon, Auguste Comte, Charles Fourier, and Félicité de Lamennais.[14] The brothers began to show less devotion to theology and scorned their superiors who demanded greater attention to the curriculum: students "were supposed to succeed in their various bourgeois careers, as property-owners, employees of the state, stockholders with easy consciences."[15]

The boys lived with their aunt in Sainte-Foy, and she was anything but sympathetic to radical political attitudes. The young men resented the intrusion of their aunt and her husband into their affairs, and they reacted rebelliously to their uncle's advice to seek "wealth and honours" and "admiration of the hierarchy among men." Their lives after 1851, according to their uncle, were "the abomination of desolation."[16]

Although both Elisée and Elie were highly critical of religion, they chose, interestingly, not to abandon religion, but rather to become more involved. When in 1847 Elie began his theology studies at Geneva, the original home of Calvinism, Pastor Reclus, although somewhat pleased, was nevertheless perplexed: he found it difficult to understand how his son, who was "outside grace," could study theology yet reject religious faith.[17] He must have been doubly shocked when, the following year, Elisée decided to study theology at Montauban in the Tarn-et-Garonne department in southwest France.

Elisée's decision to study for the ministry was probably bound up with youthful idealism about redirecting the church to a vigorous pursuit of Christian ideals. He clearly resolved to move beyond what he saw as the shallowness characteristic of religion. What is interesting, however, is the spirit of proselytism which struck deep roots at an early age and which pervaded Elisée Reclus's entire career. "[T]he very sight of a pulpit makes me palpitate," he said in 1851, "and I have rarely been happier than I was on that day when I preached at Montauban in front of two teachers, my brother, and the empty pews."[18]

In 1848-49 Elisée was once again the companion and school comrade of Elie, who had returned from Geneva to continue his theology studies at Montauban. By early 1848, economic and political grievances had led to unrest throughout Western Europe. The brothers soon looked anxiously to Paris for "news of political battles."[19] Though Louis-Philippe attempted to suppress radical movements, he had not been able to halt their spread underground. The round of "banquets" that began in 1847, led by such public figures as Adolphe Thiers and Odillon Barrot, intensified the political climate and drew attention to the need for electoral and parliamentary reform. When the government banned the banquet planned for 22 February 1848, the barricades went up in Paris and did not come down when Louis-Philippe tried appeasement by dismissing Guizot. Deserted by the National Guard, the king was forced to abdicate two days later, and a Republic was successfully proclaimed for the second time in French history.

An Englishman to whom Elisée would give French lessons in 1852 later recalled that his tutor "often spoke of that marvelous dawn, stormy day, and most unhappy sunset."[20] The excitement that Reclus felt in 1848 was still at a peak in 1851 when he wrote:

> For eighteen years a hideous wave of... egoism crept over France. At last there arrived the Revolution of contempt, the throne disappeared, and the bourgeois began anew to celebrate the magnanimous people, the magnanimous people who would have been shot down if they had been defeated... It was a beautiful day when the king paled at the approach of the people and looked for a dungeon in his splendid castle, a king who thought that he could, just once more, imprison the rioters.[21]

The 1848 upheaval was not restricted to France. In January there was a popular uprising in Palermo, Sicily, against the abuses of Ferdinand II of Naples, and similar agitation took place in other parts of Italy. Demonstrations in Mannheim in February were followed by uprisings throughout the German states, leading to the convening of the Frankfurt Vorparlament. In Vienna, Metternich was forced to resign, and the March Laws, which assured Hungary of virtual home rule, were a triumph for Louis Kossuth. That same year, there were disturbances in Belgium and England and revolt in Switzerland.

While many of these uprisings included strong national overtones, it is clear from what Elisée wrote shortly after 1848 that he saw them as attempts at emancipation from oppression.[22] He regarded his own feeling of local patriotism as an emotion to be used against oppression within France.[23] It is not surprising that he reacted favourably to the movement for national liberation at this time, for it was widely perceived to be an integral part of the struggle against autocracy. In February 1848 Elisée shared the view expressed by Karl Marx when he identified "the cause of nationality with the cause of democracy and the enfranchisement of the oppressed class."[24]

The Reclus brothers, meanwhile, were growing increasingly restless as theology students in Montauban, which, they complained, was totally devoid of intellectual stimulation.[25] As their social and political views crystallised, their attitudes and appearance grew "republican" and "aggressive."[26] They decided to distance themselves from the direct tutelage of the teachers at Montauban, and with their friend Edouard Grimard moved to a house four kilometres away, where, unobstructed by the daily routine of seminary life, they voraciously read a wide selection of material.[27]

This defiance finally led to their being expelled in the spring of 1849, after taking a trip to the Mediterranean[28] instead of attending a meeting at which speakers from Paris addressed the students. Elisée later claimed that the prefect of the department had discriminated against them for their political beliefs and put pressure on the school to expel them.[29] It is unlikely that the prefect would have intervened in such a minor matter, although it is possible that the principal, anxious to rid himself of three trouble-makers, used the prefect's putative dissatisfaction to strengthen his case. Elie then left for Strasbourg to resume his theology studies.[30] Elisée spent some time in Orthez and Sainte-Foy before going on to Neuwied in the autumn of 1849 to teach at the school of the hated Moravian brothers, of all places—a position no doubt secured through the intercession of his father.

Elisée's experiences at Neuwied soon led to a reaffirmation of his earlier impressions of the Moravians. While relations were more relaxed this time, they were generally superficial. He saw more clearly that any religious faith that the brothers may have once possessed now consisted in habit, that the name of God was no longer an inspiration but was mentioned only at the appointed times. Such attitudes caused friction, and he wrote in 1850: "If I appear a heretic to them, at least my heresy is dear and profound to me."[31] Unhappy with an emotionally and intellectually unsatisfying position, Elisée resigned and set out in January 1851 to study at the University of Berlin.[32]

There is evidence in a letter written shortly thereafter that his interests were changing from the sacred to the profane. While Elisée retained an interest in theology—parental preferences and personal inclinations being difficult to dismiss—in Berlin he attended courses on political economy, the history of diseases, and geography. The well-known geographer Carl Ritter sparked his imagination and would influence the development of his career as a geographer.[33] A growing interest in social and economic matters likely led him to contact German socialists in the capital, although there is no proof of this. At any rate, Elisée was aware of socialist ideas then developing in Germany.

He also made a final decision not to join the ministry. In a letter dated April 1851 he told his mother that although he was excited at the idea of preaching to the faithful, the formalities which went with the life of a pastor would weigh too heavily on him: "I do not wish to be, nor am I able, nor ought I to be a pastor."[34] The year of interruption in his studies had put an end to all his hesitations, and he resolved in a manner surprisingly reminiscent of his father to spend the rest of his life heeding nothing but "the cry of my conscience."[35] As will become clear later, Reclus's rejection of authority was accompanied, paradoxically, by an uncompromising inflexibility characteristic of his father.

In 1851 Elisée Reclus was twenty-one years old. Almost as a declaration of his adulthood, he set down a systematic account of his social and political views in the form of an essay entitled "Développement de la liberté dans le monde."[36] The essay was put aside and forgotten until it was discovered among old papers by his sister Louise many years later. While the anarchist theory which Reclus developed in the 1870s bears striking resemblance to his position in 1851, the importance of such similarities should not be exaggerated.

The title "Development of Liberty in the World" is misleading. While Reclus set out to show that the quest for liberty is inherent in the development of human beings, his notion of liberty quickly becomes subordinated to the ultimate aim, love and universal brotherhood. "For each particular man liberty is an end, but it is only a means to attain love, to attain universal brotherhood." Reclus saw it as wrong to view liberty as an end in itself, since the pursuit of liberty for its own sake would lead to nothing but egoism. His concept of liberty was based on an individual's coming to a consciousness of the need not only for personal freedom, but also for brotherly love. The Declaration of the Rights of Man erred because it liberated (or at least called for the liberation) of men as citizens rather than men as men, "since it accords to the citizen the right to liberty in such a way that this liberty is not limited by love, but by duties." Reclus rejected a negative liberty which posits others as restricting the scope of one's actions and expressed the hope for a positive liberty in which fulfillment as a loving human being is possible only within a community of equals.

The essay might have been entitled "Development of Love (or Brotherhood) in the World," since liberty was subordinated to love and brotherhood. But for Reclus the question of liberty had to be posed within the context of the struggle for a just society. The essay reflects the young man's concern about how a "communistic" brotherhood might be established without effacing the individual. He was critical of pre-1848 "utopian" communism which threatened to limit rather than increase freedom and which maintained that individuals "ought to become absorbed in the mass and to be no more than the innumerable arms of the polyp." A person "is not an accident, but a free being, necessary and active, who though united with his fellows, remains distinct from them."

For Reclus, communism had to free the individual while guaranteeing the well-being of all. People were perceived as forming a "human association"; each member of the association must "develop freely according to his means and his faculties, without being hindered in any way by the mass of his brothers," while the work of each person must contribute to the welfare of the whole association. This criticism of "utopian" communism is important because it demonstrates aspects of central concern to the theory of anarchist communism formulated in the 1870s.

Reclus was interested in neither laissez-faire liberalism nor utopian communism; liberty without equality was the mistake of the former, just as equality without liberty was that of the latter. In his critique of utopian communism he also showed a deep suspicion of attempts to put practice at the service of theory, and he questioned the notion that the ideas of major thinkers should constitute the blueprint for socialist communities. He must have had in mind the several famous attempts in the first half of the nineteenth century to establish communities based on the ideas of Charles Fourier and Robert Owen. Socialism, Reclus said, was not to be found in books, not even in those of men like Proudhon and Louis Blanc, but "in the hearts of the people... in the hearts of those poor naïve and artless peasants."

He saw history as a struggle for an equality that enhances liberty. Primitive society was moved by selfish drives and egoisms and ignorance of anything but martial values. Each stage in the rise and fall of civilisations, however, represented a step towards the wider dissemination of the idea of equality. Christianity played a crucial role. The development of feudalism with its order of institutionalised inequality had been unable to overcome the victory of Christian ideals. At least in the sight of God, master and serf had continued to be "equal." And the great French Revolution, with its ideals of liberty, equality, and fraternity, held out the promise of a kind of earthly order which Reclus was convinced could and would be established.

Writing in 1851, when reaction was successfully reasserting itself throughout Europe, his optimism remained undaunted. While he believed that the movement of history was sometimes progressive, sometimes regressive, he insisted that the former elements were always stronger than the latter, and therefore "it is incontestable that humanity advances in the direction of progress." For Reclus, progress was linked to a growing consciousness of the value and potential of humankind, but the whole point of a consciousness was to prepare the way for the new. Violence and revolution might be necessary to conquer the forces of habit, egoism, and the past. "Peaceful democracy is utopia," said the young man, whose childhood sensitivity to the cruelty he witnessed in the slaughterhouses of rural France led to lifelong vegetarianism.[37]

The ultimate aim of revolution was the creation of a universal Republic. Even though he saw some liberating effects in nationalist movements, he believed the beginnings of a new era were at hand in which nationalism would become a weak and unnecessary force. Carried away with enthusiasm for the future, he declared that national hatreds were on the wane and that people were being seen more for what they were than whence they happened to come. While France may have been viewed as progressive from police states like Prussia or Russia, Reclus maintained that French oppressors were indistinguishable from those of other countries. It was possible, therefore, for those who shared the common denominator of their oppression to look upon one another not as members of antagonistic groups, but as people united in their suffering and in their struggle.

> We democrats are united in spirit... with all you rejected peoples, with you oppressed of all nations, wretched of all climates, with you against your German oppressors, against your French oppressors...
>
> Our destiny is to live in an ideal state where nations no longer need to be under the tutelage of a government or another nation. It is the absence of government; it is anarchy, the highest expression of order.

There is similarity between this last expression and the title of Anselme Belligarrigue's journal which appeared in April and May 1850: *L'Anarchie, c'est l'ordre* and *L'Anarchie, journal de l'ordre*. Reclus was acquainted with the writings of Proudhon and in all likelihood was familiar with his *What is Property?* in which Proudhon proclaimed "I am an anarchist" and explained how "society looks for order in anarchy."[38]

The matter of what Reclus was thinking when he used the term "anarchy" in 1851 and how this relates to his views in the 1870s will be taken up later. Here it may be noted that the young Reclus was one of the few people who envisaged anarchy as a goal. He did not as yet reject the idea of working through state structures. He was excited about the opportunities that came with the establishment of republican government in 1848, but, as we shall see, he was positive even about the limited possibility for practical politics under the rule of Napoleon III. It was not until 1871, and after his bitter experience in the Paris Commune, that he became opposed to working within state structures of any kind.

Reclus's comments in these early years suggest a continuing belief in God, but in his 1851 essay he found it difficult to fit God into the analysis. Some attempt was made to reconcile religious and radical political beliefs.

It is then ridiculous to admit... that the hand of God directs the universe... All events proceed from the free development of man, all from irrevocable destiny... Man and God each have a real existence; let us therefore be neither fatalists nor atheists.

But then again Christianity was also a means by which the ideal of brotherly love might be inculcated in the hearts of all. "Tomorrow is the great day of combat," he said, "the day when Jesus will come to reign over his enemies and impose upon them brotherhood and the adoration of his God." He spoke of the "Christian Republic," "the day when all brothers of Jesus Christ are equal and free, when each person's conscience is the rule of religion, when there are neither priests nor shackles nor limits, but love only and forever!"

There is an understandable reluctance to dismiss God, even though he believed that people were—or could become—"free" beings. At one point God was simply equated with love and liberty. It was only later, when travelling in the United States, that he indicated in a letter to Elie that he had finally turned his back on his religious past.[39]

In late summer 1851 Elisée left Berlin for Strasbourg to meet Elie, who, on completion of his theological studies, immediately resigned from the ministry.[40] At the beginning of September the brothers left Strasbourg with little more than thirty francs in their pockets and with their dog at their heels. They spent the next twenty-one days making their way across France, living on bread and sleeping in the open air. They were continually suspected of being "false vagabonds," for it was less than three months before the *coup d'état* of Louis-Napoleon and security was tight. In late September they reached friends in Montauban, and some days later were in Orthez with their parents.[41]

Elisée recorded that the evening following the *coup d'état* of 2 December, the republicans of Orthez had gathered around a deputy and demanded resistance, but that the deputy had pleaded with them not to act hastily. Elie, Elisée, and a few others decided to take matters into their own hands. What support they won dwindled until they were reduced to a handful of friends outside the town hall.[42] Within the Reclus family it was accepted as fact that both brothers were threatened with arrest, and this was documented by Elisée later in life.[43] There is no official record of any protest in Orthez following the *coup*, however, and no report of orders to arrest the brothers. Whether the mayor managed to prevent anything worth reporting and merely indicated the possibility of arrest cannot be substantiated. For whatever reason, it was thought advisable that the brothers leave France, and Madame Reclus quickly raised the money necessary to get them out of the country.

Elisée and Elie had already been planning "to continue their apprenticeship of life and their sociology studies" in England, and they now happily put their plans into effect.[44]

Elisée Reclus's early years culminated in a rejection of his father's sacred trust, the Christian faith. A somewhat vague notion of socialism provided him with a framework in which to try to resolve vexing questions. He rebelled against a religion which postulated that all people would be equal in a life after death but which sanctioned the existence of social-economic inequities on earth. Many years later, in 1884, he condemned Christians who called men "brethren" and then proceeded to turn a blind eye to the poor. "The very life of humanity is but one long cry for that fraternal equity which still remains unattained."[45]

Rejection of Christianity was not rejection of Christian ideals, however. The life of Reclus may be seen an attempt to fulfill the promises of brotherhood and equality, to create a Christian society without a God, an earthly brotherhood of equals, without fathers, spiritual or otherwise! Anarchism became the struggle for the "conquest of bread," the "daily bread" that the Heavenly Father failed to provide. In 1904, the year before his death, he conceded that in many respects it was right to emulate the Christian of the bible.

> Thus, I should call no one "master," nor see myself as master of anyone; I should attempt to live in conditions of equality with everyone, Jew or Greek, property-owner or slave, millionaire or beggar, without making exceptions for alleged superiorities or presumed inferiorities.[46]

"No one could be more in harmony with the spirit of early Christianity," said a lifelong friend, "Jesus Christ would, I believe, have regarded him as a brother."[47] Elisée Reclus's religious yearnings were redefined and redirected.

Two

Beyond Earthly Paradise

It was, auspiciously, New Year's Day 1852 when the Reclus brothers arrived in London.[1] For Elisée, it was the beginning of a five-year absence from France. His odyssey, which took him to the United States and South America, provided the opportunity to come to terms with some important questions. He saw racism up close while living on a slave-holding plantation in Louisiana; a trip to Colombia and an (abortive) attempt to establish a colony high in the mountains of Sierra Nevada de Santa Marta provided the basis for the elaboration of his views on the founding of anarchist "colonies." He decided that such retreats from the world to earthly paradise had no value for anarchist theory and practice. It was also at this time that he worked out the broad outlines of the geography projects that were to occupy him from his return to France in 1858 until his death in 1905.

Elisée and his brother were among the many political refugees from France after the *coup d'état* to arrive in London almost penniless. Elie has left a depressing description of one early lodging, "the smallest imaginable—a mere dressing-room over the door-light." There were times when he tried to "find a sheltered corner on one of the bridges."[2] Elisée had some difficulty getting employment in London and was supported largely by his more fortunate brother.[3] It is clear that the two—and especially Elisée—saw themselves as persecuted French republicans, tolerated but not welcomed in London. Wrote Elisée:

[T]he questioning eye of the mistress of the house rigorously surveyed the clothes of each intruder, especially if he was from France, that "country of corruption and frivolity"... That was the period in which a Stuart Mill refused to receive a Pierre Leroux, in which the *Times* boasted of the superior way in which Britain treated refugees as opposed to continental practice: was it not better to let them die of hunger under the contempt of all than to put them in a prison from which they would one day be released as heroes or martyrs?[4]

Elisée saw his experiences in political terms and later reflected on their significance. Whether he was actually "persecuted" as he claimed is neither here nor there; in point of fact, he rather relished the thought of having been singled out as an enemy of the status quo, even something of a martyr. We have already come across a number of incidences—Neuwied, Montauban, Orthez after the *coup*—for which Elisée's claims cannot be substantiated by surviving evidence. While this does not mean that the claims are false, it does suggest that caution is warranted at least with respect to the degree of persecution. Throughout his life he evoked the image of victim of social injustice and made references to the "joy of suffering for a good cause." His tendency to "politicise" likely led him to find evidence of being singled out rather than overlook the matter.

In that first year in London Elisée made little personal contact with well-known revolutionaries. In a letter dated 2 March 1852 he told his brother that he had spent his last shilling to attend a meeting addressed by Louis Blanc and Pierre Leroux.[5] He may have become better acquainted with Leroux, whom Elie met at about this time,[6] and he may have met Ernest Coeurderoy,[7] who settled in London in 1851 after being expelled from Switzerland. There is a good chance that he also met the Russian exile Alexander Herzen.[8] Many people who fled the continent after the revolutions of 1848 lived in anticipation of another uprising and meanwhile squabbled among themselves about the relative merits of their theories.[9] Elisée maintained at least a spectator's interest in such political bickerings. He did not sink into despair, but took comfort from any sign that things would soon take a turn for the better.

The year before he went to London Reclus felt that nationalism was in decline, even while he recognised the revolutionary potential of nationalism in liberation movements. In 1852 he discerned from across the channel that Napoleon III was inadvertently playing a "revolutionary" role by setting in motion the forces of nationalism.[10] Heightened nationalism as fostered by Napoleon could lead to liberation if it gave rise to a revolution that promoted greater self-esteem among the French people, along with genuine respect for all peoples of the world. He continued to believe that the will of the people could not be subverted indefinitely, and he focused on aspects of the unhappy situation that seemed to contain the seeds of progress.

> Yes, you are right, great things are being prepared; everything was badly begun... until today love and liberty were not strong enough to transform society; but the governments are making a tabula rasa of all our feeble beginnings, and when they are finished we shall be able to begin again on a new scale.[11]

The nature of the reaction and the unlikelihood of change in the near future did not escape him, and he turned away from Europe in search of other possibilities.

By mid-1852 Elisée had secured a position on a small farm just south of Dublin with help from Elie, now a tutor in Ireland. Later that year Elisée, who was growing restless for adventure, left for the New World.

A combination of factors led to the decision. He was influenced in part by an interest in an agricultural experiment of some sort. A survey of his letters to Elie in the 1850s reveals that a general plan was probably being worked out by the brothers before Elisée left England.[12] Elie in particular was impressed by Fourier's ideas,[13] and in spite of the reservations expressed by Elisée in 1851 regarding utopian communism, he was now enthusiastic about establishing a community. There was at the time considerable support for such projects among refugees in London. While there were strong elements of a personal quest for an immediately realisable "utopia," leaving for the New World did not necessarily represent total abandonment of the old. There were some who hoped to set up alternative societies in America as models for the (eventual) reorganisation of European society, but many "Red '48ers" simply hoped to find a place in which to express themselves more freely.

Reclus's interest in geography provided another motive for the voyage to America, and he must have been excited at the prospect of the trip. He had always been fascinated by the natural environment. He was overcome with excitement on his first trip to the Mediterranean, in 1849. "When we saw the sea," recalled Elie on his deathbed in 1904, "you were so moved that you bit me on the shoulder until the blood came."[14] In a letter to Elie in 1852, Elisée described the area around the River Shannon in Ireland,[15] and this impression was later recalled in the preface to his *La Terre* in 1868. Elisée said that the inspiration for his geography came not from textbooks but from his own travels and experiences. His first major geographical work was commenced

> not in the silence of my room, but in the open air. It was in Ireland, on the top of a small hill which overlooks the rapids of the Shannon... It was there, in that charming spot, that I conceived the idea to tell the story of the phenomena of the Earth, and, without delay, I sketched the plan of my work.[16]

He wrote to his mother from New Orleans in 1855:

> ...to see the earth, for me that is to study it. The only truly serious study which I would undertake is that of geography, and I believe that it is much more worthwhile to observe nature herself than to imagine her from one's room.[17]

In another letter of that period he wrote that he had been "pregnant for some time with a geographical little rascal" (Mistouflet) that he wished "to bring into the world in the form of a book." He had already done enough scribbling, he said, and that did not satisfy him. "I also wish to see the Andes, in order to throw a little of my ink on their immaculate snow."[18] It would not be long before Reclus would work out the relationship between his social and political theories and his geography.

He formed many lasting impressions during a stay in the United States, and, not surprisingly, given his commitment to the notion of universal brotherhood, the experiences which affected him most were those associated with slavery. As tutor on a plantation near New Orleans, he was confronted with the reality of institutionalised inequality; after returning to France in 1857 he would write much on the question.[19] Although the members of the family with whom he lived in Louisiana were not harsh with the slaves and even developed close relations with some of them, Reclus was deeply troubled by the debasement inevitably involved in such relationships, and his sudden departure from the plantation in early 1856 was due largely to his scruples about slavery. Almost as a penance, he felt the need to go hungry and to sleep by the side of the road; it grieved him, he said, to be forced, through the salary he received as family tutor, "to cheat the negroes who, by their sweat and blood, have more than earned the money which I put into my pocket."[20] Looking back many years later, Reclus said that he had perhaps fled because of the impending Civil War in which he, as an abolitionist, would have had to take sides against his friends.[21]

He saw only one solution to the problems arising from slavery, and that was fusion of the races. Reclus was certainly aware of the distinctive features and unique qualities of different nations, races, and societies, but he believed that the mixing of peoples would strengthen rather than weaken the generations of the future. He was totally opposed to people like Gobineau,[22] who postulated that race was the all-important factor in human development and that the "superior" races were those which guarded their racial purity.

Early in life, Reclus had claimed—with more than a trace of French chauvinism—that the French had a greater instinct for sociability and were more "advanced" in their views; even then, he had attributed this superiority to the peculiar mix of people who had founded the country. "And now it is France," he wrote, "from which originate all those new ideas whose foreboding alone causes the old world to crack."[23]

As disturbing as Reclus's encounter with slavery was, his disgust was matched by an exhilaration over efforts to abolish the institution.

> It is beautiful to see this relentless war of the press, the discussion, the conversation day and night, all the moments against that elusive phantom of human freedom; every negro, every white who voices protest in favour of the rights of man, every word, every line in the south affirms that man is the brother of man.[24]

From New Orleans he wrote of the "most interesting ethnographic question of the century, that of the fusion of the races." In France one observed the fusion of "classes and principles," in America the fusion of armies. While the French dreamed of the brotherhood of souls, across the Atlantic the brotherhood of colours was being prepared by the "brutal force of gravitation."[25] Reclus enjoyed a good fight, and the nobility of the cause caught his imagination.

Although the solution to social problems would obviously depend on the actions of individuals, a considerable degree of determinism crept into his analysis:

> Fortunately, each problem contains the key to its solution within itself, and, indeed, it will not be due to the Americans if mixing of the races takes place, if negro, Indian, and white end up resembling each other, physically as well as morally, and blending together in one nation.[26]

43

The fusion of the races had already begun as the planter assumed the habits, character, and language of the negro, and sexual intercourse across ethnic boundaries was producing the copper shade of the "typical" American face.[27] Reclus also saw black emancipation as inevitable. The sheer weight of numbers was on their side: "...the *proportion of negroes and whites is constantly being displaced in favour of the former.*"[28] Slave-owners continually undermined their position by invoking the principle of authority. The attempt to place hitherto unquestioned authority on any kind of rational basis would be self-defeating, because, in the process, blind faith would be destroyed and authority weakened.[29]

Reclus's views in 1851 had already contained an element of teleological determinism. His experiences in the United States reinforced his conviction that progress could be halted only temporarily. As he wrote in 1855:

> But the great progress is almost totally independent of their [the Americans'] will. This progress has to follow the new relationships of man to the Earth and of races to races, because these new relationships have posed for humanity new questions which have to be resolved whether we like it or not.[30]

Reclus was critical of the institutions of the New World and the general way of life. He wrote to Elie:

> You judge the United States well, but not severely enough. It is a great auction hall where everything is sold, slaves and owner into the bargain, votes and honour, the Bible and consciences. Everything belongs to the one who is richer.[31]

He saw that profound questions were being raised, nevertheless, and he saw the peculiar virtues of the Americans as they faced these questions. In particular, he focused on the indomitable energy and boldness with which they plunged into investigations of traditional "lies." Moreover, the idea of the fundamental equality of all people was breaking through obstacles placed in its path, and, willy-nilly, "all Yankees" became "the apostles of civilisation."[32]

While admitting that these people were dealing with questions of great importance, however, Reclus was far from relinquishing the leadership of the French in the revolutionary struggle. Americans were still country bumpkins compared to the French, who would offer them guidance and a sophisticated framework in which to come to an understanding of change.

> The education of the Americans resembles that which we give the pedants in France: they know the name of things; they talk of the blunt fact to the entire world, and, later, we shall

44

come to demonstrate the idea behind the fact. To use an Anglo-Saxon comparison, they put their glasses on the table and wait for us to fill them.[33]

From early 1856 until he returned to France in the summer of 1857 Reclus travelled in Colombia, where he waited for Elie. He made elaborate preparations. He wrote his mother in June 1855, "Believe me, dear mother, the little colony we are going to establish will be charming and my brother's family will be happy there."[34] After Elie had returned to France from Ireland and married his cousin Noémi, Elisée urged them to join him.[35] But they did not arrive, and nearly a year later Elisée still implored his brother to come, promising that they would enjoy great "freedom of action."[36]

In spite of all efforts, the establishment of a community did not materialise.[37] For one thing, Elie never came. But beyond that, Elisée had limited financial resources. A relationship he had struck with an old Frenchman with whom he planned to start the plantation turned out to be "the most foolish episode of my life... the old man talked too much, was a liar, a busybody, bad-tempered..."[38] (He was reluctant to end the friendship because he felt a sense of responsibility to the man and the project.[39]) Even the site for the little colony was not well chosen: it was high in the mountains and communications were difficult. Finally, in the winter of 1856-57, Elisée came down with yellow fever. "Instead of beginning by establishing a serious plantation at Sierra," he wrote in February 1857, "we have allowed both time and money to run out; we have arrived in the mountains without a sou..."[40] In the same letter, he reflected playfully:

If we half succeed in our coffee plantation, if communications are easier as a result of the invention of some new steam engine, and it is possible to reach the delightful climate of Sierra Nevada by travelling rapidly through the tropics, then we can have our town house in Paris and our country house in Sierra Nevada. Are not all the forces of air and water, of matter and science working together to bring us closer to this little earthly nest?[41]

Elisée decided to give up the project and return to France. His letters from the summer of 1857 suggest excitement at the prospect of seeing his family. However, moving back to France involved more than a desire to be with his family. Reclus also put behind him the search for a freer way of life through flight from European civilisation. The quest for alternatives such as that offered in Sierra Nevada was abandoned, and projects of this nature were never again undertaken.

45

He retained throughout the 1850s a faith in some kind of inevitable progress. Despite the oppressive nature of European society, Reclus did not doubt that history provided evidence of human accomplishments, both material and cultural. These advances were linked in his mind to the evolution and dissemination of the ideas of liberty, equality, and fraternity.

It is interesting, however, that each move he made from 1852 (London to Ireland, Ireland to Louisiana, Louisiana to Colombia) was to increasingly "underdeveloped" areas. It is tempting to speculate that his effort to establish a little colony was an attempt to incorporate the achievements of Western civilisation (and none of its evils) into an alternative society. To what extent Reclus saw his plan for an "earthly paradise" in political terms is unclear; he may simply have wanted to experience the adventure of living in the wild. Whatever his motivation (a question that is of no particular concern here), he certainly drew lessons. The New World taught him that only with difficulty could the accomplishments of "advanced" societies—that is, those of Western Europe—be transplanted to those that were "underdeveloped."

Reclus continued to be interested in politics and concerned about injustice. He would have found it difficult to continue living in a small, isolated community. He was outraged by slavery in the southern United States and moved by the pernicious effects of the white invaders on the native Indians in South America. In 1856 he described the Indians of Sierra Nevada as

> poor children, very sweet, who... observe everything with the unintelligent curiosity of the bird... It is said that they originally lived on the plain; the barbarism of the Spanish drove them to seek refuge in these mountains... the woman is the slave of her husband and every poor girl who does not find a master becomes the rightful slave of the nearest rich man.[42]

These remarks painted no pretty picture for anyone thinking of fleeing "developed" society for "idylls." In fact, Reclus was struck by similarities between Europe and the mountain villages of Colombia: "The social system of Europe is duplicated here, but is incomparably simpler and freed of all the complications which disguise it at home."[43] His experiences in Colombia clarified such matters considerably and led him to see social injustice in Europe as never before; he began to view social evils in universal terms.

Reclus also remarked on the effects of the continuing expansion of the European economic system, and he gained a clearer vision of the struggle needed to bring the economy under democratic control. In answer to Elie's description of corruption in France, he wrote:

Viewed from afar, the spectacle of this corruption has something grandiose about it and provides a magnificent response to the question of competition, such as it was posed in 1789. Everything universalises, and when these gigantic companies, organised for *profit*, extend over the entire society, one will at least know that it is by joining together that great things are accomplished.[44]

This passage reveals excitement at the thought of the battle ahead. He would hardly have been content for long in distant Colombia, even had the colony flourished. During his stay in Louisiana, he had already realised that a colony in the mountains would be little more than a temporary respite from a world dominated by Europe. "Come," he coaxed Elie's wife, "it will be delightful. Later, when three or four years of paradise have tired you out, it will be time to see the old world again."[45]

Reclus's first book on geography, *Voyage à la Sierra-Nevada de Sainte-Marthe*, published in 1861, drew upon experiences in South America. By the 1880s it attracted the attention, ironically, of a number of people interested in founding communities, among them members of the Société anonyme de colonisation de la Sierra-Nevada.[46]

Beseeched for advice, Reclus calmly insisted that while he had confidence in the initiatives of the indigenous population and acclimatised foreigners, he doubted that such projects directed from afar could be successful. He also warned of technical difficulties, communications, and climate.[47] As for establishing a more just society through such communitarianism, Reclus's statements were quite categorically negative. Regardless of the motives behind the experiments, any proposal to get people to establish their relations according to some preconceived plan was *ipso facto* "authoritarian." One should not delude oneself into thinking that such communities could be established without force. Communitarians could not help but rely on authoritarian principles to guide their activities, and such experiments were therefore doomed to failure. As he wrote elsewhere:

It is to live in conditions of equality and escape from the falsehoods and hypocrisies of a society of superiors and inferiors, that so many men and women have formed themselves into closed corporations and little worlds apart. America abounds in communities of this sort. But these societies, few of which prosper while many perish, are all ruled more or less by force; they carry within themselves the seeds of their own dissolution,

47

and are reabsorbed by Nature's law of gravitation into the world which they have left.[48]

These conclusions were based on more than calculations of their success. Even if they were successful, he argued, even "if man enjoyed in them the highest happiness of which his nature is capable," such communities would be "obnoxious" in their "selfish isolation" from the rest of humanity. The hopes and dreams of such people were "egotistical" and "devotion to the cause of humanity" would draw the best of them, even in a successful community, back to the "great struggle."

> Never will we [anarchists] separate ourselves from the world to build a little church, hidden in some vast wilderness. Here is the fighting ground, and we remain in the ranks, ready to give our help wherever it may be most needed.[49]

The question of "colonies" emerged at the very end of the nineteenth century, when the anarchist movement was reduced to impotence. Rejected by the socialists who rapidly assumed a parliamentary identity, some anarchists believed that the creation of (non-urban) communities throughout Europe would provide an opportunity to put theory into practice, if only on a small scale. Reclus's response was decidedly negative. While he sympathised with the motives of such endeavours, he made it clear that he could in no way support them. Colonies, whether at home or abroad, said Reclus at the turn of the century, had very little chance of survival, as could be seen from experiments in France, Russia, the United States, Mexico, and Brazil. They failed because they were infected from the outset with bourgeois attitudes and institutions, such as legal marriage and paternity, subjection of women, private property, buying and selling, and the use of money. The enthusiasm of the members might hold the colony together for a while, but disintegration was inevitable, even without attack from outside.

People persisted in such efforts to establish colonies, he believed, because of a mistaken assumption that if they worked harder than their predecessors, they would be able to remove themselves from society and overcome its values and prejudices. For Reclus, there had to be social change before a successful colony could be established. Of course, by that time there would be no need to found colonies.[50]

Settlements of this kind had nothing at all to do with anarchism as Reclus understood it. Those who were attracted to the idea of a paradise, he said, suffered from the illusion that anarchism constituted a "party" outside society. Such a notion was sheer folly.

Our joy, our passion, is in putting into practice that which seems egalitarian and just to us, not only with regard to our comrades, but also with regard to all men... In our plan of existence and struggle, it is not the small chapel of comrades which interests us; it is the entire world.

Anarchists had to stay in the civilised world and continue their propaganda in shops and factories, homes, army barracks, and schools. Their enemies understood this well, sneered Reclus. They were already saying it would be convenient if all anarchists fled to some utopia, and some were even bold enough to suggest that assistance should be provided. Colonies did not point the direction of the future; they recalled the past. Their establishment was akin to the creation of monasteries in the Middle Ages.[51]

ZÉLINE RECLUS
Elisée's and Elie's mother

PHOTOGRAPH BY A. PERLAT

Pastor Jacques Reclus
Elisée's and Elie's father

PHOTOGRAPH BY BONNAL

The Reclus Family Group

From left to right standing:— 1- Onésime Reclus; 2-A friend; 3- Armand Reclus; 4- Zéline Reclus-Faure; 5- Husband of Ioanna Reclus-Bouny; 6- Marie Reclus; 7- Paul Reclus; 8-A friend; 9- Louise Reclus-Dumesnil; 10- Elisée Reclus; 11- Husband of Loïs Reclus-Trigant; 12- Elie Reclus; 13- Madam Elie Reclus; 14-A friend; 15- Husband of Zéline Reclus-Faure; 16- Trigant's son. From left to right seated:— 1-André, son of Elie Reclus; 2 Noémi Reclus; 3-Ioanna Reclus-Bouny with her child; 4-Loïs Reclus-Trigant; 5-Mother of Elie & Elisée; 6-Father of Elie & Elisée; 7-Jeannie, Elisée's daughter; 8-A friend; 9-Trigant's daughter. First child from left to right:— Elie Faure, now the famous French art critic, the second, a child of Ioanna Reclus-Bouny.

ELISÉE RECLUS

PHOTOGRAPH BY J. H. TOURTIN

Three
Affirming Differences

The France to which Elisée Reclus returned in 1857 was dominated by Napoleon III. In the face of limited scope for political expression he was consoled by his reunion with Elie and by the "atmosphere of art, science, and life, which I did not experience for such long years."[1] In the years ahead Reclus would associate with radical groups of all kinds. At this point his anarchism was not opposed in principle to republicanism, and he believed that some good could come of the French government's "liberal" policies in the latter years of the Empire. He sought a balance between personal independence and the commitment demanded by the various radical circles in which he moved. He refused to succumb to the dominating personalities of either Karl Marx or Michael Bakunin. While Marx wrote Reclus off as a Bakuninist, the infamous Russian radical was bewildered by Reclus's reluctance to become involved in his secret societies and concluded that this reluctance signified bourgeois sympathies.

Shortly after Elisée returned to France, Elie's wife Noémi introduced him to Clarisse Brian of Sainte-Foy, the mulatto daughter of a French sea captain and a Senegalese woman. They were married in a civil ceremony at Sainte-Foy on 14 December 1858. Elisée had persuaded Clarisse to marry without a religious service, and this apparently caused her some discomfort. He also insisted that their children not be baptised. They had two daughters, Magali, born 12 June 1860, and Jeannie, 1 March 1863.[2]

When Eliséee and Clarisse joined Elie and Noémi in Paris in late 1858, just after their wedding, Elie was working in the Crédit mobilier, a bank founded by the brothers Isaac and Emile Péreire in 1852 to put Saint-Simonian ideas into practice. Elisée contributed to the household by writing articles and reviews for geographical journals. Some of these, which were based on his observations in Colombia, were revised and published as a book in 1861.[3] In the early 1860s Elisée spent long periods away from Paris conducting research for a number of travel guides published by Hachette, a firm with which he would have professional relations for more than thirty years.

This period was important to his development as a geographer. The relationship between Reclus's geography and his anarchism is taken up in a later chapter. Here, it is worth tracing his involvement with the various individuals and groups that explicitly set themselves against governmental structures. Some were revolutionary and went so far as to demand the overthrow of the state; others merely advocated alternative ways of living.

The brothers Reclus had some contact with republicans and socialists in these years. Elie's son Paul would later write that there were visits with the notorious Auguste Blanqui, who was permitted to return to France after the amnesty of 1859, as well as with Proudhon.[4] Elie retained an interest in the work of the Fourierists,[5] and Elisée waged a war of words from afar against slavery during the course of the American Civil War. His marriage to a mulatto was something of a political statement. Paul would maintain that after his uncle's experiences in Louisiana he was particularly attracted to the idea of marrying a "daughter of a spurned race."[6]

Elisée continued to oppose the principles upon which the Second Empire was based, but he still believed that some of Napoleon's policies were breaking down the old order and thereby furthering liberation. He felt that the national self-determination of the Italians against their Austrian oppressors represented a step in the direction of their ultimate emancipation. Thus, unlike Proudhon,[7] he found himself among the republicans who reacted favourably to Napoleon's decision to take France into the Italian war against the wishes of his ministers, the clergy, and the well-to-do. While travelling in Italy in 1860, Reclus chanced to see King Victor Emmanuel and confessed:

> ...to my shame perhaps, when I saw him go past, that man excommunicated by the pope, enemy of Austria, betrayed at Villafranca, that stout hunter of men, whose name has become the keynote of policy for all of Italy, I believed I owed it to Italy herself to hum my *Evviva* too. The man is not much, but the Italians have made a principle of him. Through revolutionary *esprit de corps* I act with them.[8]

The more liberal policies adopted by the Second Empire in the 1860s fostered a climate conducive to political debate and helped release forces for change within France. The motives behind Napoleon's moves have become the subject of controversy, but there is some support for the contention that he wished to offset erosion of the popular support begun in the 1850s. There had been indications, in 1857, of a shift in public opinion away from the widespread support he enjoyed in the early years of the Empire. Turnout at the polls that year was considerably lower than it had been in previous elections, and republicans made limited gains. The 1863 elections voted in opposition candidates in eighteen of the twenty-two largest towns in France, and eight republicans were elected in Paris. The following year Napoleon countered by initiating a series of reforms. The November 1849 law forbidding collective industrial action was removed from the Penal Code, and although organised trade unions were still illegal, there were signs that they would be tolerated.

These reforms had a pronounced effect on Reclus's political views. Changes in the political climate form the backdrop against which the burgeoning socialist movement must be considered. Before returning to matters in Napoleonic France, let us examine his participation in socialist activities.

The most important socialist event of the day was the founding of the International Working Men's Association (IWMA), or the First International. Napoleon subsidised the attendance of French workers at the London International Exhibition of 1862,[9] and they made important contacts. The London Trades Council extended a welcome to the French, who then sent a delegation to the mass meeting on Poland in London the following year.[10] Shortly afterwards, George Odger, Secretary of the London Trades Council, drafted an address entitled "To the Workman of France from the Workingman of England," proposing the creation of an international association of workers. On 28 September 1864 a meeting was held at St. Martin's Hall in London, and the IWMA was born. Henri Tolain, Charles Limousin, and E.E. Fribourg, three of the

Frenchmen who took part, were followers of Proudhon. Other French participants included Eugéne Varlin, who pursued a more trade-union (syndicalist) approach.

While documentation is scant, it is certain that Elisée enlisted in the Paris section of the IWMA in 1865 or shortly thereafter, and that Elie probably did as well.[11] For Elisée and others in this period, membership in the IWMA represented no more than a gesture of solidarity. In the early years of the IWMA he did not become actively involved and was not well informed about its internal affairs.[12] This may have been due to poor relations with Tolain, who controlled the Paris section; certainly there were personal conflicts between Elie and Tolain in 1865.[13] Some republicans, dissatisfied with Tolain, withdrew their support for the Paris section while simultaneously declaring sympathy for the aims and principles of the International. In March 1865 Henri Lefort made this clear in an announcement in a newspaper with which the Reclus brothers were closely associated.[14]

Once Tolain's influence had waned, Elisée took a more active interest in the Paris IWMA. Although Tolain continued as French spokesperson at IWMA congresses and conferences, his position was gradually undermined in Paris by Eugéne Varlin and Benoît Malon. On 11 June 1868, in the company of Aristide Rey, Reclus met Malon[15] and became more enthusiastic about the Paris section, which now seemed to be in the hands of a new group.[16] The initial mutual respect between Reclus and Malon grew into a close friendship,[17] and it seems certain that Reclus joined the Paris Batignolles section of the IWMA in which Malon was a leading figure.[18]

His closer contact with the Paris IWMA led Reclus to look up members of the General Council while visiting London in the summer of 1869. In early July and mid-August he participated as a "visitor" in the meetings of the General Council.[19] He met Marx and on 27 July was presented with a copy of his "Eighteenth Brumaire of Louis Bonaparte."[20] While the first meeting of Reclus and Marx may have taken place the summer of 1869, they had in fact already made contact.[21]

Marx wanted *Das Kapital* translated into French because he considered it "of the greatest importance to emancipate the French from the false views in which Proudhon buried them with his idealised lower middle class."[22] Negotiations began between Paris and London, and it was hoped that Reclus and Moses Hess would translate the first volume.[23] Marx judged Reclus to be the right person to act "as French translator with German cooperation"[24] and he requested that his publisher send Reclus a copy of the book. Negotiations soon broke down, however, when Reclus and Hess became unwilling merely to translate the book but wanted "to shorten it and to modify it for the French public."[25] There was also some question about the amount of money they should receive.[26] The French translation of *Das Kapital* finally appeared in 1875.[27]

By the time Reclus and Marx met in the summer of 1869, it was unlikely that Reclus would continue with the translation. However, Marx's remarks to Engels leave no doubt that the meeting was relaxed and friendly, and the two had some fun mocking the sometime radical republican Louis Blanc. According to Marx's report:

> When Reclus was here, he also went to see LB[lanc] and said to me after his visit: The little fellow shits in his pants from fright at the mere thought of having to return to France. He feels himself bedeviled here, no doubt as a "little big man" who has been removed from danger and has—as he said directly to R[eclus]—lost absolutely all faith in the French.[28]

There is no no record of Marx's opinion of Reclus until 1876, just after Bakunin's death. Reclus was now a prominent figure in a (new) rival revolutionary organisation, and Marx began to discredit him. He alleged that both Elisée and Elie had been members of Bakunin's "secret" alliance and scoffed at their religious origins.[29] Engels mentioned to Wilhelm Liebknecht in 1877 that Elisée was "politically confused and impotent,"[30] while Marx referred to the Reclus brothers as the "souls" of the (rival) Swiss revolutionary periodical *Le Travailleur*.[31] Despite their differences, however, Reclus continued to have a high regard for Marx's contribution to socialist thought.[32]

In the 1860s the brothers were also involved in the cooperative movement. Elie was a founder of La Société du crédit au travail, established in October 1863 and directed by J.P. Béluze, son-in-law and disciple of Etienne Cabet. Elie was active in the association, as was Elisée to a lesser extent, until it was liquidated in late 1868. They helped found the first Paris cooperative of the Rochdale type, L'Association générale d'approvisionnement et de consommation, which was based on the Fourierist notion of the phalanstery. For a time Elie was director and editor of the cooperativist journal *L'Association*, published in Paris and Brussels from late 1864 to summer 1866. The Reclus were also associated with the Parisian journal *La Coopération* which appeared from September 1866 to June 1868.

Producers' cooperatives enjoyed a brief period of success in France after 1848. Much of their inspiration came from Louis Blanc, who advocated state-subsidised producers' societies in his *Organisation du travail* in 1839. Even after the June days of 1848, producers' cooperatives were grudgingly supported by the National Assembly, partly because it was thought that they would provide an alternative to the radical threat, and partly because it was the view of the Assembly that cooperativism would prove itself inadequate. In the 1860s, however, the authorities generally began to adopt more positive attitudes towards cooperatives. The principles of cooperation had by then been endorsed by liberal economists such as Léon Say and Léon Walras and were supported by republican politicians like Jules Simon. Some liberals believed that cooperatives—whether of producers or consumers—could perform the useful function of giving the workers a stake in society, and thereby tie them more securely to it.

Elie's experiences with the Saint-Simonian Crédit mobilier grew increasingly disappointing. He became restless when he saw that the business affairs were conducted not unlike those of other banks, and in 1862 he left to write for the Russian journal *Dêlo* and the newspaper *Russkoe Slovo*.[33]

The founding of Crédit au travail represented a determination to overcome Crédit mobilier's "bourgeois" shortcomings, to make headway in the emancipation of the working class. The underlying principles of every school of cooperation, according to Elie, were mutuality, independence, and solidarity. Every type of social reformer—Fourier, Comte, Saint-Simon, Cabet, Proudhon, Blanc, Leroux, and (although he is not usually considered a social reformer) even Frédéric Bastiat—made important contributions, and while all held opposing views, at one time or another each stumbled upon some truth.

Elie believed that the cooperative movement could carry out tasks begun in 1792.[34] Elisée later said that Crédit au travail was "to contribute in every way to promotion of relations between the republican bourgeoisie of good will and the world of the workers."[35] The organisation's purpose was to get involved in existing workers' associations, to help form new cooperatives, and to develop and publicise the principles of mutuality and solidarity.[36] Elie embraced a movement which held out the promise of change without violence, and he believed that cooperatives would "strongly encourage social evolution."[37] It is likely this attitude which led "the people of the International" to paint him as "that anti-socialist and anti-revolutionary patriarch."[38]

It is more difficult to isolate Elisée's views on cooperatives in this period. He leaves a general impression of scepticism, his participation motivated by support for Elie,[39] and he made no firm decision on the value of cooperativism until the following decade, and, as we shall see, that was totally negative. Another avenue explored by Elisée was that of Freemasonry.

Until the mid-1860s in France, Freemasonry was under the undisguised direction of Napoleon III, who personally selected the men at the head of its official organisations. Beginning in 1865, however, a number of factors combined to mitigate this influence, and the lodges adopted a more liberal policy toward social and political matters, thereby attracting the attention of young people interested in change. Alongside the recognised groups, however, there existed a masonic-like organisation dedicated to the overthrow of the Empire, and this arm was persecuted by the government. It was made up of groups which called themselves the Loge des Philadelphes.

Reclus's interest in politics led him to Freemasonry—very likely both varieties, although this is difficult to trace: not only is the history of Freemasonry itself obscure,[40] but there remain only scattered references to Elisée's participation. Although the nineteenth-century masonic press claimed him as a member, his participation was so limited that even his membership has been questioned.[41] A December 1894 letter does indicate that he went through the masonic entrance rites; he had become a mason, but had had only a "brief experience" with the organisation.[42] The editors of the anarchist paper Les Temps nouveaux stated in 1896 that Reclus had had nothing to do with the "closed society" after 1866.[43] It may therefore be concluded that Elisée was a more or less active mason, at least in the period 1865-66.

Elie was a member of the lodge La Renaissance—a fortuitous link, as it turned out, for through these connections he managed to escape from Paris after the suppression of the Paris Commune.[44] There is also some evidence to suggest that for a time both belonged to another lodge, Les Elus d'Hiram.[45]

The brothers may also have had experience with the Lodge of the Philadelphians in London, at least informally. This lodge, which was established late in 1850, was reserved for French émigrés, although in practice anyone who spoke French was admitted. In any event, while in London in 1852, the Reclus met Alfred Talandier, who was to hold a high position in the lodge and who would be a friend for many years. In the late 1860s, Elisée was close to several Philadelphians, including Charles Bradlaugh and Louis Blanc. He claimed that while he was initially attracted to Freemasonry, it had not held his interest:

> On the contrary, it found itself then as it does today [1894] in
> a period of evolution, in which, having fallen into the hands
> of an haute bourgeoisie, so-called liberal, it does not have any
> aim other than to deliver to its members the conquest of political
> power and, by consequence, wealth.[46]

He was not doctrinaire in his rejection, however, and accepted the hospitality of a group of Freemasons in Brussels who offered him the use of a hall, in 1894, for his geography lectures, nor was he averse to addressing Freemasons on the subject of anarchy.[47]

This limited association with Freemasonry was followed by an attraction to the Freethinkers. Reclus had close relations, in 1868, with Agis comme tu penses,[48] which was founded by French students and involved people like Aristide Rey and Georges Clemenceau as well as groups of workers. The statutes of the organisation proclaimed the law of reason and science and rejected all religious ceremony at birth, marriage, and death—"an association whose law is science, which is based upon solidarity, and which has justice as its aim."[49]

Reclus participated in Freemasonry and Freethinking as a way in which to meet people interested in the discussion of pressing contemporary issues. It is likely that he was also attracted by the atmosphere of intimacy and brotherhood. His comment on a banquet he attended in the summer of 1869 indicates just how interconnected were his feelings on Freethinking, republicanism, and socialism: "We were there, one hundred and twenty men and women, all united, freethinkers, republicans, socialists, and were happy to be together."[50]

The IWMA, cooperativism, Freemasonry, Freethinking—they all had something to offer, and although Elisée was quite aware of their contradictions,[51] he did not feel that participation in one necessarily precluded participation in another.

His most important personal contact in the late 1860s was Bakunin, anarchist of legend and antagonist of Marx. Having made his famous escape from Siberia, the gregarious Russian arrived in London in 1861, undaunted in his enthusiasm and no less disgusted by the reaction in Europe which followed the failures of mid-century uprisings. Marx gave Bakunin a warm welcome and wrote to Engels: "On the whole he is one of the few people who after sixteen years I find not less, but more fully, developed."[53] Bakunin may have been made aware of the interests of the Reclus brothers through mutual friends in England, such as Talandier or Herzen. At any rate, in an effort to recruit members for the International Brotherhood that he founded in Florence in 1864, he looked up the two while visiting Paris in November of that year.[54]

Elisée and Elie are named historically among the members of the International Brotherhood.[55] They also presumably joined Bakunin's Italian Alliance of Social Democracy in 1865, which appears to have been virtually identical to the International Brotherhood.[56] Certainly Elisée, who travelled to Italy after the eruption of Mount Etna in Sicily,[57] went to Florence to visit Bakunin in April 1865 and was introduced to the local circle.[58] Furthermore, Elisée's correspondence contains an apparent reference to his and Elie's involvement in Bakunin's societies.[59] It is likely that both were members of the International Brotherhood and the Alliance of Social Democracy. However, because so little of the correspondence between Elisée and Bakunin has survived, it cannot be established with any certainty what part the brothers played in the web of secret societies said to have been founded by Bakunin.[60]

While Elisée enjoyed Bakunin's confidence and had access to his circle, there is no detailed record of their relations until 1867, and then only in connection with yet another organisation, the League of Peace and Freedom. Elisée was among the first supporters of the League, which had been created at the initiative of the former Saint-Simonian Charles Lemmonier and which aimed to combine peace talks with the question of European unity under republican government.

The League was supported by a heterogeneous group, including members of the left, literary figures, and radical politicians, and it held its first congress in early September 1867. Although Marx dismissed it as a "futile gathering of impotent bourgeois ideologues,"[61] most of the delegates at the Lausanne Congress of the IWMA in 1867 decided to support the Geneva Congress of the League in its struggle against war. Ultimately, however, the message delivered by James Guillaume to the Geneva Congress contained a direct challenge to the political views of the League's middle-class sympathisers, and also struck a blow at the organisers, who were anxious to obtain working-class support.

Although Elisée did not attend the 1867 Congress, he followed developments with interest. He counselled Elie to accept the offer from the Central Committee of the League to act as French editor of the proposed journal *Les Etats-Unis d'Europe*, and he was disappointed that his brother wished to concentrate instead on a newspaper in Saint-Etienne.[62] This difference of opinion represents a changing, though never hostile, relationship between the two and is a sign of Elisée's growing desire to become more involved in revolutionary politics.

His enthusiasm was strengthened through correspondence with Bakunin, who was a member of a committee charged with drawing up a draft programme to be presented at the League's 1868 Congress.[63] Bakunin routinely sought the opinions of his friends, and several letters were exchanged between Berne (where the committee meetings were held) and Paris. Alfred Naquet and Elisée insisted that the word "republican" be inserted. "Perhaps," wrote Elisée, "on the eve of the day when the masses cry out the word, it is fitting for us to say it under our breath."[64]

Elisée was an enthusiastic participant at the Berne Congress of the League, held in September 1868,[65] but he was disappointed at the negative reaction of the IWMA, as expressed at its recent Brussels Congress. The IWMA had been invited to send a delegation to Berne, but chose instead to nominate three of its members to instruct the League to the effect that there was no basis for its separate existence and to invite its members to join the IWMA.[66] Reclus believed that the League was working in conjunction with the IWMA, not in competition with it, and he attributed the attitude of the IWMA to the Proudhonists, with whom there had been some friction. He contended that the Proudhonists, who had been defeated in Brussels on the question of collective ownership, were also responsible for the IWMA's attitude towards the League.[67] Such meddling by the Proudhonists he considered simply childish, but agreed with Bakunin that it would be better to let the matter rest and avoid a hostile encounter.[68]

At the League's Berne Congress, Reclus was a member of a committee set up to study and report on the "social question." The committee failed to reach agreement, refusing to adopt the programme by which Reclus (and Bakunin) supported "as ideal 'the equalisation of classes and individuals,' understanding by that equality as the point of departure for all, in order that each person might follow his career without hindrance."[69] Bakunin was so disgusted at the results of the vote, which left the question undecided, that he was ready to break away immediately. However, he was influenced by Reclus and Rey, who insisted on the value of staying until the end and putting forth their opinions. Reclus wanted to clarify his own views, which in the heat of debate were becoming more precise.[70] In fact, the Congress caught his interest to a far greater degree than he had expected. He described to Elie how he had been drawn into the discussions:

> My intention had been to write you a very detailed account of the Berne Congress. I had even drawn up three pages, which I have since lost; but [it was] impossible to continue my work because, my role of observer having from the beginning become that of participant, I could not find the time. Committee meetings, congress meetings, drafting of projects and redrafting followed without respite and until well into the night: at two or three o'clock the conversations were still going on. At the end of the week I was exhausted.[71]

Reclus delivered a speech on federalism the fourth day of the congress[72] in connection with a resolution on the "United States of Europe."[73] He felt it important to be explicit on the nature of the federation: it should not be assumed that a United States of Europe would represent an improvement over what existed already, and it should not be overlooked that unity might be won only at the expense of general subservience to a gigantic, centralised state. He was reluctant to envisage the creation of a united Europe as anything but a step on the way to the ultimate aim of the "federative republic of the entire world." He therefore insisted that the word "provisionally" be inserted into the resolution so that it would read: "The Congress is able to propose provisionally no better example than the Swiss and American confederations." Reclus was far from satisfied with existing federations and was determined to specify the differences between these and the "ideal" federation.

Carlo Gambuzzi spoke of the abolition of states, said Reclus, without noting that national borders were artificial lines established by force, war, and the "cunning" of kings. Federalism would be acceptable only if it represented an upward extension of administrative units into a federal republic; the people would have to decide with whom to federate and if and when to alter their alliances. Thus, the people of Alsace should have the right to decide whether to join the Germans, and the Basques should be left to establish their own relations. Just as national boundaries should be dependent on the will of the people, so should provincial boundaries be determined by the inhabitants. In France, Germany, and even Switzerland, existing provinces could be considered nothing more than the feudal possessions of dukes, counts, and barons—as relics of a bygone age.

Reclus attempted to show that the system of local units imposed from above was a tool of despotism, especially in France. There existed at every level representatives of the central government: at the level of the marshals (military divisions); prefects (departments); subprefects (*arrondissements*); mayors and local councillors (communes). These officials, among whom was the parish priest, were servile to their superiors and scornful of their subordinates—administrative techniques to enforce the will of the central authorities. At the bottom of the social ladder, of course, came the citizen. But Reclus was confident that the powerful apparatus of the centralised state could be broken, and that the "social Republic" could be realised. He was less precise on the question of what means the people would use to rid themselves of despotism. He was also vague about how long this process might take, although he saw as an integral part of this emancipation the raising of consciousness.

Reclus articulated the nature of his "social Republic." It would take the form of small groups or associations whose relationship to existing communes would depend on the people involved. While each association would be independent and self-administering, the people of one, acting out of a sense of brotherly love rather than competition, might well join the people of another to form a larger association, and these would vary in size. Any group could decide whether to associate with another and whether to withdraw. The association would change according to need, and it would assume different forms according to the kind of work to be undertaken—be it the construction of a city neighbourhood or a railroad. Workers unhappy living and working in one area would be free to move. Work, as an enriching experience, would occupy a central position. Idlers and parasites, while tolerated, would be made to feel uncomfortable.

Reclus also pointed out the need to emphasise "the autonomy of productive associations and groups formed by these associations." These words were suggested as an amendment to the resolution, which read "the autonomy of the communes and the provinces," a wording proposed by Bakunin and supported by Reclus himself a year earlier.[74] Reclus likely felt that "communes and provinces" implied the retention of existing boundaries and that "productive associations" would avoid giving this impression. In later years he rejected this concept as also inadequate (all people in a community are not equally productive) and returned to the idea of the commune as the basic social unit—a community of people that might only incidentally coincide with an existing administrative commune.

These ideas on decentralisation were not new, and one suspects that Bakunin played an important part in their advocacy by Reclus.[75] A detailed discussion on the question cannot be found in Reclus's later writing, although such ideas would crop up from time to time and were even given some prominence in the theories of his friend Peter Kropotkin. The disappearance of these concerns from Reclus's writing very likely indicates a reconsideration of the value of such "blueprints." It will become clear in later chapters that his determination to be "scientific" led him to emphasise the *fight* for a socialist society and to avoid detailed discussion on the society itself.

Bakunin and Reclus had wanted to push the League of Peace and Freedom in a radical direction, but their failure to enlist the support of the IWMA undermined such hopes, and they were unable to convince fellow members to endorse an advanced social programme. Along with friends like Aristide Rey, Giuseppe Fanelli, and Albert Richard, they signed a statement declaring their secession from the League.[76] The question then faced by this group of less than twenty was what to do next. Bakunin wished to take his "brothers" directly into the IWMA, but it was decided to found an "open" international organisation.[77]

Reclus favoured the decision, but it is not certain that he attended meetings in Geneva to discuss the founding of yet another organisation, the International Alliance of Socialist Democracy.[78] This group sought the IWMA's permission to affiliate as a distinct international body, and after being refused admission on this basis on 22 December 1868[79] dissolved itself as an international organisation and advised its sections to join those of the IWMA. As a "non-international" association, the Alliance applied for admission to the IWMA, and, as requested by the General Council, revised a phrase in its statutes to read "abolition" rather than "equalisation... of classes." The section of the Alliance at Geneva was finally accepted by the General Council as a section of the IWMA on 28 July 1869.[80]

Both Reclus brothers are usually linked to Bakunin's Alliance of Socialist Democracy.[81] Marx was convinced they were members of a secret alliance that, it was claimed, Bakunin continued to lead within the IWMA.[82] Regardless of membership in any of Bakunin's societies, secret or otherwise, from 1869 to 1872 Elisée had little contact with Bakunin, and Elie even less. In fact, in late 1868 there developed a strain in relations between the brothers and Bakunin. The story, insofar as it can be reconstructed, directly concerns only Elie, but both were grouped together in Bakunin's estimation and each was considered guilty of the same offence—namely, courting the bourgeoisie. The first indication of a difference of opinion can be traced to autumn 1868.

On 22 September that year, while the Congress of the League of Peace and Freedom was in session, a telegram arrived with news of the overthrow of Queen Isabella and revolution in Spain. There was talk in Bakunin's circle of joining the insurgents.[83] Fanelli, an Italian engineer, was entrusted with the mission of spreading Bakunin's ideas in Spain. It has been claimed that Elisée went to Spain under Bakunin's orders but that he was soon recalled.[84] Another account has it that he was unable to make the trip—for unspecified reasons—and that he sent Elie instead.[85] Bakunin asked Elisée to go, but, in the latter's words, the request was met with "a very categorical no."[86]

Elie eventually went to Spain, but paid little attention to Bakunin's "orders"[87]; instead, he met with Spanish republicans, in particular Fernando Garrido, a leading Fourierist and the person credited with introducing cooperatives into Spain. Disregarding the wishes of Fanelli, who considered him morally obliged "as a member of the Brotherhood" to help evangelise Spain, Elie and Garrido made a political tour of the country. Elie Reclus would tell Max Nettlau years later that he deeply resented Fanelli's interference in his affairs and the Italian's "Machiavellianism."[88]

Bakunin's disappointment with Elie's "non-revolutionary" activity in Spain was exacerbated in early 1869. In the first issue of the Mannheim newspaper *La Fraternité*, Elie was listed as one of its collaborators. In the 20 February issue of the Swiss revolutionary paper *L'Egalité*, Bakunin called the Mannheim paper "a new organ of bourgeois socialism." Only too aware of what Elie was up to in Spain, Bakunin publicly expressed astonishment at his decision to collaborate with La Rigaudière, organiser of *La Fraternité*.[89] Elisée came to his brother's defence with a letter to *L'Egalité* expressing resentment at the "mendacious assertion" in *La Fraternité*. He and Elie, he claimed, had refused an invitation

to contribute to the newspaper.[90] In March, in another letter to
L'Egalité, he took back the words "mendacious assertion" and
admitted that Elie's reply to La Rigaudière had been "evasive and
dilatory."[91]

Elisée was now suffering personal pain. His third child, Anna,
died shortly after birth, and his wife took ill and died of consumption
on 22 February. His two daughters stayed for a time with relatives;
Jeannie was cared for by Elisée's sister Marie in Nîmes and Magali
by her grandparents in Orthez.[92]

While Elisée was involved with family matters, Bakunin witnessed yet another example of Elie's "bourgeois socialist" leanings.
Elie was one of four signatories of a declaration in support of
Madame Champseix, the novelist who wrote under the name André-
Léo, shortly after her letter appeared in *L'Egalité*[93] suggesting a
rapprochement of the various democratic parties, views which were
denounced in the same issue of the paper. A further letter from
Champseix defending her point of view, and a letter of support,
were refused publication, in a note almost certainly written by
Bakunin, because of "lack of space."[94] The two letters, it was
claimed, were

> inspired by the same spirit of conciliation *vis-à-vis* that good
> bourgeois class which devours us so calmly every day, as if it
> were the most natural and legitimate thing in the world, and
> [by the same spirit] of protest against the tendencies of our
> paper, because, having raised the flag of the true politics of
> the proletariat, it does not wish to make any deals.[95]

Elie's letter has not survived, and so it is impossible to establish
the nature of his support for Champseix. He likely insisted on her
right to express her views. Bakunin was in no mood for such open-
mindedness, however, and condemned both brothers. He wrote
in 1871 that the Reclus and Champseix believed, at least in 1869,
"in the possibility of conciliating the interests of the bourgeoisie
with that of the legitimate revindications of the proletariat. They
also believed, like Mazzini, that the proletariat ought to join hands
with the radical bourgeoisie."[96]

Elisée and Elie may have been "bourgeois" to Bakunin, but
their positions were by no means identical, as he would have it.
They disagreed especially over Spanish events in 1868. Elie was
anxious to work for the republican cause, while Elisée was convinced that the whole project was a waste of time. There was
plenty to do in Paris, he said, in preparation for the coming revolution in central Europe.[97] Elie went to Spain regardless, and
Elisée did nothing to encourage him in his "compromising" with
moderates. The republicans might as well at least have "the merit

of having been honest in battle," he declared, since they had no chance of success.[98]

Elisée and Bakunin also clearly differed on the Spanish question. There were more than personal considerations behind Elisée's refusal to make the trip, as his attempt to discourage Elie from going clearly indicates. Criticism of Bakunin is barely concealed in his statement that revolutionaries were too eager to believe the great day had arrived, leading to mistakes which slowed down the revolutionary process.[99] Priority, he maintained, should be given to less spectacular activities in the advanced European countries. It may have been his opposition to Bakunin's plans for Spain that led to Elisée's detachment from the Alliance of Socialist Democracy formed after the Berne Congress of the League of Peace and Freedom.

Elisée's position *vis-à-vis* both Bakunin and Elie was based on the calculation that great dividends could be expected if they worked within centres of traditional revolutionary agitation. An examination of his correspondence from the late 1860s reveals that as the "liberal" Empire progressed in France he lived in anticipation of ever more wide-ranging political change. "You are not unaware of how serious the circumstances are and of the political turmoil in which we are living," he wrote to Elie in the autumn of 1867. "The Empire is committing suicide, and Garibaldi is perhaps at Rome. We must prepare for great things."[100] Suicide was being committed through the liberal reforms, in the 1860s, that made the regime vulnerable to its republican critics. Elisée did not believe that a liberal Empire could survive for long, and he became more certain of it as the restrictions on free speech were lifted and there opened up opportunities for the spread of revolutionary propaganda. A law passed in 1868 brought an end to tight administrative control of the press, and as a result France was flooded with journals opposing the regime, among them Henri Rochefort's *La Lanterne*.

Reclus probably saw a gain for workers in such legislation as that abolishing the article of the Civil Code by which a master's word was final in a wage dispute. He eagerly attended the meetings held following passage of the May 1868 Freedom of Assembly law. In "coarse words spoken by men without education, incorrect language, foolish remarks, passionate cries," he found confirmation of his youthful belief in the elemental power of the masses. "Pressed one against the other, breathing an atmosphere of sweat and dust, they are there for hours in the hope of hearing a word of justice and liberty, small compensation for the miseries of each day."[101] With great satisfaction he saw that most speakers respected their audience and that some of them earnestly spoke from their hearts or sought to back up arguments with "solid discussion of facts."

Although Reclus by no means rejected Bakunin, and actually joined the International Brotherhood, he came to question the usefulness of secret societies in working for social revolution. While they might have once had certain advantages, their hierarchical structures and removal from the people were serious weaknesses in an age of "free speech." It was probably this view that led him to support the foundation of an "open" alliance rather than what would have amounted to the continued existence of the (secret) Brotherhood inside the IWMA. He emphasised later that socialist theories must be developed in the context of public discussion. "To be sure, if our doctrine is... a secret doctrine, it will be stillborn."[102] In the relaxed political climate of the 1860s, Reclus chose to avoid clandestine activities against the Empire and to make use of the existing social-economic and political structures. While he anticipated the end of Napoleon's rule, he viewed the "liberal" Empire as an improvement over what had gone before.

His views in this period are summarised in a letter to his brother-in-law, Pierre Faure.[103] It contains traces of ideas expressed earlier, but represents a fairly clear statement of the theory of evolution and revolution that he would formulate in the late 1870s and would revise thereafter until it appeared in expanded form in 1898.[104] According to this theory, the social revolution would be achieved through an interrelated process of evolution and revolution rather than through a single revolution. Evolution consisted in countless small revolutions; a great outburst, on the other hand, or a "revolution," represented a speeding up of the process of evolution and was thus a form of accelerated progress. By the late 1860s Reclus was looking forward to the next great revolution which would aim "to ensure equality, to suppress the privilege of material life and intellectual life... to end the terrible antagonism between employers and wage-earners, between the bourgeoisie, the workers, and the peasants."[105] He was under no illusion, however, that this revolution would bring equality overnight. "Alas, no, but in working for our children, we take yet another step forward... perhaps in blood."[106]

Reclus was not willing, in 1869, to sit back and wait for a revolution (much less *the* revolution), which, in any case, he did not believe would be the final answer. In sharp contrast to his later negative attitude towards the vote,[107] he wrote to Faure that he wished to undermine the government by supporting the "most revolutionary" candidate in the May-June 1869 elections. In the first round he supported an old Fourierist, Cantagrel, in the second the republican Henri Rochefort, who ran against the moderate Jules Favre. Reclus insisted that even the victory of Thiers, Garnier-Pagés, and Favre (moderate liberals) could not suppress the thirty thousand "revolutionary" votes for opposition candidates. "Those who have the most resolution, the most love of progress

69

and justice, those whom the government detests the most, those are the zealots who have voted for Rochefort, for Raspail, for Alton-Shée."[108] The tactic of supporting the most revolutionary candidates was called "negative voting," and Reclus was for a short time much attracted to it. This "party-political" activity could still be reconciled with his revolutionary beliefs. As Reclus put it:

> If I write my little note on Negative Voting he [Faure] will believe that I am following his advice and letting myself be overtaken by the fever of ambition; but he will be a little deceived in thinking that I speak of things which do not comply with revolutionary fervour.[109]

Reclus came to the conclusion that revolutionary agitation could be effective if practised within the rules of the existing order and almost certainly would bear more fruit than a direct assault, Bakunin's suggestions to the contrary. The task which loomed large was hastening the destruction of the Empire, and this was already well under way. In the long term his fervent hope was for a social revolution; in the meantime he struggled in his fashion for a regime in which there would be more channels to work for greater gains. He was working for the establishment of a Republic—albeit for the moment a "bourgeois" Republic—which would represent a step in the direction of the universal social Republic.

Even before the cataclysm that befell Europe with the outbreak of the Franco-Prussian War of 1870, Reclus considered himself a revolutionary socialist; and although there is no reason to believe he had strayed from his conviction that anarchy was the socialist goal, he had not yet become an anarchist in the sense of rejecting all practices associated with parliamentary structures. After the Commune he became far more selective in his choice of political agitation.

Four
Republican Battles

The Franco-Prussian war which erupted in July 1870 found Reclus in a quandary. His activities during the war, as well as in the early days of the Commune, are difficult to explain. He had long since rejected all boundaries between nations. However, the events of 1870-71 seemed to sweep him away and he took up arms in defence of his native land. By January 1871 he was a passionate advocate of "a fight to the death," or what the French called *la guerre à outrance*. He not only cooperated with bourgeois republicans; he was antagonistic toward revolutionary agitators such as Auguste Blanqui and Charles Delescluze, and at one point said flatly that he would support even Adolphe Thiers, the proven "enemy" of the working class. In the February 1871 elections he even offered himself as a candidate.

One writer believed that Reclus continued to be "a slave of national vanity for a long time."[1] However, as plausible as such a contention might seem at first glance, it can be shown that during the Franco-Prussian War, Reclus saw himself as working to consolidate the newly established Third Republic and thereby to create an atmosphere which would ultimately help the development of a universal social Republic. His conduct during the Commune was based on the same principle.

Napoleon III's *coup d'état* had erected an insurmountable barrier between himself and the republican tradition, and regardless of subsequent reforms most republicans were still irreconciled to his "liberal" Empire. Reclus shared that view. Napoleon's democratic reforms were seen as a tactic to stave off revolution rather than the product of any real sympathy for democracy. In 1868 the new Press and Freedom of Assembly laws served to unleash the flow of republican hatred for the Empire.

Napoleon's hand was forced in 1869 when the republicans, who had made gains with every election, captured Paris and most of the larger cities. The January 1870 decree which appointed the new ministry of the former anti-Bonapartist Emile Ollivier was followed by a new constitution, which established a degree of cabinet responsibility to parliament. These concessions to democracy were fairly successful in helping Napoleon maintain his position, even if the regime continually modified them. The May plebiscite showed overwhelming public support for the Empire, and, despite opposition in the towns, it was regarded by many republicans and monarchists as a triumph for Napoleon. Reclus later contended that the Empire had been cornered into a truce with democracy and that it viewed the war with Prussia as an opportunity to undo the recently enacted liberal reform.[2]

Reclus's initial reaction to the outbreak of hostilities in early July 1870 and the official declaration of war by Napoleon on 19 July is not known. If anything, the war came as a surprise to Elisée. While Bismarck and Napoleon conducted their dangerous but secret diplomatic games, he was in the midst of affairs of the heart. In the spring of 1870 he was renewing his friendship with Fanny L'Herminez whom he had met many years before and who was at that time a tutor in London. On 26 June he was at Vascoeuil, the country estate of his brother-in-law Alfred Dumesnil in eastern Normandy, where he and Fanny pronounced their "marriage" before family and friends, without religious or civil ceremony. Apparently they returned to Paris soon after, and when war broke out Fanny and the children left for Sainte-Foy.[3]

There is evidence that Reclus was in Paris on 4 September[4] for the proclamation of the Third Republic; in any event, he was there shortly after and remained for the duration of the siege which followed. As a resident of the fifth arrondissement, he enrolled in the 119th Battalion of the National Guard and was assigned to guard duty around the Paris fortifications.[5] While he volunteered for active duty in late October[6] and in early November came before the recruiting board,[7] there is no evidence that he took part in the fighting.[8] Soon after the launching of the balloon post on 26 September, Reclus enlisted in the company of balloonists led by the photographer Félix Nadar, but while he underwent some training, he did not leave Paris via this early air transport.[9]

Until early February 1871, Reclus apparently agreed with the position of certain groups within the Paris IWMA. Although he had probably joined the IWMA in 1865, he had not been active in the Paris section, partly because of differences of opinion with Tolain, who had control of the section until 1868,[10] and partly because personal affairs and geographical pursuits (he was becoming a geographer of some renown) kept him away from Paris for long periods during 1869 and the first half of 1870. After September 1870, however, residence in Paris brought him into closer contact with the Internationalists there.

As the siege drew on, many Internationalists came to associate with the Batignolles section of the Paris IWMA, which was largely under the influence of Benoît Malon, deputy mayor of the seventeenth arrondissement.[11] Reclus was a close friend of Malon, and he was probably a member of the Batignolles section.[12] The Paris IWMA helped set up the Vigilance Committees of the twenty *arrondissements* in early September, but largely abandoned them and started on a period of "reconstruction" of the sections in November. Fragmentary evidence suggests that the Paris IWMA now split into two groups: those who continued to support the Vigilance Committees and to follow the "old policy," and the majority—including Varlin, Malon, Léo Frankel, and Reclus—who opted for the "new policy." From early January 1871, there were apparently two rival central councils, with the majority belonging to what it naturally enough termed the "real" one.[13]

Reclus's view of the proclamation of the Republic was not unlike that of those people in the Paris IWMA who, in a note to the German workingmen drawn up on the night of 4-5 September, suggested that war against Napoleon had become an assault on the French people and the Republic.[14] In that the Prussians were enemies of the French Republic (and not only of France), Reclus felt compelled to fight them. It was the "final irony," he declared, that the Prussians and Bonaparte, both enemies of the Republic, would impose war and peace on it.[15] From the outset he saw little hope of victory[16]; he took up arms as a gesture of support for the infant Republic. But what was the nature of this Republic and what could be achieved by supporting it?

Reclus theorised that the revolutionary struggle of 1870-71 was a new phase of the conflicts raised in 1789. He complained that the revolutionary journals had not adjusted theory to the new practice, that the old vocabulary was still being used as if the situation had not changed.[17] He saw the French workers as more sophisticated and far shrewder than those of 1848. If they secured

73

a position in the Republic, they would have the freedom to make even greater advances. The new Republic was no more than a "suspension of arms between the parties"; it had been proclaimed "the means of supreme salvation"—"through the instinct of preservation." Under the circumstances, revolutionaries would gain more by playing along with the old parties than by insisting on the immediate establishment of a just society.

> Orleanists, legitimists, simply patriotic bourgeois have said to us: dream now, guide us, triumph for us, and we shall see what happens! Let us accept the dream, and if we carry out our mandate, if we save France, as we are asked to do, then the Republic will be secured and we shall have the pleasure of beginning for our children an era of progress, justice, and well-being.[18]

It followed that Reclus dismissed accusations that he was collaborating with the bourgeoisie. The path he advocated was risky, but he saw no contradiction between an unswerving loyalty to the revolutionary cause and support for the Republic in its moment of birth and crisis. He wrote to his brother-in-law:

> Thus, Faure, my friend, I who am more revolutionary than you, I who am a frightful communist and an infamous atheist, I do not fear the bourgeois element in the economy: I would even accept Thiers... However, do not get the idea that I do not intend to keep up my propaganda for the social Revolution continuously and forever.[19]

Reclus had no intention of undermining the existing Republic and earnestly hoped it could be consolidated.[20] While Thiers had accepted no office in the new Republic, he had acquiesced in its existence. In Marx's "Eighteenth Brumaire"[21] Reclus read that in the Second Republic "Thiers had professed to Louis-Philippe's family that 'it was... wholly in accord with the tradition of their forefathers to recognise the republic for the moment and wait until events permitted the conversion of the presidential chair into a throne'."[22] There seemed every reason to believe (as later events showed) that Thiers could be persuaded to tolerate the Republic. Reclus was aware that a Republic headed by Thiers would be a very different affair than the social Republic, but he was convinced that it would be more acceptable than the Empire or a Restoration under either Orleanists or Legitimists and would lead to even better things in the future.

Determination to consolidate the republican form of government was the overriding consideration governing Reclus's acts during the siege and makes sense of several curious episodes—for example, his reaction to the 31 October uprising by those in favour of *la guerre à outrance.* The uprising was provoked by news of the fall of Metz, the loss of Le Bourget, and popular consternation at the idea of peace negotiations with the Prussians. For its part, the IWMA refused to sanction the planned demonstration and ruled that Internationalists who participated would be acting as individuals,[23] not as members of the association.

Reclus agreed with this view—though not necessarily for the same reasons—and divorced himself from Pierre Flourens, Blanqui, and Delescluze, all of whom clung to the hope of military victory. A letter dated 6 November[24] reveals satisfaction with government victory in the plebiscite three days before and the municipal elections which followed, as well as greater confidence than ever in "the final upholding of the Republic." He hoped that the Republic would make peace, for only thus would it ensure its existence. It would ultimately mean very little even if France lost Alsace and Lorraine, he felt, for if the Republic endured, Germany herself, along with those provinces, would eventually enter "the confederation of free peoples." Nationalist pride may have been implicit in Elisée's initial opposition to peace imposed by Prussia. This sentiment passed, however—although nationalism of sorts persisted in his obsession with the idea that the existence of the French Republic was crucial to the establishment of a universal Republic.[25]

Reclus's political position in early 1871 can be deduced in part from a review of *La République des travailleurs*, the paper launched by the Batignolles section of the Paris IWMA and published six times in January and February.[26] A programme in the first issue was signed by several people, including Elisée and Elie, Malon, and André-Léo (the pseudonym of Madame Champseix). One of its unique features was an "anti-programmatic" tone. It did not offer a neat formula for revolution. On the contrary, it said that strategies would emerge in the course of struggle when theory and practice would be united.

> It is in attaching ourselves to revolutionary principles, in studying them profoundly, in constantly returning to them, in always applying them to real life, in pointing out every violation of these principles in political and social deeds, it is by this constant elaboration, by this reciprocal penetration of action and idea, that we shall arrive at unity, our only force and one which would render us invincible if we knew how to acquire it.

The struggle itself would determine the course of the revolution, provided there was sufficient dedication in the ranks, a will to win, and a desire to think through the theoretical implications of action. The precondition for the establishment of the "social"

Republic was the defence and consolidation of the already existing "political" Republic.

While the programme did not elaborate a precise definition of "worker," the term was used synonymously with "people" and the "disinherited." Workers had a special role to play in the struggle, both in France itself and against Prussia. They would be the vanguard of a two-pronged struggle and the mainstay of the existing "Republic of liberty." Having consolidated their position, they would play a major role in founding the "Republic of equality." The programme was an appeal to the Parisian people "to work, to fight, to battle! with all your strength, with your whole heart, with your whole mind! because life or death, rebirth or decomposition are at the end of this trial."

From early January, therefore, Reclus moved steadily towards accepting *la guerre à outrance*. The "Bulletin" section of the first issue of *La République des travailleurs*, which he wrote in early January, provides an even clearer account of his position. "We would like to speak of work, peace, liberty, justice," he began, "but the war, the atrocious war, is there, with its hideous continuation of hatred, massacre, destruction, infamy of every kind." Most German soldiers, he believed, wanted peace, and thousands of them were aware of their complicity in the "crime" of attacking the French Republic, but they were slaves of Bismarck and William, and were enemies of the republican cause. Just as the German soldiers were at fault in acquiescing to their masters instead of resisting them, said Reclus, so the people of Paris were wrong to entrust their fate to General Trochu and Jules Favre, as if these men were infallible. Trochu was no more capable of saving them than Napoleon had been; nor would a Flourens or Blanqui dictatorship be any more effective. Everything accomplished so far (since early September 1870) was a result of "public opinion alone"—the fortifications, requisitions, military engagements.

According to Reclus, such pressure from below must enter the departments of government and inspire "magnanimous resolutions, worthy of a people that claims to fight not only for the salvation of a city, but for that of the universal Republic." The victory of Paris would also be "the salvation of the world," and the people of Paris were enjoined to rise to the great task prepared by destiny. They were fighting not only for the French Republic, Reclus reminded them, but also for the future German Republic.

In the Reichstag of Berlin, the deputy Liebknecht has protested against the empire of William and his infamous victories. In the Parliament of Stuttgart, seven deputies, out of about a hundred, did not want their names to appear on the list of imperial lackeys. In the streets of Dresden, workers have torn up the bulletins announcing Prussian victories, knowing that

76

every defeat of the French Republic is a disaster for the future German Republic.

An examination of his newspaper writing in early January suggests that although Reclus may have doubted military victory, he felt there was no choice but to urge his countrymen to heroism in the name of the Republic.[27] As the Germans bombarded Paris, he pointed to the sympathy being extended to its beleaguered inhabitants by the outside world and to the courage of the provincial armies. By late January he was more determined than ever to pursue *la guerre à outrance*, even though the bombardment, the failure of the 22 January uprising, and the subsequent defeat of the provincial armies made military victory much more remote. The armistice signed by Favre on 28 January was proof that the Prussians would not, after all, negotiate with the French Republic, for it allowed three weeks for a newly elected National Assembly to meet at Bordeaux and assume responsibility for the terms of peace.

In preparation for the elections of 8 February, the Batignolles section met, the first of the month, with three other sections of the Paris IWMA, Ternes, Grenelle, and Vaugirard, and decided on a list "of amalgamation and conciliation" with the republican bourgeoisie.[28] Two days later there appeared a list entitled "Four Committees" comprising the IWMA and three radical groups, the Alliance républicaine, the Défenseurs de la République, and the Union républicaine.[29] The rival federal councils of the Paris IWMA held a joint meeting, the following day, to seek agreement on a list of "pure revolutionaries" to be supported "without compromise with the bourgeoisie,"[30] and shortly thereafter "rectified" the IWMA's position concerning the four committees.[31]

Reclus never felt bound by party discipline, and it is unlikely that the agreements reached by the IWMA would have led him to reverse his decision to support the republicans. He chose to abide by the principles underlying the agreements between the four committees, and on 3 February, before the proposed meeting of the IWMA, left Paris for the Lower Pyrenees where he hoped to stand as republican candidate—"knowing that the position of deputy is morally the most perilous."[32] His name appeared on at least two radical republican lists, those of the Comité républicain radical du XIe arrondissement[33] and the Liste des candidats proposés par les Comités républicains radicaux de la Rive gauche et de la Rive droite.[34]

In contrast to his hostile reaction to the groups that engineered the 31 October uprising, in February 1871 Reclus did not hesitate to take up the republican stand for *la guerre à outrance*, since he became convinced that the defeat of the republicans in the 8 February elections would mean the end of the Republic. He saw the elections as a plebiscite in favour of peace or war, and to side with the "honourable" peace faction was simply to support the anti-republicans, Legitimists, Orleanists, and the few Bonapartists who remained. "Elisée thought," wrote Elie shortly afterwards, "that the triumph of Thiers and the assembly would be the triumph of reaction and sooner or later the reversal of the Republic."[35] The preservation of the Republic was Elisée's main concern at the time of the elections and during the early days of the Commune.

Although the letters in which he offered himself for election in the Lower Pyrenees arrived after the candidates had been chosen, a short stay convinced Reclus that "these gentlemen" would not have preferred his *guerre à outrance*, that "a so-called ʻhonourableʼ peace" would have been much more to their taste."[36] (In fact, the Lower Pyrenees voted in a fairly moderate republican fashion.) Travelling to Paris via Sainte-Foy where his wife was living, Reclus was disappointed in the political attitudes of the French peasants, especially the richer peasants who had enthusiastically voted for the Legitimist-Orleanist-Bonapartist list,[37] but also the mass of peasants who seemed annoyed that the Republic had not immediately disappeared with the electoral results.[38] The new National Assembly would be dominated by monarchists. Under the circumstances, it was important, he wrote Elie, to organise a "Defenders of the Republic" committee in every town, with a representative in every village.

Before returning to Paris, he stayed in the area around Sainte-Foy and spoke for "the cause of the Republic," although he was reluctant to follow his brother Paul's advice to begin a campaign in Orthez for the next elections to the National Assembly:

> I replied that when I thought of standing as a candidate, I reflected on the terrifying responsibility which deputies have to assume. But I do not know what the task of the future Chamber will be, and therefore I cannot consider keeping my candidacy open on a permanent basis. I take back my liberty completely.[39]

An example of his patriotism appears in a letter of this period to Félix Nadar: "Since all is lost, let us begin life with a fresh start; let us act as if, waking up from a sleep of a hundred thousand years, we perceive that there is everything to win: fatherland, liberty, dignity, honour."[40] Reclus and many other republicans convinced themselves that their patriotism carried revolutionary implications; "fatherland, liberty, dignity, honour" were identified with the French Republic, which after the February elections was in grave danger of assault from the monarchist Assembly. He was determined to stay on: "If exile or misery do not force me to leave France, I shall remain: here is my battlefield."

78

Before the outbreak of hostilities in 1870 Reclus believed that there could be genuine progress towards revolution by working within a "liberal" order. It was essential, he reasoned, to protect civil liberties even while exploiting them on behalf of the revolutionary cause. His every move during the siege of Paris was motivated by a determination to consolidate the new Republic and to contribute to a style of politics in which there would be opportunities to work for the social Republic of the future. There is no indication that he supported any French military undertaking directed at the German armies until after the proclamation of the Republic in September. From then on, he maintained that while the Parisians were struggling to defend the French Republic, they were also fighting on behalf of the future German Republic.

That his political goal was the defence of the Republic, and not simply France and French soil, is borne out by his favourable reaction in the autumn of 1870 to the possibility that Bismarck might negotiate with the infant Republic, and thereby give it recognition. In January 1871, as French military victory appeared less and less likely, Reclus became more emphatic that republicans make greater sacrifices to avert military defeat, which, he believed, would spell the end of the Republic. At the end of January he came out decisively in support of the republican stand for *la guerre à outrance*, for he had become convinced that defeat in the February elections would amount to the Republic's death warrant.

At some point Reclus decided to return to Paris.[41] He may have been present for the demonstrations of the National Guard which began around the Place de la Bastille on 24 February and continued for two days when the guns earlier placed in various artillery parks were taken to Montmartre[42] for fear that they would fall into Prussian hands when they entered Paris in Triumphal Procession on 1 March. In any event, the reluctance of the National Guard to disarm on government orders led to bloodshed and the proclamation of the Commune on 18 March.

After Thiers ordered the transfer of government agencies from Paris to Versailles on 18 March, the "moderate" Central Committee of the National Guard emerged as the only political force left in Paris. Unwilling to act without some kind of popular sanction, it restricted its activities to carrying out essential services and arranged for elections to take place on 22 March. Three days before, Thiers instructed the mayors of the twenty *arrondissements*, whose political views varied according to district represented, to mediate with the "insurgents."

Under the lead of the radical mayor of Montmartre, Deputy Georges Clemenceau, a series of meetings took place between the Central Committee and the mayors and deputies of Paris. On 20 March the Central Committee agreed to hand city hall over to the mayors and to postpone municipal elections until the Assembly in Versailles, through the intercession of the mayors, had voted a municipal law for Paris. However, the following day the Central Committee, under pressure from the Vigilance Committees of the twenty *arrondissements*, informed Clemenceau that it had decided not to hand over city hall, although it would postpone the elections.

Thiers reacted by preparing the reorganisation of military forces to meet the challenge from Paris, and the Central Committee, in turn, did its utmost to destroy the last vestiges of his support. The municipal buildings of the conservative Tirard, and even those of Clemenceau, were occupied.

There was also mounting unrest among the moderate elements of Paris, who were less concerned about revolution than about the decisions of Versailles regarding the lifting of the moratorium on rents and promissory notes, decisions which meant economic ruin for many in the lower middle class. This opposition to more radical elements led to demonstrations by the "Friends of Order" on 21 March and the massacre in (ironically) the rue de la Paix the following day. Impatient at the lack of response from Versailles for municipal elections in Paris and encouraged by the sympathetic uprisings in centres such as Saint-Etienne, Le Creusot, Marseilles, Lyons, and Toulouse, the Central Committee went ahead with the postponed elections anyway.

The first days of the Commune left the IWMA bewildered and indecisive about the position which it should take *vis-à-vis* the proposed municipal elections. At a general meeting of the Paris IWMA on 23 March Léo Frankel said that the municipal council would represent nothing more than a "supervisory council" in an association, and the decision was taken, albeit reluctantly by some, to support the Central Committee of the National Guard and to call for municipal elections. An IWMA manifesto issued the following day called for a "communal revolution" which would ensure the "independence" and "autonomy" of the Commune.[43]

Such an optimistic assessment of the Commune elections was not to be found in the statement of 25 March signed by Elisée Reclus, his brothers Elie and Paul, and F.D. Leblanc.[44] It echoed the statement issued the same day by the deputies and mayors and the Central Committee[45] in its insistence on avoiding bloodshed and consolidating republican government as the main aims of the elections to be held the next day. However, the Reclus brothers also charged the mayors and the Central Committee with responsibility for the confusion that could lead to civil war. Parisians were beseeched to end the struggle between their representatives and to render a verdict at the polls. The deputies and mayors and the Central Committee had already compromised the Republic through their "clumsiness" and did not have the right to expose it to a "street battle." They quibbled about legal questions which had no place in a "full revolution," said the brothers. These "authorities" were an obstacle to revolutionary change, although to challenge them directly would be to jeopardise the Republic's chances of survival.

The conciliatory tone of this statement indicates that Reclus had generally not changed his views since the first siege. Throughout the entire period his aim was preservation of the Republic, and he was ready to advocate conciliation to achieve that end. He even associated with the republican Groupe de la conciliation par l'action, which chose him as a candidate for the sixth arrondissement in the by-elections to the Commune on 16 April (although he would then be in prison).[46] The day after the earlier Commune elections, Reclus had commented briefly in a letter to his brother-in-law Alfred Dumesnil that he considered 18 March to be "the greatest date in the history of France since 10 August [1789]."[47] It saw both the triumph of the "Workers' Republic" and the inauguration of the "Communal Federation." He referred to the birth of the Commune as "a change of this scope" that "has been able to take place almost peacefully."[48] A week later Reclus expressed disillusionment with the behaviour of politicians, but he was not yet ready to abandon faith in the electoral process.

His experiences within the Commune were cut short when he was arrested on 4 April by the Versailles forces. With the cooperation of Bismarck, Thiers managed to muster more than sixty thousand troops at Versailles by early April. A reconnaissance on 30 March by the Marquis de Gallifet was followed by a strong attack on Courbevoie on 2 April which resulted in the seizure of the vital bridge at Neuilly. The following day units of the Paris National Guard set out to march on Versailles in three columns, Bergeret and Flourens heading on either side of Mont-Valérien towards the village of Rueil, Eudes advancing via Meudon and Chaville, and Duval, whose task was to secure the left flank by an attack on the Châtillon plateau.

Elisée and his brother Paul were among the men installed by Duval on the Châtillon plateau the night of 3 April.[49] In the early hours of the next morning, the Versailles troops counter-attacked, and Duval was forced to surrender. Elisée was among the prisoners who witnessed the brutal slaying of Duval and suffered the indignity of the march to Versailles and the trip to Brest.[50] Paul Reclus, who accompanied the battalion as a medical doctor, returned without news of his brother. With help from Edouard Charton,[51] as well as through the efforts of an American medical student, Mary Putnam, and very likely American Ambassador Washburne, the Reclus family learned of his whereabouts.[52]

Reclus was imprisoned at Fort de Quélern until late July or early August when he was transferred to Trébéron. At the end of October he was taken back to Versailles, this time to stand trial, and on 15 November was sentenced by the Seventh Council of War sitting at Saint-Germain-en-Laye to "simple deportation," a decision which destined him to a stay at New Caledonia. Reclus was found guilty of carrying and using arms in the "insurrectional movement of Paris," but not guilty of wearing a uniform in the movement, nor, significantly, of participating in "an attempt to destroy or to change the form of government."[53]

By 1871 Reclus had already become a well-known figure in international geography circles. In the late 1850s and 1860s he had published articles and reviews in several major journals, including the *Bulletin de la Société de géographie, Le Tour du monde,* and *La Revue des deux mondes.* He wrote some of the travel guides published as the *Guides Joanne* and collaborated on several others. His first important geographical work appeared as the two-volume *La Terre* in 1868-69. Probably his best known book of the day, *Histoire d'un ruisseau,* was also published in 1869. At the time of his imprisonment, *La Terre* was being translated into English.

The world of geography took notice of Reclus's plight, and French and English friends and scholars commenced petitioning for his release before the trial, but it was not until after his trial and conviction that agitation began in earnest. Henry Woodward, a member of the London Geological and Zoological Society and editor of the English translation of *La Terre,* sent a petition from London in late December.[54]

In the meantime, Reclus was moved to Mont-Valérien and on to the Maison de correction de Versailles. On 3 February 1872 the sentence was commuted to ten years in exile. He was transferred from Versailles to Paris and then taken to Pontarlier where he spent four days before being released on Swiss soil on 14 March 1872.[55]

The theme which runs through Reclus's prison letters is determination to act according to his conscience. A letter written in early January 1872 represents a kind of personal testament for the years 1870-72. It brings to mind the young student at Berlin and is indicative of the priest-like attitude which marked all his activities.

> I have certainly suffered very much since my imprisonment and earlier during the Franco-Prussian War and the Commune, but... my great consolation has been to be able to act according to my conscience. More than once I have had to question my sense of duty, but I have not hesitated to obey, at the risk of compromising life or liberty. For this today I have the satisfaction of having won the respect even of my political adversaries.[56]

Although there are occasional allusions to the uncertainty of his future, the letters abound in examples of his refusal to compromise in order to get a release. In the latter part of July 1871 Reclus received a letter from the secretary of the Geography Society of Paris requesting a statement or at least "a word of allegiance in a private letter" that could be used to get him Society support, but this request was flatly refused.[57] In October Reclus again showed stubbornness, as well as pride, when Pastor Berth, a friend of his father, suggested appealing to Casimir Périer: "Of course... What I want is to be free, as my comrades are, without condition, without a promise that could be offensive to my dignity." He wrote a declaration "weighing every word. I explained what are in my opinion the legal reasons which should ensure my liberty, but naturally I did not stoop to ask for it."[58]

Reclus was also determined to live as "normally" as possible even in prison, and doggedly continued his intellectual pursuits.[59] In early June 1871 he began work on *Sol et les Races*, which was probably incorporated into his later geographical work. He also began "a purely literary little work" which was very likely the beginning of *Histoire d'une montagne*. In July he corrected the proofs for the second volume of the abridged edition of *La Terre*. In reply to a letter that same month from the editor of *Le Tour du monde*, he submitted a plan for "a kind of geographical encyclopaedia, divided into instalments costing three or four sous each." In August there came favourable news from Emile Templier of Hachette, with whom there had been some disagreement. "If I stay in France—which is what I believe—I shall be able to continue my work, and perhaps undertake great things which are still only a dream,"[60] Reclus wrote to Alfred Dumesnil, referring to what would become his multi-volume *Nouvelle Géographie universelle*.

His continuing commitment to republicanism, his concern for the intellectual and moral welfare of the inmates, and his status in the scientific and literary world placed Reclus in an influential position among the prisoners, especially during the "free mutual instruction" sessions that were arranged at Quélern and probably at Trébéron. A prisoner at Quélern reported in April that Elisée Reclus

> is making a great contribution to making our sad stay more endurable with his daily discussions, as interesting as they are instructive, always stressing the idea of right and justice. He supports our republican faith, and several of us owe it to him that they will leave prison better than they were when they came.[61]

At Quélern Reclus had been in charge of the small prison library and spent his time giving English lessons and holding seminars.

He took lessons in Flemish from the Belgian socialist Victor Buurmans, a fellow prisoner.[62]

The authorities were rather embarrassed at having incarcerated such an eminent figure as Reclus and gave him every opportunity to express his "regrets." However, his influence among the other prisoners and his refusal to "compromise" intensified their resolve to deny pardon unless he professed his guilt.[63] A report of 16 January 1872 from the Ministry of Justice declared that Reclus's ideas made it impossible to commute his sentence, much less pardon him, unless he promised to stay away from political activity in future. The commander of the Seine-et-Oise subdivision said that there were no grounds for clemency, given the absence of repentance. "Under these conditions, his knowledge and his intelligence only render him more dangerous."[64]

But his iron will was counterbalanced by black moments. Reclus was often disappointed with the behaviour and attitudes of his fellow inmates,[65] and, like most prisoners, he occasionally became paranoid and depressed, as revealed by his relations with Jules Simon. In July 1871 Simon, who was on a routine visit to Brest prisons, asked to see Reclus and showed a concern for his welfare. Reclus refused to meet him and later claimed that because of this slight, Simon had him transferred from Quélern to Trébéron and ordered the authorities "to keep a sharp eye on my doings and to have me shut up in my room."

When he was treated kindly, he attributed his good fortune to the marine doctors and officers in charge (his brother Armand was a marine officer) who disobeyed Simon's orders.[66] Reclus had misjudged Simon, who had said that in spite of Reclus's attitudes he would provide him with some comfort,[67] and, according to the evidence, that is exactly what he did.[68]

Some idea of Reclus's state of mind can be gathered from the opening pages of *Histoire d'une montagne*, which were written in prison. Men whom he had called friends had turned against him, he claimed, when they saw his misfortune; human beings were motivated by self-interest and possessed by uncontrolled passions, which struck him as "ghastly." When questioned about these lines many years later, Reclus answered that at the time "I felt around me a thick, almost impenetrable wall of hate, the aversion of the entire world to the Commune and the Communards. Perhaps I braced myself and that movement suppressed my true nature."[69]

The prison experiences were deeply distressing. It pained Reclus to see the "weaknesses" of the many communards who were unable to achieve a level of dignity and resignation. His own reaction was one of surprising calm as he tried to keep up his friendships and carry on with his career. In spite of everything, he did not flinch from the decision to work for the overthrow of the social and political order. Working through the "bourgeois" Republic had ended in catastrophe, but revolutionaries would strike again. Reclus concluded that since parliamentary institutions were bound to fail, alternative methods of struggle must be found.

Five
Communard's Wrath

Disillusionment with parliamentary politics was evident among radical republicans in France as far back as the bloody repression of June 1848. However, despite the mistrust and even hostility directed at the National Assembly, many radicals continued to believe that a popularly elected body could help bring about social justice. Until 1870 the loosely organised International Working Men's Association was able to contain a whole range of conflicting opinions; the role of the state was not yet a crucial issue. It was in the mid-1870s that the question of the state came to a head and was "settled" with the adoption of a position that united anarchists in their isolation within the social-democratic movement.

Reclus's politics conform to this pattern. His correspondence reveals how eagerly he participated in the mid-nineteenth-century debates on the social question and how anxious he was to express his stand. While some early views suggest important aspects of his later anarchist theories, nothing in principle precluded at least temporary accommodation to the parliamentary system. In the period immediately preceding the débâcle of 1871, moreover, Reclus was convinced that reform was possible. There is no doubt that his experiences in 1870-71 constituted a decisive turning point. Though a self-professed revolutionary socialist until 1871, in the period after the Commune he became implacably opposed to all party-political activity and an anti-authoritarian in every respect.

It might be expected that as the years passed Reclus would comment profusely on the significance of the events of 1871. After all, he was a noted scholar and a highly regarded anarchist theorist, a participant in the Commune who suffered imprisonment and banishment. Yet he was extremely reluctant to make a statement. Although he was the "soul" of the Geneva-based *Le Travailleur* (1877-78),[1] the paper which did so much to create the "myth" of the Commune,[2] it carried nothing by Reclus on the subject. He mentioned in 1877 that he refused a request for an article on the Commune[3] because he was not qualified[4]; the following year he admitted that he was working on a piece entitled "Experiences of a Prisoner."[5]

But except for a few brief comments written near the end of his life, Reclus could not be coaxed, even by his friends and colleagues, to provide the analysis of the Commune it was in his power to write. In 1905 he said that he could not find the "personal impressions" which he once wrote and did not have time to compose another account.[6]

This silence on the Commune is so conspicuous that it invites speculation. Reclus pleaded ignorance. "I do not know the history of the Commune: I was so small an actor and spectator that that does not count. To improvise that which one does not know is a bad thing."[7] But this is hardly an explanation. He wrote prolifically and unhesitatingly on many subjects, and he was especially interested in examining contemporary politics. There had not been such an important event since the great French Revolution, as he himself claimed from the first days of the Commune, and, furthermore, many people spoke out who had been less involved than had Reclus. Reclus may have been reluctant merely to rhyme off his experiences as he remembered them for fear that he might call into question the myth of the Commune which took shape from the first day of the bloody repression. Since he could not or would not falsify, Reclus said nothing. We can, nevertheless, reconstruct his general critique.

One of the striking features of Reclus's political outlook after the Commune is the violent rejection of the Third Republic that he had initially struggled to defend. Simultaneously, there was an unmistakeable and passionate devotion to the memory of the Commune. The Third Republic's Assembly of "gunmen," he wrote shortly after arriving in Switzerland, was a hopeless mirage and ceased to exist for him: "...I dissolved it. It is in spite of us that it holds together."[8]

While his correspondence from 1872 to 1874 avoided contemporary politics (partly out of a fear that it might fall into the hands of the police), his attitude oscillated from repugnance to bitter curiosity. According to a letter written in October 1873, French politics had fallen upon "very sad days." "When the republicans lent their hands to the extermination of their own avant-garde, how could they have the naïveté to count on triumph?" he asked.[9] In persecuting the communards, the republicans were slitting their own throats; they were turning away from the hallowed goals of the Third Republic, as Reclus understood them in 1870-71. On 4 July 1874 he told a friend:

> Should the centre-left triumph, the words of Laboulaye will remain true: "We have all marched under the flag of the Republic against the external enemy; why not march under the same flag against the internal enemy?" The internal enemy—what is it, if not every man of justice and truth.[10]

The internal enemies of the Republic were the very people who had struggled to create it in 1870-71, those who had become the hated communards.

Nor did Reclus show much sympathy for moderate-left agitation in other spheres of political activity. The Labour Congress held in Rome in April 1872 was labelled a "congress of would-be workers," and two delegates who were expelled, one for his opinions on strikes, the other for his views on secular education, were lauded as "true workers."[11] A note to Elie on the Congress of the League of Peace and Freedom at Lugano in September 1872 shows the extent to which Elisée's political approach had changed from the Berne Congress of 1868 when he had been an enthusiastic participant.[12] Now he was merely an observer, and Elie was sent a cynical account of the "bourgeois" and "mediocre" congress. Something in the words of the Englishman Hodgson Pratt was found to deserve praise, though Elisée insisted that Pratt was unaware of the implications of his declaration: "...with bourgeois societies, one will never do anything; one must not only work for the workers, but also with them. Without their support, all work is stillborn."[13] Before the Commune Reclus thought "negative voting" could be a useful revolutionary tactic; afterwards there was no question of ever again participating in elections.[14] Henceforth the struggle for liberation would be carried out simultaneously against the social-economic order and the political system.

The Commune itself became a hallowed event. Reclus began his campaign to enshrine it his first day in Switzerland when he changed the "horror" felt by an old friend for the Commune into "respect."[15] His principles of brotherhood were certainly put to the test as he lived and worked in Switzerland. He remained faithful to the prison vow never to forget fellow communards; he worked among refugees in Switzerland, and, when possible, helped those elsewhere in the world.[16] Loyalty to the memory of the Commune led to uncharacteristic behaviour when Reclus fell out with his brother-in-law, the radical deputy Germain Casse. He told his unhappy sister Julie that since her husband "disowned the Commune after he had taken part in it, I shall never be able to feel friendship for him."[17]

After his amnesty on 3 March 1879 Reclus publicly reiterated his solidarity with those communards to whom the French government refused to grant freedom. The amnesty distinguished between a criminal element and the misled but guilty majority; it provided for the return from exile or release from prison of all but about a thousand communards. La Solidarité, the group of Commune refugees, held a meeting in Geneva later that month to examine the law, and signed a declaration protesting the attempt to divide them. Reclus wrote a letter to La Solidarité and requested that it be passed on to French newspapers.

> I would be a vile man if my first words were not ones of solidarity, respect, and love for those, worse stricken than me, who still inhabit the jails or the prison of New Caledonia... Their cause is always mine, their honour is mine, and every insult which is addressed to them hurts me most deeply.

La Solidarité's declaration and Reclus's letter appeared together in the form of a leaflet.[18]

His memory of the Commune was anything but uncritical, however. In a police report of December 1885 Reclus is reported to have cautioned anarchist friends that to jump into revolution would be to repeat the mistakes of the Commune, that such folly would set them back twenty years. When the next opportunity for revolution came along, he said, they would have to seize the Bank of France, the big rail companies, get the economy going immediately, and take up arms in defence of the revolution.[19]

It was not until nearly the turn of the century that Reclus spoke publicly about the Commune's "mistakes," and then only briefly.[20] Even so, it is clear that he saw it as anything but the grand affair it was supposed to have been, and he whittled away—with all due respect, to be sure—at the legend that had become an important part of leftist ideology. The Commune's military organisation, he said, had been as bad as that under the "lamentable" Trochu during the first siege: the public pronouncements as unclear, the disorder as great, the activity as ridiculous. While he believed that the "improvised ministers" had remained honest in their exercise of power, they had had neither the good sense nor the will to assess the situation correctly. They continued all the mistakes of earlier governments, said Reclus, maintaining bureaucratic structures while simply bringing in new faces, and were concerned daily with protecting the money despatched by the Bank of France to Versailles. The Commune elections voted in men who, seized by the "dizziness" of power and "stupid routine," dutifully followed the rules of traditional politics. They failed to comprehend the revolutionary movement which had brought them to power in the first place.

The only other statement of consequence was the short account of the Commune in *L'Homme et la Terre*, a six-volume work published posthumously by Elisée's nephew Paul.[21] Anyone with a notion of history, said Reclus here, could have no doubt as to the final outcome of the conflict. Everyone who acclaimed the Commune—the old campaigners of past revolutions as well as the "young enthusiasts infatuated with liberty"—knew they were doomed to defeat. Paris had no chance of winning as long as it was surrounded by German troops delighting in pillage, French troops aching to wreak vengeance on compatriots for the recent defeat at the hands of the Germans, and the masses eager to hit back at Paris for once.[22]

These words evoke the communard of 1871, even if the pitch was new. It would be an exaggeration, however, to suggest that the final outcome was expected by everyone who participated in the Commune. Any social movement not bent on suicide must contain some hope of success, even if it is merely a glimmer, and there surely was one this time.

Given the odds against them, stated Reclus in *L'Homme et la Terre*, the communards could not have been successful. Yet he was deeply disappointed at their record.[23] The principal factor in the Commune's failure was "precisely that of being a government and of substituting the force of circumstances for people."[24] He was probably also thinking of the Commune government when he wrote back in 1873 that the state had "interfered" with the natural evolution towards communal property.[25] The revolutionary potential of the people was stifled by the "natural" functioning of power and the "dizziness" of authority, both unavoidable accompaniments of all governments. He claimed in 1880 that the Paris Commune had been insurrectional below but governmental above.[26]

Reclus said that the very fact of being a government and exercising authority condemned the Commune to impotence, but also that the authorities should have taken the initiative and proceeded to systematically destroy all state institutions and suppress the obstacles preventing the spontaneous grouping of citizens. He was not unaware that a few of them saw their goal as such.[27]

Is it reasonable to expect an institution to do something of which it is inherently incapable? Was Reclus, toward the end of his life and after decades of anarchist theorising, expressing a lingering doubt about the function of government? A second point must be made. He suggested that Commune officials held revolutionary potential in check, or at least did not know how to use it. But he also said that the people did not want a social revolution. "If the citizens had been inspired by a common will for social change, they would have imposed it on their delegates, but they were preoccupied with defence: to fight well and die well."[28] In the final analysis, the people were responsible for the fate of the Commune. Otherwise they would not have reacted so naïvely and would have compelled the Commune government to fulfill its revolutionary aims.

While Reclus claimed that the state in all its forms was at fault, and he certainly witnessed the whole range of evils associated with it, he saw these commissions as less fundamental than the failure of the people to demand change. They could have "imposed" social change on the Commune delegates. In the first siege he had persuaded himself that he was part of a powerful movement for social justice, but he became increasingly disillusioned as the months passed. When he heard the news of Favre's 28 January armistice, he did not react, as many other revolutionaries did, by accusing the negotiators of treachery. Instead, he pointed to the people themselves; in the final analysis, they were responsible for the defeat.

> We are conquered, and conquered through our own fault! Since 4 September our cause has been just, but we are unworthy of it because we allowed force to surpass right. The resources at our disposal were immense, but so was our inertia, our cowardly routine, our blind confidence in certain persons. Our fate was in our own hands, and if we had really wished it, the Republic would have been triumphant. But, mealy-mouthed, we handed our future over to a little coterie of saviours, the sworn officials of the empire, and to the former aide-de-camp of Marshal Saint-Arnaud [Trouchu].[29]

The weakness of a people without resolution and naïve enough to trust their leaders became clearer to Reclus after the election of the monarchist Assembly in February 1871, and especially as he observed the Commune.

How Reclus chose to remember his initial response to the Commune can be gathered from an account written by Kropotkin in 1882.

> "I will never forget," said a friend [Reclus] to us, "those delightful moments of deliverance. I came down from my upper chamber

91

in the Latin Quarter to join that immense open-air club which filled the boulevards from one end of Paris to the other. Everyone talked about public affairs; all mere personal preoccupations were forgotten; no more thought of buying or selling; all felt ready, body and soul, to advance towards the future. Men of the middleclass even, carried away by the general enthusiasm, saw with joy a new world opened up. "If it is necessary to make social revolution," they said, "make it then. Put all things in common; we are ready for it." All the elements of the revolution were there, it was only necessary to set them to work. When I returned to my lodging at night I said to myself, How fine is humanity after all, but no one knew it; it has always been calumniated."[30]

This version of events deviates substantially from what Reclus wrote in the days of the Commune. A degree of nostalgia could have crept in, but it may well be also that the euphoria of the Commune's early days made him see revolutionary possibilities in the conduct of ordinary people and to renew a faith tested by the defeat of the first siege. What followed the euphoria, however, quickly brought him down to earth.

Then came the elections, the members of the Commune were named—and then little by little the ardor of devotion and the desire for action were extinguished. Everyone returned to his usual task, saying to himself, "Now that we have an honest government, let it act for us."[31]

For a long time Reclus was aware of a wide gulf between his ideal brotherhood of equals and flesh and blood men and women. It took the experiences of 1870-71, however, to make clear to him the real extent of that chasm. The culprits in the messy affair of the Commune were the people. They were too weak to live up to the demands of a social order based on liberty and equality; they were far from ready for society based on brotherhood.

Reclus was shaken by the direction taken by the Commune; there was a glimpse of utopia, but that was followed by confusion, weakness, pitiless repression, and less than noble defeat. Publicly humiliated and incensed by the "thick, almost impenetrable wall of hate, the aversion of the entire world to the Commune and the Communards,"[32] he came back stronger than ever. He tried to draw communards together in their dark hour, and he longed to participate in collective and massive defiance which would prove that the death of the Commune was no more than a temporary setback. Since the people were incapable of using political machinery to advantage, another way to social justice must be found. The struggle would be taken up anew, with greater vigour and no compromise.

The implications that Reclus drew from the events of 1870-71 while he was still a prisoner are summarised in a letter written in late August 1871 as the first anniversary of the proclamation of the Third Republic (4 September 1870) drew near. The suffering was not in vain; successes and failures must be assessed and lessons learned.

> Frightful have been the misfortunes; generally, however, we are indeed fortunate, because the world has learned from all this. Every generation must make sacrifices for future generations. Let us not complain, then, since the terrible lesson of history made at our expense will profit future republics.[33]

In May 1872 Reclus told his friend Félix Nadar: "Everything miserable and horrible that we have seen nonetheless contains the germ of something great."[34] Reclus had a grand vision, but it was up to the people to create this society. "I very much love my poor brothers in humanity who in general are worth so little," he wrote shortly after his release, "but with them, through affection, through incessant propaganda, one can develop such great things."[35] Reclus's object of love is not clear, whether human beings or idealised versions of them. In any event, the man whose faith in the people was expressed so joyfully and eloquently on occasion also felt disappointment in their failure to make greater advances.

As we have seen, Reclus was hardly pleased with the behaviour of some communards. In 1878 he confided to a friend that his "Experiences of a Prisoner" could not be published for at least twenty years because he remembered only too well "things of which we are not proud." These matters he was yet unwilling to make public, for "we are still in the period of struggle and before the common enemy we stick together."[36] In the years following the Commune, Reclus would later explain, the repression and outrages suffered by the communards had united them, and he declined to judge men who "had hardly been worthy of the cause they defended."[37] He was solicitous of the communards' welfare, and yet at times also reproachful. By energetically supporting them he was attempting to salvage what he could from the Commune for the revolutionary cause. Reclus was aware of the political potential of exploiting the memory of the Paris Commune; in fact, he promoted it as a central feature of revolutionary ideology. He was no less clear in his own mind that he was participating in the creation of a "myth."

After 1871 Reclus had to face the problem of seeking social justice outside the parliamentary system. He now had little time for cooperativism and trade unionism, although for a time he preferred to remain silent rather than condemn workers who struggled to better their lot.

Charting his anarchist way to socialism meant relentless propaganda against the existing order. People would have to be shown the injustices around them, and revolt could follow. Any overt rejection of injustice was viewed positively; even vengeance he saw as a form of primitive justice. Terrorism, or propaganda by the deed, as the anarchists called it, had serious ramifications. It would appeal to Reclus, however, because it exposed the vulnerability of the state and raised the hope of anarchist revolution. Unlike prominent anarchists such as Jean Grave and Peter Kropotkin, Reclus would see revolutionary implications in *la reprise individuelle* (individual recovery of the fruits of one's labour), or theft, and positive gains in accepting it as a principle. Even violence could be justified, and his defence of the attentats in the 1890s caused concern among some anarchists. The suppression of the Paris Commune represented a declaration of war, *la guerre à outrance.*

Six
Anarchy and Theory

Anarchist theory, as it developed in Europe in the latter part of the nineteenth century, flowered first in Switzerland. It emerged, in the post-Commune decade, from the debates of the small groups of socialists who in 1872 established a federalist wing of the International Working Men's Association. After the Hague Congress that year, the IWMA split into two groups, a federalist or "anti-authoritarian" International which gravitated around the Jura Federation in Switzerland, and a less successful "centralist" International which followed Marx's call for party-political action and tighter control of the IWMA General Council over the various sections.

The term "anarchist" has been applied to so many people and their various and countless acts that it has nearly lost all meaning. In the 1870s it referred to members of the federalist International; in the first half of the 1870s it was sometimes used pejoratively to denote socialists who refused to engage in party-political action. The term was being used by some of these people themselves in

1876, but it was not adopted on any scale until after the collapse of the federalist International in 1877.[1]

While acceptance of the fundamentals of anarchism was often decisive and clear, adoption of an anarchist programme was invariably halting and uncertain. By the late 1870s, however, those socialists who professed "anarchist" principles felt compelled to clarify their position. Elisée Reclus played an important role in this process.

Reclus's first two years of exile in Switzerland were marked by political inactivity. Lugano, where he set up house with his wife Fanny and their two daughters, was a political desert. He spent much time writing and doing research for geographical projects,[2] but was nonetheless kept under official surveillance. A police report in early January 1874 referred to him as "a very learned man, hard-working, with regular habits, but very much a dreamer, bizarre, obstinate in his ideas and with a belief in the realisation of universal brotherhood."[3] For years, certainly since 1869, Reclus had been estranged from Bakunin, who, with some justification, had detected "bourgeois" tendencies in his friend's approach to questions of revolutionary activity. However, his decisive stand against collaboration with the bourgeois order after 1871 impressed Bakunin:

> ...excellent Elisée... with whom I get along better and better. There is the model of a man—so pure, noble, simple, modest, selfless. He is perhaps not so completely the devil of a fellow, as might be desired, but that is a question of temperament... He is a valuable, very reliable, very earnest, very sincere friend and completely one of us.[4]

Reclus could not be content for long if he was not involved in politics, and in June 1873 he wrote to the Belgian socialist Victor Buurmans: "We are still living very much in retirement, watching the world from a distance... the great human comedy. Don't think, though, that we've become sceptics. We take very much to heart everything that happens on the world stage."[5]

A turning point, no doubt, was 14 February 1874 when Fanny died in childbirth. Fanny had been a match for her husband in obstinacy, idealism, and courage, and had been a great source of strength during his imprisonment. Given the times, the marriage ceremony itself had been very definitely a political statement, for their simple declaration before family and friends had defied the authority of Church and state. Elisée was deeply attached to Fanny, and her death was a great tragedy for him. Four years later he described her in moving terms:

> ...the woman who, during the siege and the Commune, defended my honour so admirably, the woman who made me love life,

of whom I was proud because she always gave me courage and rectitude and because she was the better part of my being... I have changed a great deal. In animated conversation, when it is a question of the cause, I am still the same: but in day-to-day life I am the most taciturn of men.[6]

But Reclus was no ascetic. He married Ermance Beaumont Trigant in 1875, although the memory of Fanny stayed with him, and in his fashion he grieved for many years.[7] In 1880 he confided to a friend that he was very unhappy: "Life has been so difficult for me that I very often ask myself if it would not be better to go to bed and die." But at least he was blessed with family and friends, and, above all, there was the "joy of fighting and suffering for a good cause."[8]

In 1874, with his personal life in disarray, Reclus turned his attention to the "cause." Since arriving in Switzerland, he had often rubbed shoulders with members of the federalist International, but the earliest surviving reference to formal membership is an August 1874 circular of the Jura Federation in which he is mentioned as a "central" member—that is, not connected with a specific section.[9]

Some time before mid-April 1875 Reclus joined the section at Vevey, where he then lived.[10] This section, actually little more than a handful of friends, was an active group whose prominent members included a carpenter (Samuel Rossier), a cook (Joseph Favre), and Charles Perron, who had moved to Vevey in 1875 to work as cartographer on Reclus's *Nouvelle Géographie universelle*. The group showed a keen interest in the local workers' movement and contributed to the Jura Federation's *Bulletin*. Reclus helped it "organise" such that it anticipated later anarchist groups. There was no central office, and each member was free to act independently in all matters. Correspondence was to be addressed to Reclus, not because he held some position but for the convenience of those wishing to contact the section.[11]

Reclus became more deeply involved in Jura politics in the late 1870s, and this behaviour is reflected in the changing attitudes of the police towards him. Prior to 1875 they reported that despite his "advanced" views, he lived a quiet life and was not active in politics.[12] In June 1876 the French ambassador in Berne informed the French Minister of Foreign Affairs that Reclus, then giving geography lectures in Geneva, "conducted himself very well."[13] According to a police report of May 1877, however, "since his arrival in Switzerland [he] has not ceased to encourage actively all the intrigues of the revolutionary party."[14] Two years later he was singled out as "one of the most ardent propagators" of the federalist International.[15] And it is true that Reclus played an important part not only in the elaboration of anarchist theory, but

97

in building the momentum necessary to sustain interest in a set of principles that were eventually embodied in a movement of consequence.

There is some confusion as to European anarchism and its relation to socialism. From shortly after the Paris Commune socialists were seen as divided into two camps—the anarchists and the others; according to the various accounts, these "others" have encompassed everything from revolutionary Marxism to various forms of social democracy. The rift between the anarchists and the "others" has been perceived as so deep that the anarchists continually risk being rejected as socialists. There has been a tendency to regard the anarchists as a distinct species and to link them with every conceivable belief or theory that expresses anti-authoritarian, anti-statist, or anti-government sentiments. But socialism continued to be a tenet of late-nineteenth-century European anarchism.

Reclus said in 1851 that anarchy was the highest expression of order, but it would be a mistake to assume that he was articulating the later anarchist position. His self-proclaimed early "anarchism" was an expression of what he and many others saw as the goal of revolutionary activity. Anarchy represented a society "without masters," which was also the goal of virtually all nineteenth-century socialists. Marx's "withering away of the state" evoked similar images of a self-directing society with no authority imposed from above. In 1872, in fact, the General Council of the IWMA felt compelled to reassure its recalcitrant sections that anarchy was the goal of all socialists.[16]

Such reassurances came in response to demands for immediate decentralisation of authority and decision-making within the IWMA. The General Council insisted that decentralisation could not destroy the existing order, that only political power could make the repressive machinery of the state yield to the administrative functions of government. Marx believed that authority must be met with authority; some disagreed, and to make their point they called themselves the anti-authoritarians. These were a heterogeneous lot—English trade unionists, for example, and Belgian socialists who supported the federalist Jurassians and Italians out of a conviction that the Council had no right to assume wide-ranging powers. The spectre which loomed large in the early 1870s was the Council's tyranny in attempting to discipline IWMA members and threatening to continue doing so even after the revolution. The anti-authoritarians protested. At St-Imier they insisted on autonomy for the sections and utterly rejected the notion of revolutionary government after the overthrow of the existing order.[17]

Resistance to Marxist "authoritarianism" is contained in several varieties of socialism, as the history of the past century clearly demonstrates. Thus, while a non-authoritarian approach to the struggle for socialism is fundamental to late-nineteenth-century European anarchism, it is not enough by itself to characterise the historic anarchist position. One can strive for a society "without masters" yet engage in parliamentary politics, as such prominent social democrats as Jean Jaurès and Léon Blum bear witness. It is not clear that the federalist objections to Marxism would have led to the development of anarchism had there not also existed an intense hostility to the state, and specifically revulsion to party-political activity.

The relative importance of politics and economics was a delicate issue from the inception of the IWMA, but in the 1860s there were few critics who could not be persuaded that party-political activities might be used "as a means" to achieving "stateless" society. Bakunin's "anarchist" programme of 1868[18] upset this balance, but its effect on the development of anarchism in the late 1870s should not be exaggerated. Bakunin continued to inspire the anarchists; for a time he fascinated most socialists, including Marx. But the anarchists did not emerge out of personal loyalty to Bakunin. When the Russian "retired" from politics in 1873, there was no clearly articulated anarchist position. Only after his death in 1876 was the theory of anarchism formulated, and then by people who rejected important aspects of his theories. Marx's paranoia over Bakunin's conspiracies led him to see Bakunin behind the federalist International.

Anarchism was not merely a continuation of the legendary Bakuninist opposition to Marx. Reclus, for example, was not moved at all by the Marx-Bakunin debate, yet he became a leading theoretician of nineteenth-century anarchism. His post-1971 stance represents not the return of a wayward Bakuninist to the fold, but a rupture or significant shift in nineteenth-century European radical politics.

The major factor in the emergence of an anarchist position in the 1870s may have been not Marxism but distrust of the politics then emerging as more countries introduced the franchise. This distrust grew into bitter hostility. In the case of Reclus, after his experiences in 1870-71 the negative attitude towards the state that he shared with all radicals was transformed into the relentless hostility that became characteristic of the anarchists. Any contact whatsoever with the political order was thought to be contaminating. His objections to the question of revolutionary government were rooted in the "lessons" of the Commune. If the revolution established any sort of government, he said in 1878, that government would necessarily cease to be revolutionary and become conservative. Defenders of the oppressed would inevitably become oppressors. It was essential that revolutionaries stay among the people and not be tempted by the pretext of serving them.[19]

Anarchists were revolutionaries who constantly sought unattainable purification. Reclus's friend Carlo Cafiero went insane, haunted by the notion that he might be enjoying more than his fair share of sunlight. Cafiero's madness demonstrates, in exaggerated form, the psychological propensity implicit in the quest for purity. This should not be viewed as a peculiar or distinctive feature of anarchism, however. There had to be objective historical conditions contributing to this particular form of the quest for purity.

Their intransigent opposition to parliamentary politics had important implications for the anarchists' attempt to work out a theoretical basis for revolutionary action. Having rejected Marxist authoritarianism and bourgeois party-politics, they came to support a strategy resting on the precept of "natural" social progress. The notion of socialism as natural to humankind had for decades been common to the thought of countless revolutionaries, including both Marx and Bakunin.[20] It became a recurrent theme in the writing of Reclus that if people were allowed to make decisions for themselves, then society would naturally develop in the direction of socialism, just as children naturally grow into adults.

This view would have profound consequences for the development of anarchist theory, as succeeding chapters will show. At this point let us examine some general concepts developed by the anarchists in the 1870s, as they sought to define themselves *vis-à-vis* the state and other socialists.

The participants at the federalist or "anti-authoritarian" St-Imier Congress of 1871 did not believe their position represented a break with IWMA policy. On the contrary, they were convinced that they were merely enunciating what the International had stood for all along. A great deal of the ambiguity in the anarchist ranks at the time can be traced to their insistence that their theories were a logical extension of IWMA principles, and that their "socialism" therefore did not require any special definition. The federalists' Geneva Congress of 1873—to which were invited all sections opposed to the IWMA General Council (i.e., Marx)—was called the "Sixth Congress of the International" to stress that the resolutions of the IWMA Hague Congress the year before were not recognised and that the meeting was carrying on IWMA business begun in 1864. It took time for the anarchists to distinguish themselves from the wide assortment of groups making up the federalist International. This process was in part a response to the public service theory of the state put forth by the Belgian socialist Caesar de Paepe.

At the federalists' Brussels Congress in 1874 De Paepe argued that even in post-revolutionary society it would be necessary to organise public services such as communications at the level of local commune or federation of communes; that administrative structure would have to be imposed by a "collective dictatorship." The notion of a dictatorship, argued his opponents, that would impose a structure upon a free society—or one struggling to become so—was totally contradictory; it was essential that people associate as they wished and that communes federate freely.[21] This argument was taken up at the 1876 Lausanne anniversary reunion in honour of the Paris Commune. Gustave Lefrançais and Nicholas Joukowsky, according to Paul Brousse, defended the public service theory of the state, while he and Reclus attacked it.[22]

The federalist International embraced many organisations espousing a wide variety of theories. Until the mid-1870s most were content to share labels like "collectivist," "revolutionary," "socialist," and "libertarian." Generally, they advocated collectivised property, abolition of the state, and spontaneous revolution. A serious debate over labels and doctrine began in 1876, when the terms "anarchist" and "anarchy" were being used to refer to certain groups and individuals, though not always without strong opposition. James Guillaume argued that it would be unwise to adopt negative and ambiguous labels, and he reminded the readers of the Jura Federation's *Bulletin* that it would be more appropriate to call attention to the collectivist theory as formulated in the congresses of the International.[23]

Back in 1851, Reclus had used the word "anarchy" to refer to a harmonious stateless society based on the principles of justice, equality, and brotherly love.[24] He apparently called himself "an anarchist" in public at the Lausanne anniversary reunion in 1876.[25] A year later he delivered an address entitled "Anarchy and the State" at St-Imier,[26] and in 1878 defended the use of "anarchy" and "anarchist" on logical and practical grounds.[27] Etymologically, he argued, the words expressed the desired goals perfectly—did not socialists strive to achieve anarchy?—and the terms were distinctive enough to draw public attention. In any event, he said, there was little point worrying about the matter, since the terms were already being used by friends and enemies alike.

The sources for documenting Reclus's anarchist theory in this period are his address at St-Imier in March 1877 and articles in the revolutionary journal *Le Travailleur* (1877-78), particularly its programme and two essays it published in early 1878.[28]

The St-Imier address traced the forms assumed by the state from earliest times: theocracy, monarchy, aristocracy, and democracy. Democracy, he said, professed to be government of the people by the people, but, of course, it was nothing of the kind. If that were the case, anarchy would already be reality. The modern European state was part of an evolution, he suggested, and contained the seeds of progress. While Kropotkin tended to see the European state as an artificial creation imposed on an idealised mediaeval decentralisation, Reclus regarded it as a further embodiment of authority, and in a way an improvement over the political institutions of the past. In the Middle Ages, Reclus had said many years before, master and serf had been equal before God; in the 1870s, he asserted that all men were equal under the law. The task of the anarchist was to make real this theoretical equality.

Although the historical survey tried to show that there had been progress towards anarchy, said Reclus, only by abandoning the state would it ultimately be achieved. Decentralisation was impeded by existing states with a counter-revolutionary tendency to centralise. Modern states had completely outlived their usefulness, although advocates argued that they performed essential directing or policing functions. [29]

The *Le Travailleur* programme, which Reclus probably had a large part in writing, saw the state in several forms (political, juridical, religious) and as a governmental machine which reflected the economic system while also reinforcing and protecting it. Contrary to what has become the popular conception of the anarchists, the state was not seen as the source of all evil. It was economic inequality that was isolated as "the most powerful instrument of oppression."[30] The revolutionary struggle was directed against the social-economic system as well as the state, as the weapon of privilege.

Reclus was one anarchist who did not simply believe—in what is commonly referred to as the "Bakuninist" tradition—that on abolition of the state people would spontaneously develop their natural ability for friendly cooperation. Removal of the state, he said at St-Imier, would not necessarily lead to transformation of the social-economic order.[31] Even control of the means of production would not be enough to bring about a just society: such control must be enhanced by a development of intellectual and physical faculties. The question of consciousness would become more important to him in the years to come.

Anarchist rejection of the state did not rule out the establishment of a coordinating body in an anarchist society. Such "government" was seen in terms of people sharing communal responsibilities. Government structures would be based on "natural" communities and would take shape from the bottom up. Reclus had made similar points earlier, and they were explicit in much of Kropotkin's writing. In 1877 Reclus maintained that the law must be replaced by "free contract" and the constraints of the state by "free association of the forces of humanity."[33]

After the 1870s, however, Reclus showed little interest in exploring this question. He would not deny that in the post-revolutionary age, government coordination might be useful, desirable, and even necessary. Nor would he object to the establishment of institutions created by people to serve their own needs. However, given the existing circumstances, said Reclus, it was pointless to advocate the immediate restructuring of society. Not only must they concentrate on ousting the incumbent power-holders, but until people reached a level of intellectual and moral development, they would be incapable of controlling any "governments" they created.

Reclus insisted that people alone could make a successful revolution and that it was important to choose their means carefully. He found it easier, however, to say what these means were not. Certainly, participation in parliamentary politics was anathema, but participation in such non-parliamentary enterprises as co-operatives was also ruled out. By the 1870s Reclus had shed his ambivalence toward cooperativism. Cooperative undertakings, he stated in 1878, far from being socialistic, were even counter-revolutionary; successful cooperatives earned money, became property-owners, were forced to conform to the conditions of capital, and became "bourgeois." Thus removed from the people, they entered "the great brotherhood of the privileged." If it happened that a cooperative failed, at least the participants might see the light and return to the revolutionary struggle, but success would pave the way for integration into bourgeois society, and members would be lost to the revolution forever.[34]

In politics and economics Reclus saw what amounted to "iron" laws. Just as participation in party politics produced integration into the existing political order, so too would anarchists be co-opted through any form of participation as entrepreneurs in the economy. Liberal economists who advocated cooperativism as a means of ensuring the stability of the system were, in his view, correct in their analysis.

Workers and peasants were the two groups isolated by Reclus as agents of revolution. Both suffered the demoralising effects of social contempt for physical labour.[35] He suggested, although he did not make it clear, that the full equality that anarchism demanded would come about through the emancipation of society's lowliest members. Reclus saw an unbridgeable gulf between those who supported privilege-inequality and those who supported equality. In contrast to what he had advocated in 1870-71, he now insisted that nothing could be gained by joining forces with the "caste" of the bourgeoisie, because as a caste it felt entitled to privilege. The anarchists were levellers; both caste and state and traditional and legal inequities must be abolished. For the same reasons, it was illusory to support the petite bourgeoisie, even if it had cause for grievance.[36] Elsewhere he suggested that revolutionaries should not be deceived into thinking that workers could be emancipated through reconciliation with the capitalists, since existing society was based on private property while the route to justice and liberty

103

consisted in an attack on private property, not support for it.[37] Further questions dealing with the social-economic order will be taken up in a later chapter.

The revolutionary, according to Reclus, must work relentlessly at spreading propaganda among the people, to awaken in them a thirst for the great task that lay ahead. Yet he was at a loss to say what could be done beyond spreading the word through the press and public meetings. He must have sensed the limitations of this strategy when he said that it was better for anarchists to march directly toward their goal, even if this meant proceeding more slowly, than to use "circuitous" routes through parliamentary politics and cooperatives which would make them lose sight of it altogether.

> In continuing to be sincere anarchists, enemies of the state in all its forms, we have the advantage of deceiving no one, and especially not ourselves. Under the pretext of realising a small part of our programme, even with the chagrin of violating another part, we shall not be tempted to address ourselves to power or to take part in it. We shall spare ourselves the scandal of those retractions which so many ambitious people and sceptics make and which so deeply trouble the conscience of the people.[38]

Such idealism was of paramount importance, but it likely did not prove emotionally satisfying for a man of Reclus's spirited temperament and he soon placed his hopes in the revolutionary potential of propaganda by the deed, a new approach that would strike terror into the hearts of many Europeans in the latter part of the century.[39]

His refusal to work within the existing political order was final. The world was divided into good and evil, friends and foes. On the one hand there were those who would profit from injustice and inequality, and on the other those who struggled for liberty.[40] Reclus said in 1882 that there was always an elemental clash of opposites at work, and this conflict must always be kept in mind.

> There are socialists and there are socialists, it will be said, and of the different schools, which one will prevail? Of course, in appearance, there is a great diversity of forms, but that is only an illusion. Fundamentally, there are only two principles: on the one side, that of government and authority; on the other, anarchy and liberty... All revolutionary acts are, by their very nature, essentially anarchical, whatever the power that seeks to profit from them.[41]

Unlike Bakunin, Kropotkin, and Brousse, he preferred to see the post-1871 period as a new stage in revolutionary politics rather

104

than a continuation of old battles. It was new because of the war against the state and government, but also because of the universal nature that the struggle for socialism assumed.

According to the *Le Travailleur* programme, the most significant development of the 1870s was the fact that the localised commune (Paris Commune) had given way to a wider, working-class struggle. Everywhere one looked in Europe (Italy, Spain, Germany, Greece, Belgium, Switzerland, Russia), workers were responding to the challenge. Regardless of differing strategies, all had the same aim: to emancipate themselves from the employer. And questions of production and consumption were universal; boundaries, mountains, and oceans did not change the fact that workers were exploited everywhere.[42]

The Marxist attempt to capture political power was a backhanded recognition of the importance of states. Anarchists, on the other hand, were revolutionaries who committed the state to the dustbin of history. For Reclus, this led to a partial renunciation of French nationalism, and he attempted to formulate a theory which could somehow get round the necessity of working through existing states, even in order to destroy them—which was the Marxist position.

In this "new" period Reclus was not inclined to get involved in "old" politics, and he saw no value in working with an anarchist "party." He chose to associate with the motley Geneva group of French and Russian exiles, communards, and others, instead of moving in the sectarian circles of the Jurassians in Neuchâtel. Reclus was a curiosity; the most anarchist of the anarchists, as often as not he could be found with non-anarchists, and would thus raise the ire of those whose outlook was closest to his. And true to form, much of the hostility directed at Reclus in the 1870s came from people who would later become his closest associates. This was especially true with regard to Kropotkin.

Kropotkin left England for Switzerland in late 1876. He hoped to renew his acquaintance with Guillaume and the Jura watch-makers who had so impressed him on his first trip in 1872. A visit to Belgium, to "spy out" the land for Brousse in early 1877, had convinced him that little could be accomplished there unless he stayed at least a year. On arriving in Switzerland finally in February 1877, he seems to have been captivated by the romantic notion of working for a "pure" anarchist party. He was uneasy about the "learned" Reclus, but was reassured on meeting him. "I liked him very much," Kropotkin wrote Paul Robin. "...I was pleasantly surprised to see a true socialist."[43] However, as Kropotkin became beguiled by Brousse's vitality and his "extreme" position, he aligned himself with the Jurassians in opposition to Reclus and the Genevans. There were disagreements over the value of projects connected with "scientific" education which Reclus was anxious to pursue (see chapter 7), and the dispute came to a head when the Genevans decided to publish *Le Travailleur*.

This move was a response to hopes aroused by the revival of the working-class movement in France. By 1876, the labour movement, which had collapsed with the defeat of the Commune, began to recover. There was a workers' delegation from France at the Vienna International Exhibition in 1873, and another at Philadelphia in 1876. Also in 1876, the first Labour Congress was held in Paris, and although it was quite moderate, its very existence was considered significant. January elections that year returned a Republican majority, and as republicans became more confident, there began agitation for general amnesty for the communards. These events took place as the myth of the Commune was being established. France was now more accessible to propaganda, and by early April the Geneva exiles decided to publish a periodical that could exist openly in Switzerland and be smuggled into France.

Not only Reclus saw the possibilities for agitation in France. Brousse planned to bring out *L'Avant-garde* as an organ of the French Federation with which he had close contact, and he saw *Le Travailleur* as a conspiracy against both *L'Avant-garde* and the Jura Federation's *Bulletin*. He wrote to Kropotkin about the risks involved in dealing with the varied opinions of those behind *Le Travailleur* (the Jacobin Gambon, the anarchist Reclus, and the De Paepist Lefrançais). The letter shows that Brousse was concerned about the ambitions of the Geneva group and the consequent threat to his own position in Berne. The "friends" in Geneva were involved in the *Almanach* and were making plans for a socialist dictionary; "now it is a question of a periodical; tomorrow it will be a question of a newspaper."[44]

Kropotkin sided with Brousse, and in a letter to Paul Robin explained his version of the "split" between the south (Geneva, Lausanne, Vevey) and the north (Neuchâtel, St-Imier, Berne, La Chaux-de-Fonds). The leader in the south was Nicholas Joukowsky, who chattered a lot, said Kropotkin, but did nothing useful. Next came Reclus, who, it was claimed, contributed little more than his name. Then there were the easily led Perron and Ralli. The only good word was reserved for the "likeable" Kahn, who, alas, let himself be exploited. Because these people never associated with workers, he explained, they scribbled and used up precious funds. Kropotkin refused to deal further with them, and claimed that the Free Tribune section of *Le Travailleur* was an "open door" for Joukowsky and Kahn's Jacobin friends. He maintained that the periodical was directed against the *Bulletin* and saw nothing open to question when in the same letter he informed Robin that Brousse was planning a paper for clandestine distribution in France.[45] He later said that *L'Avant-garde* was founded because the *Bulletin* had simply become "insipid."[46]

While the Geneva group's opinions on revolutionary matters caused the northerners to be suspicious, relations were exacerbated by their independent action, their propensity for propaganda, and their disagreements over money. It is likely that Brousse's ambition and his conviction that his was the true way to socialism were largely responsible for the hostility toward the Geneva group. His eagerness for action, which inclined him to resent Guillaume's cautious and conciliatory manner,[47] was also a factor in the animosity toward the more reflective and eclectic approach of the Genevans. Kropotkin, anxious to belong to a "party of pure anarchy," showed a readiness to repeat gossip. "As for me," he wrote to Robin, "I rally openly to the Jurassians of the north, the party of pure anarchy, of agitation in the workplace, of action." He was attracted to this group, he said, because it had an "intimate relationship" and represented a "compact party with a determined programme."[48]

Reclus preferred, for the sake of the "cause," to say nothing. Beneath the calm exterior, however, he was critical. Two years earlier, in 1875, Bakunin had commented on the "heroic patience and perseverence" of the Jurassians and the Belgian socialists, but Reclus responded by expressing concern about their lack of cohesion and their whims.[49] This opinion was no doubt reaffirmed by the petty squabbles in the Jura. Reclus went his way, refusing to submit to "authority" but also refraining from attack. When Madame Champseix complained in April 1877 of the treatment Benoît Malon was receiving at the hands of Guillaume and asked him to defend Malon, Reclus remained silent.[50] And yet, as exasperating as he could be in self-styled "martyrdom," he also showed childlike glee at signs of mended quarrels. At about the time of Champseix's letter, he wrote that Brousse and Guillaume seemed to be getting on. "No rivalries, no gossiping!," he exclaimed joyfully, "that is vital. 'Oil! oil!' as [Félix] Nadar said to me when we went up in a balloon..."[51]

Reclus avoided direct confrontation with the Jurassians, as well as with non-anarchist groups, but unobtrusively held to anarchism and kept his own counsel. When Caesar de Paepe wondered if he would be a suitable collaborator for a proposed journal, *Socialisme progressif*,[52] Malon replied that he did not think he would do it, even if asked directly, because he was "an out-and-out anarchist, the most anarchist of the *Le Travailleur* editors and a great friend of the Jurasso-Italian enthusiasts."[53] A note in *Le Travailleur* announcing *Socialisme progressif* as a journal of the statist school of socialism expressed Reclus's general outlook. "Our duty, as revolutionary anarchists, is to welcome this socialist organ of free and cordial discussion. It is up to the readers to study it and to judge for themselves."[54] In a similar spirit, *Le Travailleur* would be devoted to study: all questions would be raised and solutions examined; the discussion would be frank and the criticisms fair. Serene in its detachment, the journal said simply that the question of self-esteem did not exist for revolutionaries, whose cause was that of the workers of the world.[55]

As far as Brousse and Kropotkin were concerned, such open-mindedness left much to be desired. They were more in tune with the line of the French Federation in *L'Avant-garde* which stated that the first duty of the people was to rise up and overthrow the state by violent revolution.[56]

When the federalists' Verviers Congress was held in September 1877, the anarchists had become an identifiable group in the Jura Federation. At Verviers, the intransigents—Brousse, Andreas Costa, and Garcia Viñas—managed to silence the more conciliatory delegates represented by Guillaume.[57] Shortly afterward, at the International Socialist Congress in Ghent, anarchist policies led to a rejection of the proposed pact of solidarity between all socialists.[58] Reclus stood firm, but off-stage. He likely responded cautiously to any formal agreement for fear of compromising anarchist principles. In any event, the defeat of the pact led to virtual isolation of the anarchists within the European socialist movement.

Verviers was the International's last annual Congress. Having failed to establish a popular base and losing support through a crisis in the watchmaking industry, the Jura anarchists faced bleak times. The *Bulletin* closed down for lack of funds in March 1878, and shortly thereafter Guillaume himself left for France. The April-May issue of *Le Travailleur* announced that it, too, was in difficulty. At a joint meeting held 9 June at Neuchâtel it was decided that *L'Avant-garde* would carry on the work of *Le Travailleur*. Factional disputes abated somewhat at the meeting, and there were signs that some "anarchists" were becoming less strongly opposed to working within the political order![59] At a Federal Congress held at Fribourg in August of that year, the intransigent Brousse even questioned the advisability of abstention from electoral activity.[60]

Collapse of the federalist International softened the rigidity of the "pure" anarchists and led to dissolution of the animosity aimed at Reclus. He described the June 1878 Neuchâtel meeting as a "gathering of friends. We were about fifteen, full of good will towards each other."[61]

There was some contact between Reclus and Brousse in 1878. Brousse stayed briefly in Vevey before being arrested by the Swiss authorities on Boxing Day and charged with responsibility for the allegedly subversive nature of certain articles in *L'Avant-garde*.[62] Only Reclus and Brousse's friend Natalie Landsberg were permitted to see him in the following weeks. Reclus's support of Brousse is suggested in a letter dated 18 January 1879 from Kropotkin to Robin.[63] In February and March there were trips to

Lausanne, where Brousse's lawyer Fauquiez lived.[64] Reclus was in the Pyrenees at the time of the trial in April, but in early May thanked Fauquiez for handling the case.[65] Brousse succumbed to this concern for his welfare, and late in 1879 hoped to secure Reclus's collaboration on a newspaper project.[66] Brousse's arrest and trial had provided Reclus with the chance to help a like-minded countryman and to show the power of socialist solidarity. It set the pattern for action throughout his life.

More important to the history of anarchism was the *rapprochement* between Reclus and Kropotkin. Early in 1879 Kropotkin reported to Robin that relations with the *Le Travailleur* group were improving.[67] He made some mildly sarcastic remarks, but these were reserved for Gustave Lefrançais and Joukowsky, not Reclus. By this time, moreover, Kropotkin was adopting a more reflective position on anarchism and the social revolution. To what extent this was a result of discussions with Reclus is difficult to ascertain.

When Kropotkin decided to publish a new anarchist paper, it was to be "moderate in tone but revolutionary in substance."[68] The paper was called *Le Révolté*, and it appeared on 22 February 1879, at the point when the anarchist movement seemed to have fizzled out. The paper's success therefore came as a pleasant surprise, for its circulation quickly surpassed that of all other Jura anarchist papers.[69] Reclus began almost immediately to support financially *Le Révolté*,[70] and his address on the abolition of capital punishment was published as a pamphlet by the *Révolté* press.[71]

A few disconcerted revolutionaries in the Swiss Jura had been responsible for the elaboration of the anarchist position, but, finally, when some "anarchists" were changing their minds about working within the political order, the message began striking a responsive chord. Anarchists close to *Le Révolté* were heartened by signs of support and began once again to refine their theories. In 1880, before organisational ties disappeared altogether, the theory of anarchist communism was officially adopted by the Jura Federation Congress at La Chaux-de-Fonds.[72]

The major innovation of anarchist communism concerned the issue of distributing goods in post-revolutionary society. According to the Bakuninist tradition of collectivism, distribution would be based on labour; according to the new theory, the products of labour would be distributed according to need. The term "anarchist communism" was first used in a pamphlet signed by François Dumartheray on behalf of a group of refugees from Lyons in 1876. Entitled *Aux travailleurs manuels, partisans de l'action politique*, it was the third in a series advocating electoral abstention. A fourth pamphlet was to define the theory of anarchist communism more precisely, but this has never been traced. That same year the theory of anarchist communism was propagated among the Italian sections of the International by Errico Malatesta, Carlo

Cafiero, and Andreas Costa. They were instrumental in persuading the Italians to accept it at the Federal Congress of Florence in the autumn, and in December the *Bulletin* carried a report signed by Malatesta and Cafiero.

Reclus is said to have been one of the first to advocate the theory of anarchist communism. In May 1927 the eighty-five-year-old Dumartheray recounted to Max Nettlau that Reclus's Lausanne address in March 1876 had been "a completely anarchist communist speech."[73] His influence among the Geneva refugees, moreover, led to the belief that Reclus had collaborated on Dumartheray's 1876 pamphlet.[74] He was certainly among the first to adopt the principles of anarchist communism. As for formulation of the theory, it would be a mistake to try to establish authorship; several people came to roughly the same position almost simultaneously. The 1876 report of Malatesta and Cafiero indicates the thinking that was beginning to take hold in anarchist circles.

> The Italian Federation considers collective ownership of the products of labour a necessary component of the collectivist programme, *the cooperation of all for the needs of each* being the sole rule of production and consumption that corresponds to the principle of solidarity.[75]

Reclus likely played a prominent role in convincing Kropotkin of the theory's merits. The Russian was reluctant to endorse it because he worried about the difficulty of distributing scarce resources after a revolution that he expected within a few years.[76] In 1879, at the Jura Federation Congress, Kropotkin relented somewhat by proposing communism as the aim, with collectivism as the transition stage. A year later, however, at La Chaux-de-Fonds, he put forward the case for anarchist communism, suggesting that this theory came closest to expressing anarchist aims.

Reclus supported Kropotkin. The products of labour, he said, could not be apportioned strictly according to labour, for they were the result of the combined efforts not only of existing generations but also of those which had preceded them. It would therefore be right for individuals to draw from the common stock, with no other principle to guide them but "that which grows out of common interest and the mutual respect of [their] associates." There was no reason to fear the problem of scarce resources, for there would be plenty for all when commercial waste and private appropriation came to an end.

No mention was made of individual need. Cafiero, who spoke later, stressed the slogan "from each according to ability, to each according to need." Reclus preferred to say that distribution would be regulated according to the principle of solidarity, rather than that of individual need.[77] This important point is not stressed in studies of the theory of anarchist communism. For Reclus, need was a crude measure of what an individual ought to take from the common stock, indicating an egotistical mentality. Solidarity, or consideration of one's own needs in relation to those of others, on the other hand, represented a higher stage in human development.

In the twenty years or so following these debates the anarchist movement assumed a character broadly different from that of the earlier movement which had revolved around the IWMA. The Jura Federation continued to hold congresses for a few years, and there was the famous London Anarchist Congress of 1881. However, after 1882 the movement consisted of small groups scattered throughout Europe. These groups maintained only informal contact with each other and with sympathisers in other parts of the world. They met irregularly, their membership changed continually, they kept no records, and as a matter of principle they recognised no leaders. In 1883 Emile Gauthier spoke of "simple meeting places where friends gather each week to talk about things which interest them. Most of the time, however, one sees only new faces, with the exception of a small nucleus of four or five faithful."[78] There was no office in the anarchist group, no fixed membership fee, and everyone acted independently.

The aim of all socialists was a state of anarchy, a society in which people would no longer be subject to "masters," social-economic or political. Those socialists who became known as anarchists also insisted on an anarchist way to socialism.

Seven

Science and Rebellion

Nineteenth-century socialists rejected the structures of the social-economic and political order, but they rallied, ironically, to the faith in science proclaimed by that order. By the 1890s Marxism had become the dominant socialist theory, and its precepts were presented as grounded in "scientific socialism." Marxism characterised anarchism as old-fashioned utopianism, devoid of scientific basis. It is a mark of the decisiveness of the Marxist victory that this could be, since the anarchists certainly acknowledged the claims of science and they worked out their own scientific understanding of change and revolution. The leading theoreticians of the late-nineteenth-century anarchist movement were, in fact, men of science: Elisée Reclus was a famous geographer, and Peter Kropotkin, despite his uneasiness about scholarship, made important contributions to geography, geology, and sociology.

Anarchism, no less than Marxism, was a product of the times: certainties based on religion and philosophy yielded to unquestioning commitment to the establishment of "scientific" bases for claims about knowledge and power. As of the 1870s, in a world of increasingly sophisticated socialist theorising, anarchists had to legitimate their position by anchoring their socialism in science.

Reclus's career as geographer and the development of his political thought were always interrelated. His interest in both geography and socialism were rooted in a left-wing commitment to the notion of universal brotherhood. His fascination with geography can be traced to the lectures of the famous geographer Carl Ritter which captivated him as a student in Berlin in 1851, the year in which he also first recorded his views on anarchy. It is clear that geography and politics combined to enrich his travels and experiences in the period 1852-57.

When he returned to France, the social question again caught his attention, and he also pursued a career in geography. After the Commune his political thought changed greatly; he also began the monumental *Nouvelle Géographie universelle*, a project which was to earn him a permanent place in the history of the field.

The parallel between geography and politics is also clear in that the idea for the *Nouvelle Géographie universelle* came to Reclus while he was in prison; and around that time he also began to develop his anarchism. He drew up plans for "a kind of geographical encyclopaedia, divided into instalments costing three or four sous each."[1] The work eventually reached gigantic proportions, the completed *Nouvelle Géographie universelle* comprising nineteen volumes, one each year from 1876 to 1894. Each volume first appeared, as planned, in weekly instalments. The methodical and systematic Reclus was a disciplined worker, pursuing his task with single-minded fervour.

By mid-century Reclus evidently felt he had exhausted virtually every avenue within the Church for a way to put his Christian convictions into practice. Theology was a last resort. But young Reclus was then inspired by the lectures of Ritter, the geographer and Christian, and his imagination was fired by the message of the earth as the common home of all men and women. Reclus found it easy to see the earth as providing for human needs, and he always kept his early belief that science and technology could greatly enhance the earth's bounty. From the beginning he was struck by the simple but significant fact that human existence is predicated on the interaction of human beings with each other and with nature. He rejected the idea that to survive one must pit oneself against nature; such aggression was counterproductive. "A secret harmony exists between the earth and the people whom it nourishes," he wrote in the 1860s, "and when imprudent societies let themselves violate this harmony, they always end up regretting it."[2]

In an 1864 article on the effects of human behaviour on geography, Reclus described how the interaction between human

113

beings and their natural environment had led historically to diverse relationships between human beings and the earth. The acts of men and women were often destructive, but sometimes the state of the earth was improved. Whether it was harmed or enhanced depended on the "social state and the progress of each people." Reclus suggested that elements of decline and revival have existed simulteaneously and in varying proportions. The vision he preached in his voluminous geographical works comes through in the following passage.

> The barbarian pillages the earth; he exploits it violently and fails to restore its riches, in the end rendering it uninhabitable. The truly civilised man understands that his interest is bound up with the interest of everyone and with that of nature. He repairs the damage done by his predecessors and works to improve his domain. As a farmer and an industrialist, he knows how to use more and more of the earth's resources; and as an artist, he also knows how to enhance his environment with charm, grace, and majesty. Having become "the conscience of the earth," the man worthy of his mission assumes responsibility for the harmony and beauty of nature.[3]

La Terre, his first major work, focused on the physical environment, human beings appearing "almost as an afterthought" in the last chapters.[4] The epilogue indicates that Reclus was now becoming more precise as to the direction of his geographical writing. He would later describe *La Terre* as a "sort of preface" to the larger work which, as the title suggests, he believed was both new and universal.

Nouvelle Géographie universelle departed from conventional studies in subject, scope, and intended readership. Reclus was not interested in citing longitudes and latitudes or merely enumerating towns, villages, and political and administrative divisions. He was anxious to study ordinary people's changing relationships with one another and with their environment—or what has become known as "human geography." By studying people from a geographical as well as historical, biological, and sociological perspectives, Reclus set out to trace the history of institutions as well as the origins of languages and race relationships. He was not content to concentrate on a small part of the earth; he would deal with the whole. A new and universal geography was needed, he felt, in order to take into account progress in the scientific conquest of the earth. New regions were opened up, and the laws "which all terrestrial phenomena obey" had to be rigorously examined. Discussion of these universal scientific laws should not be confined to scholarship; Reclus would write for the general reader.[5]

Reclus integrated the study of human behaviour and physical geography by choosing *La Terre et les Hommes* as subtitle for

Nouvelle Géographie universelle. The title of the six-volume work which later completed his great trilogy was *L'Homme et la Terre,* an indication, it has been pointed out, that humans in their interaction with the earth had now moved to the forefront of his research.[6]

The epistemology informing Reclus's geography, as might be expected from the assumptions of the period, was positivist. Part of his attraction to geography was the relative ease with which it yielded to first-hand empirical observation, and Reclus had a disdain for those who presumed to contribute to the field from the isolation of the study. Scientific method was tied to observation, and all concepts and generalisations had to be derived from empirically verifiable data. Reclus saw the globe as an historically and spatially interrelated system subject to discoverable laws.

Reclus was attracted to Ritter's lectures precisely because the great geographer managed to rescue the field from the dull monotony of textbooks. His lectures were characterised by "marvelous clarity" and he treated "the most grandiose subjects" in "language of almost childlike simplicity." Unlike Ritter's written work, in which he felt obliged to be "academic," his lectures sketched *les grands faits* (the great deeds).[7] Here is the clue to Reclus's approach to both politics and geography: to uncover and transmit to his readers *les grands faits.*

The preoccupation of Reclus the geographer with the spatial dimensions of human existence caused him to return continually to the question of state boundaries. His enthusiasm for "natural" rather than artificial boundaries led, in 1868, to a sort of blueprint for future decentralised society. In his initial (1870) support for the French Third Republic he showed some disregard for French fortunes by subordinating the fate of Alsace and Lorraine to that of the Republic. What matter, he reasoned, whether they be French or German; in the long run, they would be part of the universal social Republic. Reclus held to his 1868 conviction that these territories should have the right of self-determination. That Reclus was thinking along these lines with regard to other areas of France in the period 1870-71 is confirmed by a later letter in which he questioned the French right to keep Nice when the people preferred to join Italy. During the Franco-Prussian war, he continued, he had started to write an article "to affirm that the strict duty of France" was to "restore Nice to its autonomy."[8]

In his youth and until the 1860s Reclus hoped that nationalism would be a force of liberation. In the post-1871 period, however, he saw another side of the matter—that the spirit of nationalism might be evoked "artificially" and used to rally peoples against their neighbours. While still in prison, he began to fear the growth of this nationalist perversion and to lament the hatred then building between the French and the Germans.[9]

115

These anxieties intensified when religious struggles in Turkey led to Russian intervention, ostensibly on behalf of fellow Slavs and orthodox Christians. In late 1876 Reclus wrote to the Jura Federation's *Bulletin* suggesting that the forthcoming Berne Congress discuss the attitude of the International towards the Eastern war which he believed would prove to be worse than the Franco-Prussian war.[10] Even if the Internationalists were unwilling to dirty their hands in the world of politics, he said, they must comment on the matter. To isolate themselves from contemporary society, to remain ignorant of political crimes, would be to fall into a sort of "mysticism." The Vevey section arranged for Nicholas Joukowsky to deliver a paper on the Eastern question in late January, and in early March both Reclus and Joukowsky addressed the St-Imier and La Chaux-de-Fonds meetings.[11]

In the February-March 1878 issue of *Le Travailleur* Reclus tried to demonstrate the importance of the Russo-Turkish war. Two factors helped shape his analysis of the effect of the "new" nationalism on the formation of European states: the emergence of a centralised Russia and the dominance of Germany. The movement toward centralisation in the East fit the pattern of French unification and more recently that of Germany and Italy, said Reclus, and would lead to Slavic unity.[12] The force of "racial patriotism" and "brotherhood" of language played an important role in consolidating the German and Italian "empires," he believed, and would increase the Russian domain.[13] But Reclus was also convinced that this Slavic unity would not be the product of "free" peoples, but would be created by the "will of the masters." Moreover, Slavic unity was a misnomer, because "Slavs or no Slavs, all those whose geography encloses them within the new boundaries will have to obey and be grateful."[14]

For Reclus, the "natural" feelings of cooperation among people who shared certain social features were being ruthlessly harnessed to serve those in power. "National" unity in Russia, as elsewhere, could be accomplished only through repression of "true" nationalities. He refused to acknowledge the national status of European states, preferring to speak of empires. In the case of Italy, this would appear to be a reversal of his earlier position, which expressed some enthusiasm for Victor Emmanuel. He saw the nationalism of the years following 1871 as a new phenomenon that carried alarming consequences for the future of Europe.

In the world of great states, Reclus stressed the importance of national self-determination and did not flinch when he saw how this principle was used by the new generation of leaders. However, he became far more critical than he had been prior to 1871. He was now unwilling to support any nationalist movement, even when it emerged from below. In May 1877 he suggested that race

116

and language were not enough to unite people in universal brotherhood—this could only be accomplished by means of a higher moral, according to right and duty. A national unity movement would have to see its liberation in the wider context of the universal struggle for justice.[15] In a letter to Victor Buurmans in February 1878,[16] Reclus agreed wholeheartedly that the extinction of the Flemish communes was an evil act. There was no doubt that the communes were free "in right"; "...it is for them to group as they wish with other communes, Flemish or Dutch, of the south or the north." However, he continued, all rights were interrelated; the Flemings were making the mistake of restricting themselves to fighting for one right, their language, without relating their particular predicament to "human right." He saw this as a tragedy, for the "nationalism" of some Flemings led them to identify with the German empire and to regard Bismarck as the great champion of nationality. This wing of the movement, which even contemplated adopting high German as their literary language, facilitated German expansion. In words which by 1940 were to prove prophetic, Reclus wrote:

> The Prussian soldiers will push back their "natural frontiers" as far as Lille and Saint-Omer and Pas-de-Calais, and, in turn, will face the English as neighbours. I regret these future events because, more than any other peoples, the Germans represent discipline—that is to say death.

England was doomed, according to Reclus, not only because of German aggressiveness, but also because of the nature of the British Empire, scattered as it was around the globe. Its heterogeneity would make it impossible to secure the various parts of the Empire in the face of serious challenges (internal or external). In early 1878, before the European Accord in May, at a time when England appeared to be at the height of her power and prestige, Reclus prophesied the decline of the British Empire. The future, he forecast, lay at least for a time with the centralised military states, Germany and Russia in particular, whose power was increasing at the rate of England's decline.[17]

A positivist approach, as Reclus practised it, implied analysis that corresponded to empirically verifiable tendencies, and his accounts of European developments are striking. But a positivist framework for Reclus did not amount to recognition of laws to which people were more or less obliged to submit. He saw two sets of laws: one flowing inexorably from the logic of the existing institutional framework, and another from human nature. The second was continually threatening to burst through the institutional bounds which contained it. Positivism, for Reclus, was both an investigation of the laws contributing to maintenance of the existing order and a search for laws which challenged it.

After the disappointment of 1871 he looked to science for reassurance of the triumph of the universal social Republic. In 1875 he pointed to the "great scientific movement of the epoch" in an attempt to comfort a dejected Michael Bakunin then brooding over the evaporating revolutionary instinct in the masses. Even if the spirit which Bakunin called the great French civilisation disappeared, he said, there would be more important guides in the Darwinian theory of evolution, the study of inertia, and comparative sociology.[18]

The notion of progressive evolution was a fundamental part of Reclus's conception of history. In both their biological and social characters, people tended to move from the simple to the complex, he thought, and it was more or less assumed that the movement, unless it was diverted by "unnatural" institutions, would give rise to higher stages of development.

> But whether it is a question of small or large groups of human beings, it is always through solidarity, through the association of spontaneous, coordinated forces, that progress is made... The historian, the judge who evokes the centuries... shows us how the law of the blind and brutal struggle for existence, so extolled by the admirers of success, is subordinated to a second law, that of the grouping of weak individuals into more developed organisms, learning to defend themselves against enemy forces and to recognise natural resources, even to create new ones. We know that if our descendants are to achieve science and liberty, they will owe it to... constant collaboration, to this mutual aid from which brotherhood grows little by little.[19]

Progress was to be achieved through intensification of the "natural" inclination to cooperate—that is, through mutual aid. Reclus saw a parallel growing awareness of the bonds between all human beings: the seeds of instinctual cooperation flowered into a more fully developed and conscious variety.[20] He believed that the growth of consciousness would facilitate the development of morality, the assumption being that knowledge of how people acted "naturally" was also a guide to how they ought to act.

Anarchists are almost without exception taken to have rejected the theory of the struggle for existence in favour of one of mutual aid, which they supposedly believed was the determining factor in the evolution of the species. This has contributed to interpretations in which people like Reclus and Kropotkin are attributed a saintliness which is exaggerated even for those who devoted their lives to the idea of brotherly love. It has also led to confusion on the question of the logic by which men renowned for their benevolence could accept and even condone violence. But co-operation does not preclude violence, and their complementarity is the clue to Reclus's position.

As we have seen, Reclus argued that Darwin's theory of evolution was evidence of the inevitable success of the revolutionary cause. He later left no doubt that he could see strategic benefits in Darwin's theories. "In the history of the world all the armies of a Napoleon are not worth so much as one word of a Darwin, fruit of a life of work and thought."[21] Reclus rejected the popular notion that the theory of the survival of the fittest and natural selection could act as philosophical justification for the existing order.[22] He declared, quite to the contrary, that the theory provided ammunition for revolutionaries and that it rightly referred to the natural superiority of the stronger—the working class.

> We should congratulate ourselves that the question is thus simplified, for it is much closer to the solution. Force reigns, say the advocates of social inequality; force reigns, proclaims modern industry... But why shouldn't revolutionists talk like economists and merchants? The law of the strongest will not always and necessarily work for the benefit of commerce. "Might surpasses right," said Bismarck, echoing many others; but perhaps we should prepare for the day when might is at the service of right.[23]

Banding together in "collective defence"[24] against the bourgeoisie, the working class had to get along, and this cooperation would make them invincible. "What power do isolated individuals, however rich in money, intelligence, and cunning, have compared to the collective masses?"[25] Mutual aid pointed to the future. It was not simply desirable; it was necessary, natural, and morally and intellectually superior to primitive notions of competition. The dominant classes were denied any part in the moral and intellectual development of the human race, and, in accordance with the law of natural selection, belonged to a world that would soon pass.[26]

Mutual aid was alive and well, but before it could become the dominant social value it would have to smash the bonds that held it in check. Reclus made it perfectly clear that workers would have to fight for their liberation.[27] The competitive nature of capitalism made it difficult to respond to serious threats from a unified working class, but he felt that it could be overturned with little effort.[28] The ruling classes could hardly be expected to yield without a fight; that would run counter to the natural order. It was also inconceivable that the working class, once victorious, would revert to the primitive law of competition, since in the very act of freeing themselves workers would develop an instinct for cooperation, and this would bring about fundamental change. There was no more established fact, said Reclus, than that "external society must change in proportion to internal pressure."[29]

This notion appears in various formulations throughout Reclus's work. In the 1870s he enjoined readers "not to forget that the social ideal is always realised,"[30] and made the point in 1892 that "the first law of history is that society models itself after its ideals."[31] Society would have to be modelled on the anarchist ideal, which was not "human nature as we find it in ourselves," but rather the "noble form of self-gratification—for the general good."[32] Therein lay the appeal of mutual aid, and it had to be fostered if workers were to build and sustain a socialist society. Practice was not always a response to theory, however; Reclus insisted that there existed interaction between the two: "The deed grows out of the idea, and the idea out of the deed."[33]

Reclus was well aware of the popular belief—which has endured—that anarchism was appropriate only for "backward" areas. He objected as well to the suggestion that all countries were open to the anarchist appeal. Bakunin, he argued, became an anarchist in Paris, and although he attracted many Russians, none continued to be anarchists after his death; and while Kropotkin made contact with Russian exiles in England, all were more or less constitutionalists. The countries with the most anarchists were those which

> have long been liberated from religious and monarchical prejudice, where revolution has upset the established order, where the practice of communal life has accustomed people to working without a master, where objective study has developed independent thinkers.[34]

Reclus saw the anarchist ideal as more highly developed in those areas of the world in which education led to emancipation from religious and political prejudices: primarily in France, then in Catalonia, Northern Italy, London, among the Germans in the United States, in the Spanish-American republics, and in Australia. It was not race which determined the tendency towards anarchism: "education is everything."[35]

North Americans were not on his list. Reclus mentioned only German-Americans, and was thinking especially of those around Johann Most's *Freiheit* in New York.[36] The individualist school of Benjamin Tucker in the United States he considered totally distinct from European anarchism. "The only resemblance between individualist anarchists and us," he wrote, "is that of name."[37] The revolutionary potential of the American strike which paralysed the country in 1877 and extended to Canada Reclus saw as otherwise untapped; workers concentrated on trade-union issues like wages and working conditions.[38]

Science was for Reclus a tool with which to create the society "without masters." "I fight for what I know to be a good cause," he wrote, "because in that way I keep my sense of justice."[39] "I am far from believing in progress as an axiom," yet all persons of principle had no choice but to fight and to suffer for it.[40] "It matters little whether we succeed; at least we shall have interpreted the internal voice."[41] What are we to make of the relationship between such religious convictions and science?

Like virtually all late-nineteenth-century socialists and liberals who appealed to science to ground their beliefs, Reclus did not worry about those myths of science and rationality which trouble twentieth-century theorists. Science was perhaps the one authority he failed to question, and he joined with Marxists and liberals in acknowledging it. As we have seen, as of 1871 Reclus conscientiously abstained from participating in "bourgeois" politics and economy. It simply never occurred to him that his adherence to the tenets of Western science constituted participation in the order that he so despised.

It was through science, thought Reclus, that reality could be explained, and the chief characteristic of human beings was their position in a natural order, their conscience an integral part of this order.[42] Presumably, all who followed their conscience—that is, acted in good faith—would be faultless. According to his schema of human evolution, a primitive being reacting blindly to the demands of the environment was gradually transformed into one reacting self-consciously. In a sense, both were in tune with nature. The primitive who possessed only rudiments of a conscience should be judged in the context of what could reasonably be expected. Reclus meant not that an individual should be subject to surveillance by others, for, not fully possessing the facts, they could render only an opinion. The real judge was the individual, who could never escape the merciless demands of the "internal voice." "Do what you please!" Reclus saw as the message of "our great ancestor Rabelais,"[43] so long as you follow your conscience. It is interesting that he refused to moralise despite his own highly moral standards.

Conscience was the guide to proper conduct. "It is in each person, in his internal tribunal, in his conscience, and in his will that is to be found the spur of destiny."[44] The course of human history was seen as essentially a struggle of wills. Russia and Germany were unified under "the will of the masters." The revolutionary struggle was one of brotherhood, and as people progressed to a higher level, as their conscience became more developed, their will became more forceful. Like conscience, will was an integral part of human nature, and its potential was formidable.

It was this conviction that sustained his belief that great states could be undermined,[45] but it did not carry with it the strain of inevitability which characterised Reclus's views in the 1850s. He wrote to Bakunin in 1875 that he was very uneasy about the "definitive result"; not for a long time, he said, had he believed in the inevitability of progress.[46] While Reclus perceived the existence of a natural evolutionary process, he also saw that the success of the revolutionary cause depended on human beings. Progress was not a foregone conclusion.

Reclus explained the "natural" order represented by anarchy. The relationship between individual and society he compared to that of cell and body: each existing independently but completely dependent on the other.[47] Sociology provided anarchists with two primordial facts, he said; each person is interdependent and perishes in isolation, and social progress is accomplished by the force of individual wills. To conform to the first "law" was to become collectivist; to the second, anarchist. People must conform to both in order to be true to their nature—that is, to be free. Submission to nature was liberation, and Reclus differentiated it from the forced obedience to the laws of the state, against which the anarchists were in "permanent revolt."[48] Anarchy, wrote Reclus, was "'life without masters,' for society as well as for the individual—social accord arising not from authority and obedience, from the law and its penal sanctions, but from the free association of individuals and groups acting in the interest of all and of each."[49] Anarchists could be confident that anarchy was possible because it was the fulfillment of laws which were immanent in human nature.

A strong sense of resistance, even in the face of an apparently hopeless situation, marked Reclus's life, and this attitude helped shape his approach to the German question. After the Paris Commune he shared the prevailing anarchist concern about the possibility of another war between France and Germany. In 1887 he declared in a letter that, given the state of the world, war was to be expected.[50] To foresee events, however, was not to become resigned to them. Reclus adopted an intransigent anti-militarism to the point where the Paris police claimed in a secret document that he might be preparing "a seditious movement whose aim is to thwart the efforts of the French armies at the moment of a Franco-German war."[51] By no means did Reclus lose his thirst for war against the state; socialism continued to be a universal aim of workers and peasants. His anti-militarism was based not on pacifism, but on the conviction that war between peoples directed by "nation-states" was regressive.

His friend Jacques Gross argued that there might be the advantage in war of "mixing the races." But, asked Reclus, had the recent war of Tongking changed the locals into Frenchmen? Were the French and Germans any closer after the war of 1870? The Franco-Prussian war had led not to less private ownership or to *rapprochement*; on the contrary, the tendency had been to strengthen property and weaken reconciliation.[52] He could not support a war which would inevitably divide the working class.

On this question Reclus was also at odds with Kropotkin, whose obsession with the possibility of a European war was evident from early 1887.[53] In January of that year Kropotkin insisted that German armies would attack France no later than spring and—in the tradition of the Paris Commune—advocated that they be resisted by the creation of revolutionary communes.[54] But Reclus was impatient with Kropotkin's strategy. He wrote to Gross that the discussion of war distracted from the social question.[55]

As a scientist committed to an understanding of general laws of development, Reclus was not content to insist that the will of the people could radically alter the nature of the existing system. There had to be evidence of such opposition in the past and a pattern of behaviour for the future. Science must help uncover the laws of social change. He believed he had found these laws in his theory of evolution and revolution. The theory, contained in an address given in Geneva in 1880, was an elaboration of a letter Reclus had written to the Fribourg Congress of the Jura Federation in 1878 and drew together a number of thoughts that had germinated for years.

The theme of evolution and revolution became a leitmotif in Reclus's writings, and almost everything he wrote after the 1870s related to it. His 1880 address was published as a pamphlet entitled *Evolution et Révolution*, which went through six editions and over the years appeared in several languages. Finally, the theme was expanded to book length and published in 1898.[56]

The argument was simple. One could not assume, said Reclus, that evolution and revolution were alternative forms of social change; there existed, in fact, an interrelated process of evolution and revolution. While evolution represented a period of preparation in which development of ideas and morals took place, it could not be expected to progress significantly toward socialist society because change constantly ran up against inertia. Pressure on the existing order could not build indefinitely, however, and resolution came in the form of shocks or revolutions. Thus, revolution followed evolution logically and naturally. Change, according to Reclus, was achieved through a repeated series of evolution-revolution, and it did not really matter whether one called this process evolutionary or revolutionary, for the gradual and the accelerated became aspects of change. He also thought of the process in terms of "permanent revolution."[57]

As Reclus attempted to come to terms with personal and political tragedy in the 1870s, he was comforted by the idea that although the hour of revolution had passed it would return in a more forceful form. His stand on the question was clarified in a mid-decade exchange of letters with Bakunin. The correspondence indicates the change of direction in European anarchism which Reclus saw as "normal evolution"; the flood of the revolution had receded without having done great damage. Although there were unpleasant times ahead, at least the experience would be "conclusive and complete."[58]

Bakunin was incapable of such stoicism. While agreeing to some extent, he was alarmed by the dangers of this kind of evolution and bemoaned "the MacMahon-Bonapartist dictatorship in France, that of Bismarck in the rest of Europe."[59] At one point he accused Reclus of disinterest in events in France.[60] Bakunin, whose inspiration was rooted in the mid-century upheavals, could not understand this detached enthusiasm. While Reclus looked to science for answers, and thereby set the pace for future anarchist thought, Bakunin found a modicum of comfort in the anticlerical movements of late 1875.

Bakunin died at Berne on 1 July 1876. In a graveside speech Reclus emphasised Bakunin's personal qualities, his vigorous intelligence, and his tireless participation in revolutionary struggle.[61] Shortly after, he became part of an international committee charged with collecting and editing the manuscripts of the great revolutionary. Some of Bakunin's manuscripts on the Paris Commune were published by Reclus in *Le Travailleur*, April-May 1878, and in 1882 he and Carlo Cafiero published part of another manuscript, the most widely read of Bakunin's writings, which they entitled *Dieu et l'Etat* (God and the State). For Reclus, Bakunin embodied the spirit of revolt immanent in all social progress, but his death represented the end of an era. The future lay with science.

The analysis of social change developed by Reclus had wide-ranging implications for his anarchist theories. He confessed that anarchy was but an ideal for the distant future,[62] when there would be no fixed institutions.[63] Anarchists of his own day he saw as at a relatively low level of development; since people in the future would have further evolved, contemporary anarchists were in no position to say how they should organise their world. Reclus avoided the trap of utopianism. His science led him to admit that the more he learned about human nature, the less certain he was about the kind of society he wanted. It was discomforting to be caught between science and utopia.

Anarchists, it is frequently said, believed in an apocalyptic revolution which would transform the world totally and establish a veritable heaven on earth. As far as Reclus was concerned, nothing could be farther from the truth. And it is likely that Reclus was not the only anarchist to be misread on the question. Granted, it appears certain that in the late 1870s there continued to exist enthusiastic anarchists, even people like Kropotkin who felt that revolution was imminent; many other socialists, including Marx and Engels, shared these hopes. Such hopes never died, but they did grow weaker.

The popularity of Reclus's pamphlet on evolution and revolution indicates a break with the traditional "Bakuninist" notion of revolution. It can hardly be doubted that Reclus was an important influence. In 1905 Kropotkin attributed to all anarchists ideas that were practically identical to those which Reclus had been formulating for decades.

> In common with most socialists, the anarchists recognise that, like all evolution in nature, the slow evolution of society is followed from time to time by periods of accelerated evolution which are called revolutions; and they think that the era of revolutions is not yet closed.[64]

By 1880 Reclus's work on evolution-revolution had established a theory that insisted on a natural "unfolding" of human potential. This process could not be forced, although Reclus clearly preferred to think it could be guided and hastened. As a "conscious anarchist" he found it necessary to formulate a revolutionary strategy. In view of the theory's rejection of any organisational structure which might cramp individual initiative, and its hostility to all political processes connected with the state, the development of a revolutionary strategy was not easy. Reclus came to develop a position in which both education and violence followed logically upon his theory of evolution and revolution.

Eight
Education, Violence, Solidarity

European socialist ideologies became sharply defined in the 1870s. Anarchists grew more isolated until they emerged as a distinct group with a fairly coherent outlook, although lacking a plan of action. The effectiveness of the modern state's means of repression, as demonstrated in 1871, severely limited the value of the tradition of the barricades. Anarchists themselves dismissed any question of party-political activity, Marxist or otherwise, within the parliamentary system. This attitude did not, however, preclude activities that might accelerate the revolutionary process. Anarchists wanted somehow to inform the people and stimulate them to action. Today, such notions might sound ineffectual; but from the perspective of the established order, anarchist propaganda conjured up more frightening visions than anything the Marxists came up with.

It is worth noting that in the late nineteenth century propaganda did not carry the pejorative connotations that have come to be associated with it today. For Reclus, propaganda was simply information, communication, the "facts," rather than deliberate distortion. Anarchist propaganda could take any number of forms, from apparently harmless casual conversation with the oppressed, to newspaper articles, to acts of violence. For Reclus, propaganda, defined in this broad sense, had a place, and he had scientific justifications for it.

The decade following the destruction of the Paris Commune was one in which anarchist theory took shape. Reclus was out of step and out of favour with other anarchists. The animosity directed at him was partly personal, but there existed underlying fundamental differences about revolutionary theory and the question of strategy. While Peter Kropotkin and Paul Brousse placed their hopes in imminent revolution, Reclus believed the era after 1871 was in important respects a new one and that the struggle must reflect this. In 1878 he said the way to anarchy would be long, just how long he could not tell.[1] In the early 1880s he continued to refer to the "great revolution"[2] and to the "next revolution,"[3] but in accordance with his theory of evolution and revolution it would be only one of many such events. Revolutionaries, said Reclus, must concentrate on helping the masses prepare for the next revolution. The immediate task involved working for emancipation from prejudice, ignorance, and the past; to loosen the emotional and intellectual structures of the existing order.

Preparation was obviously crucial to success. The period at hand, when states seemed more firmly entrenched than ever, was a time of evolution; Reclus stressed the importance of education. In December 1876 the Vevey section of the Jura Federation reflected his concerns when the *Bulletin* carried an insertion on "scientific socialist education." Three related areas were presented for discussion: (1) textbooks worth recommending to friends and sympathetic teachers; (2) textbooks that could be composed from revolutionary socialist literature and those which should be produced at any price; and (3) measures to assure children a scientific education outside religious, national, and political influences.[4] There were teachers who were prepared, he believed, or who could be persuaded, to use materials more favourably disposed to the revolutionary point of view. He did not see this as indoctrination, because socialist education would be *ipso facto* "scientific"; the information would be presented in such a way that people would be able to draw their own conclusions.[5]

Kropotkin was initially supportive of the idea, partly because he hoped the project would dovetail with his friend Paul Robin's plans to publish a series of children's books,[6] but he grew impatient when he realised that Reclus was thinking along the lines of bringing out a third series of James Guillaume's *Esquisses historiques* and a collection of songs.[7] Eventually, the La Chaux-de-Fonds section, in which Kropotkin was active, claimed that education must be subordinated to the struggle for social revolution.

In an open letter to La Chaux-de-Fonds in the *Bulletin* in March 1877,[8] Vevey expressed its agreement, and went on to state that members were under no illusion that an "integral and rational" education—or scientific education as opposed to "bourgeois" indoctrination—was now possible. This was not to say that greater influence could not be exerted; the question must be pursued, because education was an "essential weapon in the battle against present society." Vevey pointed to the excellent *Esquisses historiques*, and proposed that it be used as a model for an elementary work in each particular "science." A second project might be *Esquisses géographiques*, for which a plan already existed. The geography project would reveal the laws of the earth and study the races "which quarrel over it and whose common property it is." The series would put forward a scientific argument for the idea of universal brotherhood. The Vevey section responded favourably to La Chaux-de-Fonds' proposal for a history of popular movements, but thought it better to concentrate on a collection of songs and revolutionary poems which could be more readily published.

Reclus was very serious about his educational ideas, despite the lack of support. Plans were outlined for the publication of the third series of *Esquisses historiques* and for *Esquisses géographiques*.[9] Kropotkin remained silent on the question of *Esquisses historiques* but was irritated at the plan to deal with geography.[10] The precious funds, he said, would be better spent on a more explicitly political journal. Kropotkin complained about the Geneva group's proposal for a socialist dictionary; this project, he thought, should be entrusted to people with the same beliefs, and he suggested that an outline be drawn up as a guide, although he doubted that even such precautions would be effective.[11]

In 1876-77 Reclus and Kropotkin differed on several questions, but the two would in time become close friends and the leading theoreticians of the European anarchist movement. There were differences in temperament and judgement, but they diverged most sharply when it came to what each regarded as the scientific basis for anarchism.

Reclus saw anarchism as a theory capable of being supported scientifically, so that it did not matter if people of different political persuasions joined in the theoretical disputes (as trying as this might be at times)[12]; in the end the truth would win out. As for Kropotkin, although he had engaged in scientific endeavours in his homeland he retained a strain of anti-intellectualism which surfaced in his relations with Reclus and lingered in his political writings. If Reclus was anxious to explore alternatives in search of truth, Kropotkin was convinced that it was already embodied in the policies put forward by the Jura Federation and feared lest it be lost in the eclecticism of Genevans such as Reclus. Kropotkin's anarchism, at least in the 1870s, rested largely on the faith that was guarded by the priests of the "pure" anarchist party. Reclus shared that anarchist faith up to a point, but he wanted to move beyond narrow sectarianism; he would base anarchism on science, prove the validity of its arguments, and the world as a whole would embrace it.

He was willing to overlook what he saw as Kropotkin's short-comings, but Reclus was nevertheless disappointed at the lack of support for *Esquisses historiques* and *Esquisses géographiques*, and he had to abandon both projects. A parting shot was contained in "L'Avenir de nos enfants" (The Future of Our Children, 1877), which commenced: "Egoists that we are, in our revolutionary fervour we think of others much less often than we do ourselves. When we expose the grievance of the workers it is particularly that of the men, because men are the stronger." He pleaded with socialists to "think about our children's future rather than about our own situation. We belong more to the past than to the future." Children must be saved from the evils of bourgeois education, he said; they must become "physically and morally healthy." Anarchists must strive for free society by creating free individuals. [13]

These discussions on education took place while the Jura movement was facing disintegration. Prospects in Switzerland were far from good. Police harassment conspired with the failure to establish a popular base to drive many, like Paul Brousse and Andreas Costa, away from the struggle and into the arena of municipal and parliamentary socialism.

For people whose aim it was to foment universal social revolution, the scope for action was exceedingly narrow, and it looked as though they might be reduced to a small band of impotent ideologues out of touch with modern society and politics. In the mid-1870s Reclus wrote to Michael Bakunin about the weak spirits in the movement whose wish it was, rather than their commitment, to see the struggle through. [14] By the end of the decade he grew despondent over their lack of desire for an anarchist movement. Frustrated by his own impotence, he lavished praise upon those who elsewhere struggled on against Czarist autocracy or languished in Russian prisons. [15] But Reclus lost hope only momentarily. His feisty spirit was restored, and he became more extreme than ever. This new militancy was expressed at the last Congress of the Jura Federation held at Lausanne in June 1882.

His most surprising statements at Lausanne were made in the discussion on "integral" education. Reclus warned that a precondition for such education was the abolition of property, for as long as society was divided into classes—bosses and workers—all efforts to establish integral education would be diversionary. Asked if it was wise to wait until the morrow of the revolution, whether it might be useful to take an interest in vocational education and to persuade the trade associations to become involved at the commune level, Reclus insisted that it was absolutely wrong to have anything to do with the state or the commune, to ask anything of "authority" under any circumstance. If the trade associations convinced communes to establish vocational education, he said, the most intelligent pupils would develop into "little tyrants," good foremen who would be the enemies of workers and socialists and who would one day become politicians.[16] The socialist's task was to demonstrate by propaganda "all social evils."[17] At the informal gathering after the Congress, Reclus added:

> It is only in a free society, based on solidarity, economic equality, and complete individual liberty, that there can exist the results of integral education, because... education, that is, life, is the continual physical and moral development of the individual... in a mutually responsible and free society, which we shall reach only through revolution.[18]

Ever since the Commune Reclus had been interested in a counter-educational system. By 1882 this interest had subsided, although other anarchists in the meantime had taken up the idea. As the Jura movement declined, Reclus abandoned the last vestiges of his "moderate" approach and asserted instead that society must be liberated before changes in education could be expected. The educational system, parliamentary politics, and cooperativism he now saw as "circuitous" routes that anarchists must avoid. Later in the century he would return somewhat to advocating change via educational reform.

Reclus also had more than just second thoughts about the value of working with trade associations. Some members of the Federation felt that anarchists might even help organise trade associations. Reclus insisted that it was impossible to do so without becoming contaminated by the narrow ideas of the workers, that socialists would run the risk of compromising their beliefs: "We shall not be able to unfurl our socialist flag; we shall be obliged to work at their level." Still, he thought, revolutionaries might infiltrate existing organisations in order to undermine "the old ways" and agitate from the inside.[19] Reclus's arguments were successful, and the Lausanne Congress supported his position on both education and trade associations.

> The Congress is of the opinion that without the abolition of private property and the State, its gendarme, agitation for integral education can be only illusory. The Congress, recognising the usefulness of every workers' organisation insofar as

it is a force of opposition, declares its solidarity with every strike and every economic struggle.[20]

That Reclus participated in the 1882 Lausanne Congress is surprising in view of his customary reluctance, in the post-Commune period, to take part in debate.[21] One senses an urgency to clarify issues while there was still some organisation. At any rate, a further meeting was planned, at his instigation, to coincide with the Geneva international music festival.[22] This last international gathering of anarchists for many years was held 13-14 August and was attended by the Jurassians, several Frenchmen, and one delegate from Italy.[23]

Their manifesto emphasised schism.

"Between we anarchists and every political party, conservative or moderate, whether it fights against all freedom or grants it by degrees, the schism is complete..." The groups were to be absolutely autonomous "in the means which will seem to them the most efficacious."[24] One of the defendants at the Lyons trial of anarchists in January 1883 said that Reclus had drafted this manifesto[25] and additional testimony would confirm this.[26]

At this time European socialists of all shades could usually agree on what they were against as well as their ultimate goals. It was the question of means that most divided them. For Reclus this issue was a crucial one, and in order to avoid "circuitous" routes he considered numerous alternatives. As we saw in chapter 2, he refused to retreat to some anarchist "colony," either in Europe or the New World. Perhaps out of both exasperation and determination, he welcomed acts of terrorism—then referred to by anarchists less menacingly as "propaganda by the deed."

The notion of propaganda by the deed can be traced to Italian anarchists in the 1870s. It gained recognition in anarchist circles elsewhere after the famous Benevento affair of April 1877 when Carlo Cafiero and Errico Malatesta provoked a peasant uprising in southern Italy in which tax records were burned and the overthrow of the king proclaimed. The tactic was outlined by one of Malatesta's associates who described how a small group of armed men could move

> about the countryside as much as possible, preaching war, inciting social brigandage, occupying small communes and leaving them after performing those revolutionary acts that were possible and moving to locations where our presence would be most useful.[27]

Such activities came to be considered an acceptable means of educating the illiterate masses.

In August 1877 an article entitled "Propaganda by the Deed," written by Brousse and supported by Kropotkin, appeared in the *Bulletin*. Traditional propaganda, said the article, was inherently limited in its ability to reach the masses and must henceforth be supplemented by the deed. The Paris Commune was used as a powerful illustration of what ordinary people could achieve, but even modest events like the demonstrations then being held in Berne were seen as worthy examples.[28] Anarchist ideas must be spread not only by the spoken and written word, Kropotkin insisted in 1879, but also—and especially—by action.[29]

Just what propaganda by the deed might entail was left unclear. Anarchists continued to think in terms of the uprising at Benevento; they did not foresee that such acts would be used as theoretical justification for political terrorism. There is some basis for arguing that anarchists were caught off-guard by the "terrorists." As we shall see in chapter 10, however, Reclus reacted positively and enthusiastically to the terrorism of the early 1890s. The roots of his position can be traced to the decade following the Commune.

The shift in emphasis of the Russian revolutionary movement from the peaceful activities of the Narodniks (Populists) to the terrorism of Narodnaya Volya (People's Will) had an important effect on Reclus. In December 1878 he declared: "In order to give birth to the new society of peace, joy, and love, young people must not be afraid to die."[30] The following July he told Elie that Russian nihilists were "the salt of the earth. Their devotion to duty, their contempt for death, their spirit of solidarity, their peace of mind amazes me, and I blush when I compare myself to them."[31]

Reclus had contact with a number of Russian exiles in Switzerland, including Ralli, Nicholas Joukowsky, and Kropotkin, and he probably met Vera Zasúlitch who made her way there in the spring of 1878.[32] He was heartened by people like Klementz who returned to Russia prepared to suffer imprisonment for their beliefs. Although the Jura movement was in decline, there was a revolutionary spark elsewhere—even in Russia, the darkest corner of civilisation. In 1878, for the first time in almost a decade, Reclus came out in favour of violence. If justice were the ideal, anarchists would demand it for all, he said; if, however, it were true that only force governed society, then anarchists would use violence against it.[33]

Propaganda by the deed, however imprecise it would continue to be for the time being, was recognised for the first time at the London (Black) International Congress of 14-20 July 1881, which for fairly transparent reasons suggested studying the new technical and chemical sciences.[34] There is evidence, however, that the anarchist programme drawn up in London simply reiterated decisions taken the year before. According to a police report, Reclus, Kropotkin, and Pierre Martin were among thirty-two "political agitators" who met at Vevey on 12 September 1880 for the purpose of discussing tactics. A number of resolutions resembled those passed later in London. In some instances even the wording was identical. According to the police report, the Swiss meeting called for:

1. Total destruction by force of existing institutions.
2. The necessity of propagating by the deed the revolutionary idea and the spirit of revolt.
3. Departure from legal means in order to act at an illegal level, which is the only way to revolution.
4. Since the technical and chemical sciences have already served the revolutionary cause, the organisations and individuals who make up the groups must be advised to give weight to the study and application of these sciences as a means of attack and defence.
5. Group and individual autonomy is agreed upon, but in order to maintain unity of action the groups should correspond directly with each other; to facilitate such contact a central bureau of international information will be created.[35]

Unfortunately, the police report is not dated and the whole affair may have been invented by a police agent after the London Congress. There is a strong probability, however, that the report is not a fake and that the Swiss programme was adopted in London with minor modifications. Reclus did not go to London, but as a member of the group associated with the new *Révolté* (launched by Kropotkin in 1879), he signed a statement supporting Kropotkin as delegate.[36] There is nothing to indicate that Reclus disagreed with the London resolutions. On the contrary, the record of his participation at Lausanne the following year shows that he supported them. The 1882 Congress of the Jura Federation could, in fact, be taken as confirming the conclusions reached at London, for it resolved on "the urgency of every means of action, the spoken and written word and the deed, [and] recommends that all comrades become zealously involved in incessant propaganda, especially among our brothers, the peasants."[37]

Propaganda by the deed became increasingly identified with any act of revolt, even when the act was not consciously performed to elicit support for anarchism.[38] In March 1882 an unemployed young man named Fournier shot his employer, whom he considered responsible for the crisis in the weaving industry at Roanne in France. In August of the same year there was extensive terrorist activity by the Bande noire directed against the mine owners of Montceau-les-Mines in the Lyons area. Fournier did not act under the banner of anarchism, but nonetheless *Le Révolté* referred to his act as "propaganda by the deed, the most fecund, the most popular."[39] The Bande noire terrorism was likewise considered an event of "immense significance, and hence the consequences, from the socialist-revolutionary point of view, are inestimable."[40] There is no question that the root of such unrest was a French economy that had been experiencing stagnation since 1873. To the anarchists, however, the "revolt" represented an elemental thirst for justice and was an indication of revolutionary spirit.

Although some anarchists were uneasy, in an important sense their theory demanded accommodation to acts of revolt. The Lyons trial of 1883 showed how anarchists became identified as instigators and justifiers of terrorism. It is not difficult to imagine why the Lyons authorities concluded that anarchists' "moral solidarity" was instrumental to social unrest there, if not the root cause. In an effort to control terrorism, they arrested and tried sixty-five anarchists, including such prominent figures as Kropotkin and Emile Gauthier, for belonging to an international organisation whose goal was the destruction of the state.[41] Kropotkin fuelled the allegations of complicity in crime: "I have said that when a party is put in the position of having to use dynamite, it ought to use it—as, for example, in Russia where the people [as a force] would have disappeared if they had not used the means put at their disposal by science."[42]

Shortly after the trial a poster went up around Paris, signed by a "groupe parisien de propagande anarchiste" and printed by the *Révolté* press (Reclus had assumed responsibility for the paper while Kropotkin was in prison). "Yes," is read, "we are guilty of applying our theories by all means: by word, by the pen, BY THE DEED—that is to say, by revolutionary acts, whatever these may be." In anticipation of things to come, the text continued: "Yes, we acknowledge them loudly. We claim them as ours. We delight in them."[43] The poster represented a shift in position, from after-the-fact approval to blatant advocacy. Kropotkin languished in prison, but the trial brought him and the anarchists a good deal of notoriety. In keeping with the mood, Reclus chose *Paroles d'un révolté* (Words of a Rebel) as the title for a collection of Kropotkin's essays that he published in 1885.

Once Reclus began to consider the implications of violent acts originating with the people he injected a more positive note into his theorising on the question of violence and revolutionary tactics. In February 1883 he insisted that it was perfectly just to arm oneself in self-defence: "...defence armed with a right" should not be equated with gratuitous violence.[44]

> If it is true, as I believe it is, that the product of common work ought to be common property, it is not a call to violence to demand one's share. If it is true, as I believe it is, that no one has the right to deprive another of his freedom, then he who rebels is completely within his rights.[45]

Reclus recognised that revolution would be violent, but claimed that the word "violent" originally meant "strong." The people had to use force in support of justice and goodness; it was a question of strength.[46] Acts of revolt were to be welcomed, for they showed the capacity of the human spirit. Since governments failed to check social evils, it fell to "free" people to impose justice.[47]

It was to be hoped, said Reclus, that the violence necessary for the overthrow of the existing order would stop short of vengeance, for the cause of justice would not be served if one set of oppressors were replaced by another. Anarchists should not condemn people to death, however rich and powerful they were; the society which produced such malevolents was the object of attack.[48] Nonetheless, acts of vengeance could not be eliminated altogether; Reclus saw them as "inevitable incidents of a period of violent change," the "necessary outcome" of unjust relations.[49]

> In a word, if whole classes and populations are unfairly used, and have no hope of finding in the society to which they belong a redresser of abuses, is it not certain that they will resume their inherent right of vengeance and execute it without pity? Is not this indeed a law of Nature, a consequence of the physical law of shock and counter-shock?... Oppression has always been answered with violence.[50]

In mid-1883 Reclus clearly believed that revolution would be made by those who had something to gain from it, but he preferred to say: "It will develop by the natural accommodation of men to their normal milieu."[51]

In earlier revolutions, explained Reclus in *Evolution et Révolution*, people had vague ideas but no definite aims. Now, however, they were becoming conscious of the need for a just society.

> What the worker felt yesterday, he knows today, and each new experience teaches him to know it better. And are not the peasants, who cannot raise enough to keep body and soul together from their morsel of ground, and the yet more numerous class who do not possess a clod of their own, are not all these beginning to comprehend that the soil ought to belong to the men who cultivate it? They have always instinctively felt this, now they know it, and are preparing to assert their claim in plain language.[52]

Instinct was giving way to determination, and it was accompanied by growing solidarity among the rebels. "Isolated, the rebels are doomed to death, but their example is not lost, and other malcontents rise after them. They form a league, and, from defeat to defeat, they finally arrive at victory."[53] Revolutionaries, because of their superior education, might formulate the ideas, but their theories were based on study of the masses.

> It is not they [the revolutionaries] who experience the joy of transforming ideas and passions into deeds. The Revolution is always made below. For those above there is a struggle between ideas and personal affinities; for those below, they are at one; that is where there is an immense superiority of force.[54]

Reclus maintained that as individuals reached higher levels of development, the instinctual gave way to the self-conscious. Yet the more conscious a person became, the farther removed he or she seemed to be from the scene of the battle. Revolutionary tactics were elaborated by the people as they struggled to establish the just society. As a theoretician Reclus had to discover these tactics, and to suggest improvements. He was an interpreter. It was not his business to condemn theft and violence, but to show how they fitted in with the people's struggle.

A growing fanaticism did not turn Reclus into a fire-eating radical, however. As an internationally renowned geographer who was also an anarchist committed to the idea of universal brotherhood, he appeared eccentric, and even naïve, but hardly dangerous. His scholarship and fame provided a kind of license. The French authorities kept a close watch on his activities after 1872, but they were reluctant to prosecute him without firm evidence. Reclus was not brought to trial at Lyons in 1883—although he said he would not flee[55]—even when the prosecution considered links with him as evidence against an accused.[56] One defendant charged that the authorities were afraid to arrest the famous geographer lest all manner of Europeans protest, not only anarchists and radicals. Kropotkin was also a scholar, but he was an exile and a foreigner.[57]

To his admirers, love, goodness, and tolerance exuded from Reclus's very being. When he supported violence, some people attributed even that to his goodness.[58] As he grew older, his reputation became almost mythical and was confirmed physically by the flowing white hair and beard of the sage. There is plenty of evidence to substantiate this image. We have already discussed the generosity of his reaction in the late 1870s to his detractor Paul Brousse. It is also worth noting the evidence for his subsequent relations with Kropotkin, the man who joined Brousse's "pure anarchist party."

At their first meeting in February 1877, Reclus offered to introduce Kropotkin to the Swiss Geographical Society.[59] As we have seen, however, such cordiality soon vanished. As relations slowly improved, though, the two drew closer. Kropotkin was admitted into the society in January 1880.[60] At about this time Reclus invited him to help prepare the sixth volume of *Nouvelle Géographie universelle* which was devoted to a study of Siberia,[61] and Kropotkin and his wife Sophie moved from Geneva to Clarens where Reclus had lived since early 1879.[62] In April Reclus wrote to the *Journal de Genève* in support of his "colleague and friend" whose lack of official papers concerned the Geneva authorities. Kropotkin looked back fondly on his stay at Clarens and remarked that it was then that he "worked out the foundation of nearly all that I wrote later on."[63] Kropotkin was expelled from Switzerland in August 1881 and went to live in Thonon, near Lyons; his new friendship with Reclus grew stronger.

In December 1882 Reclus hastened from Clarens to Thonon to be at Kropotkin's side when he was arrested by the Lyons authorities.[64] During the three years of Kropotkin's imprisonment (1883-86), Reclus provided both moral and material support.[65] When *Le Révolté* foundered under a manager too fond of the nearby wine shop, he approached Jean Grave and persuaded him to come to Geneva.[66] Wrote Kropotkin in his *Memoirs*: "For the first year we had to rely entirely on ourselves; but gradually Elisée Reclus took a greater interest in the work, and finally gave more life than ever to the paper after my arrest."[67]

Grave has left no doubt that Reclus contributed money as well as ideas and interest. By the time Grave arrived in Geneva, Reclus was paying for the printer as well as the manager.[68] He also assured Grave of eighty francs per month.[69] The personal account book kept by Reclus as of 1875 shows that he contributed to *Le Révolté* from May 1879, and from the end of 1880 paid generous amounts to Kropotkin, Herzig, and Dumartheray as well. As of spring 1883 funds also went to Sophie, Grave, and Clairvaux (where the anarchists condemned at the Lyons trial were imprisoned). The sums were usually one hundred francs, and sometimes two hundred, but occasionally amounted to more than five hundred in one month; this pattern continued until about 1887. (From time to time, he also financially helped other friends as well as various relatives.)[70] Small wonder that in anarchist folklore Reclus and Kropotkin have emerged as close friends and allies and that Kropotkin's initial hostility toward Reclus faded.

After his release from Clairvaux in early 1886, Kropotkin was expelled from France and moved to England. He looked warmly back on France, the land of revolution. In the winter of 1877-78 he had helped Andreas Costa and Jules Guesde create the first anarchist groups in Paris,[71] and he referred to *Le Révolté* as his "child." He probably took it for granted that he would resume control of the paper once he was free. In April 1886, three months after his release, he contemplated the future of the paper and the energy it would require. "For my child, the *Révolté*," he wrote to

Willam Morris, "I see with some anxiousness that we shall soon be compelled to make it appear weekly, and that I shall be bound to give it some two days, or more, every week, instead of every fortnight."[72]

In the meantime, Le Révolté was in the hands of Jean Grave, a man whose temperament can be gathered from his nickname, "the pope of rue Mouffetard" (where both he and the journal resided). A shoemaker by trade, Grave occupied a place of some importance in the French anarchist movement of the day, especially after 1885 when Le Révolté was transferred to Paris to avoid increasing harassment from the Swiss authorities.[73] In September 1887 Grave launched La Révolte as a replacement for Le Révolté, perhaps in an attempt to assert his own position.

The Paris police continued to speculate on Kropotkin's relations with the French anarchists. A police report of early December 1887 noted that Kropotkin complained about the stagnation of the groups and that some months earlier his wife Sophie had travelled to Paris to put things in order. She was "very irritated" with Grave who had monopolised Le Révolté, she was cool towards Elisée Reclus, and she considered Elie bourgeois. The report suggested that Sophie wanted to see the journal more fully under the control of her husband and was encouraged in this by Kropotkin's friends in the Parisian groups. According to the police, there was talk of bringing out a rival paper, and although money was a "burning question" the paper was considered a possibility.[74]

Although the police report may be pure fabrication, it is known that there did exist tensions of some sort in 1888. Reclus wrote to Jacques Gross: "The affair is disastrous, 1. because it prevents us from spending our money usefully, 2. because it keeps us from making recommendations in the future." The unpublished letter has been edited, unfortunately. It breaks off at this point, and then continues: "Tell me what to do. There will be only half an evil if solidarity is maintained between comrades and if we recover from it better comrades and better friends."[75] There is no evidence of Kropotkin's being involved in this "affair."

Despite Kropotkin's plans to devote more energy to the French paper, his efforts now went into the London-based anarchist journal Freedom, which he helped found in 1886. There is some suggestion of minor clashes between Kropotkin and Grave in the early 1890s. According to an October 1892 police report, when Grave was asked why Kropotkin no longer contributed articles to La Révolte, he replied: "Because I corrected his articles 2 or 3 times. Should there be pontiffs here, yes or no?"[76]

Reclus and Kropotkin, on the other hand, got along better all the time. Reclus wrote the preface and corrected the proofs for Kropotkin's La Conquête du pain[77] (The Conquest of Bread, 1892).[78] Tensions which might have surfaced between them were minimised because for his part Reclus wanted to present a united front. Moreover, it became increasingly difficult for Kropotkin to adopt a hostile attitude. There was no one to replace Brousse, with whom he had allied himself earlier, and in any case it would have been difficult to turn against one to whom he had become heavily indebted. Furthermore, Kropotkin's years in prison had lost him some ground to Reclus, whose stature in anarchist and scholarly circles grew steadily. For all these reasons, solidarity won the day, and as we shall see in the next two chapters, it also stood the test of time and serious differences of opinion on the questions of theft and terrorism.

Solidarity represented a peculiar type of influence which Reclus exercised over both Kropotkin and Grave. "The pope" was easily put in his place by Reclus. In 1891, for example, Grave was about to condemn the new syndicalist paper, *Le Pot à colle*. Concerned about such "excommunication," Reclus said it was no better to "make personal remarks against papers than against individuals... Let us concern ourselves with our own affairs and let others manage for themselves."[79] Grave often grew exasperated with Reclus's axiom "Let us not judge,"[80] but Reclus was determined to uphold the common front and for a long time avoided direct criticism of rival socialist theories.

Reclus may have been naïve at times, but he should not be seen as a saint. It is clear how he wished to be remembered. "I am a fighting cock," he once announced to a friend.[81] Solidarity against the enemy and a fight to the finish. To Reclus, solidarity was more than a sentiment; it was part of his revolutionary strategy.

ELISÉE RECLUS

Photograph by NADAR

Elie Reclus
Photograph by PAUL RECLUS

Nine

Property and Theft

Such anarchists as Elisée Reclus saw the society of the future as one in which there would be communism in production and distribution; solidarity would replace unfettered competition. In the meantime, Reclus regarded himself as a revolutionary as well as a scientist whose task it was to discover the laws of social-economic development. He maintained that what happened historically was not necessarily in tune with nature, and that men and women would best fulfill their potential by challenging capitalism and establishing communism. But it was not simply a question of a utopian quest, for Reclus held that capitalism was pathological to human society. If allowed to proceed on its "destined" course, it would destroy all achievements and reduce the majority to slaves, before destroying itself. His conclusions were emphatic. Private property was the heart of the system; since, he also reasoned, all property was theft, to "steal it back" was an emancipatory act. Reclus and his nephew Paul were almost the only *Révolté* anarchists to support individuals who repossessed "common property." His position on property and theft flowed logically from his theories; as we shall see, he could not condemn the anarchist "thief" short of denying the validity of his own arguments.

The post-Commune years Reclus viewed as a period of rising consciousness. There was also a change in the objective fortunes of the bourgeoisie. In 1875 Reclus wrote to Bakunin of the "normal" evolution taking place in France. It was the bourgeoisie in its "abstract state" that would reign; stripped of religious trappings and old symbols, it would soon show its true face.[1] The Republic would survive in France under bourgeois domination, he said, because there was no longer any need for a Napoleon.[2] There was also room for optimism. While the bourgeoisie had won its battle with the aristocracy, at the moment of triumph it had also become more vulnerable, since it could no longer hide behind the traditional authority represented by the Church and the aristocracy. Thus Reclus could even take heart at bourgeois domination, because the issues between capital and labour were becoming simplified.[3]

Under his influence, the small Vevey section of the Jura Federation emphasised this point, and in 1875 criticised members of the (federalist) International who allowed debate on the social question to be diverted into outdated discussion of clerical and aristocratic evils. Revolutionaries had a duty to "acquaint all workers with the arrogance of the bourgeois reaction."[4] The struggle to wrest power from the "masters" was what revolution was about; only after destruction of the capitalist economy could people build a society based on communist principles.

A hitherto neglected fragment of a letter from 1887 provides insight into Reclus's thoughts on relations between capital and labour. Apparently addressed to the Italian Oscar Bertoia, it comments on a brochure that Bertoia had written.[5] "Your thesis," wrote Reclus, "is the following: The activity of workers under one or several masters accustoms them to communism in production, which is followed by communism in consumption." The argument was flawed, he contended, because industrial production was a form of slavery, and as such could never develop in the opposite direction, towards freedom. Slavery might accustom workers to communal production, but as soon as the fetters were removed, the relationship collapsed. Freed slaves took refuge in their own little plots of land, living apart from their former comrades. Not only did industrial production under capitalism not promote association, it discouraged the natural tendency to cooperate. Capitalism brutalised workers both physically and morally through excessive use of the division of labour. How could people occupied in mindless tasks for forty years of their lives, fourteen hours a day, 320 days a year—slaves of the machine—be on the way to "libertarian communism"? Capitalists pushed the division-of-labour

143

principle to such an extreme that even scientists were reduced to assembly-line robots. Reclus personally knew one chemist who had been employed to do the same scientific experiment for five years; there were German scientists who worked alone all day, testing substances in a dark room. Industrial employees performed mindless tasks, but, worst of all, they were kept from knowing how their work fitted in with that of others.

As capitalists became more subject to the mounting pressures of competition, said Reclus, they would be compelled to introduce more efficient machines. This would result in the continual simplifying of procedures, as well as rising unemployment, which in turn would place more and more power in the hands of the employer. He would be able to reduce salaries, get rid of trouble-makers, and hire the most docile. If French workers were too independent, they could be replaced by Germans; if the Germans subsequently proved unruly, they could be replaced by Chinese.[6] Nor were these developments restricted to the towns and cities. Day by day, old farming routines were discarded in favour of scientific procedures.[7] In the agricultural sector, no less than in industry, concentration was inevitable.

> By the laws of economic development, it is the fate of small property to be devoured by large. The plots of land owned by the peasants are destined to become part of the large domains, just as the small workshops are inevitable prey for the powerful manufacturers, while the big financiers enrich themselves on the ruins of petty speculators.[8]

For the sceptical, Reclus pointed to instances of large-scale agricultural production in the United States and to English proposals to import American techniques.[9] Even the French peasant, the most tenacious of all, would not be able to hold out.

> The peasant who has a patch of earth may, like the artisan and the petit bourgeois, still own something. The time is coming when it will be impossible for him to compete with the systematic exploitation of the soil by the capitalists and the machine, and then he will have no choice but to become a beggar.[10]

Inevitable and inexorable laws governed capitalism and led to competition at the level of capital and labour. Among capitalists there would develop increasing concentration of economic power until it rested in the hands of a mighty few. Among the workers there would arise great hordes scrambling for the crumbs which fell from the tables of the mighty. The peasants and the factory workers would share the same fate, "working when the employers are interested in giving them work... then humbly asking to be hired, then even extending their hands to beg for a pittance."[11] To let capitalism develop in accordance with the laws that governed it would be to participate in the creation of a world in which the many would be the slaves of the few. Ultimately, the very success of capitalism would be its own demise, for the laws governing it doomed it to collapse; efforts to increase production and keep the work force at a minimum would lead to mass unemployment and inability to sell products.[12] But, as we shall see shortly, simply waiting for the end would prove suicidal for workers and for society as a whole.

That Reclus agreed with the arguments made in *Das Kapital* is clear, and there is little doubt that he was influenced by them. Before 1871, his relations with Marx were good, and it was then that he became familiar with Marxist ideas. While both were determined to present their views "scientifically," Reclus was less bothered about injecting a moralising tone into his work (that is not to say that Marx did not moralise). He wrote of capitalists' greed and the misery of the masses, and he equated capitalism with injustice, communism with justice. His religious roots are evident in such statements as the following made in 1884: "One capital fact dominates the history of man—that every kindred and people yearns after justice. The very life of humanity is but one long cry for that fraternal equity which still remains unattained."[13] Reclus condemned capitalism for allowing people with money, or those with more intelligence, or cunning, or luck, to control the lives of other human beings.[14]

Marxian economics was based on the British experience. In France, the land of peasants, Reclus's interest was understandably centred on the significance of capitalism for agriculture, and his contribution to the economic debate consisted mainly of a concern over the spread of capitalism to the countryside. His early years in the Gironde and Lower Pyrenees had sensitised him to the problems of rural France. In the mid-1860s Reclus worried about the political views of the peasants, their strong identification with the Napoleonic regime and their lack of participation in the newly emerging workers' movement. In 1866, he and Madame Champseix founded the Sunday paper *L'Agriculteur*, which appealed to peasants in terms they could understand.[15] He stated at an IWMA General Council meeting held in London in mid-1869 that French peasants knew very little about world affairs.[16] In the February 1871 elections, as we have seen, he offered himself as a candidate in the Lower Pyrenees, and he engaged in Republican propaganda there and in the Gironde before returning to Paris.[17]

Reclus believed it was a mistake to focus only on urban workers as agents of revolution. Peasants were not shielded from the laws of capitalist development, he argued, and they too would eventually succumb. The hope for the future lay in this very defeat, in fact, because in the struggle for survival against the threat of capitalism the peasants' isolation would give way to solidarity. Agricultural associations formed for purposes of defence would force peasants to adopt progressive attitudes and new institutions. Reclus felt that this process had already begun in England. There was hardly a word said on the subject at revolutionary meetings, he complained in 1873, but "this association of the workers of the land is perhaps the greatest development of the century."[18] Peasants and factory workers were the "true proletarians."[19] With the expansion of capitalism, all workers, be their workplace field or factory, would be dependent on the "good will of a master."[20]

With some dismay, in fact, Reclus saw the revolutionaries as playing into the hands of the dominant classes, whose power relied on hostility between peasant and factory worker.[21] The peasants would have to be drawn into the movement for communism; as all workers struggled for control of the means of production—both land and factory—they would recognise a common enemy.[22] Like Marx, Reclus felt that the petits bourgeois would surely disappear and that most would join the working class.

For Reclus, it was urgent that the message reach the ordinary folk he had known from personal experience. "It is absolutely necessary to join the people," he said. "We ought to follow the example of the Russian youth."[23] Reclus wrote two pamphlets specifically designed to stimulate ideas about and among the peasants: *Ouvrier, prends la machine, Prends la terre, paysan!* (1880) (Worker, Take the Machine! Take the Land, Peasant!); and the popular *A mon Frère, le paysan* (1893) (To My Brother, the Peasant). It was not the aim of socialists, he said, to take the land away from the peasants who had cultivated it so lovingly.

> Thus we shall take the land—yes, we shall take it—but away from those who hold it without working it, in order to return it to those who do work it... What you cultivate, my brother, is yours, and we shall do everything in our power to help you keep it; but what you do not cultivate belongs to a comrade. Make room for him.[24]

Peasants were warned of the cunning of the common enemy, the *seigneur* (read capitalist) and the state. They would be better able to ward off the enemy, they were advised, by grouping together, as did the Zadrougas, or "group of friends," in the *mir* (commune), or little "universe," in Russia. There would be no need to divide collective property into innumerable little plots of land, nor to drive the cows into different enclosures at day's end. Everyone would work together in harmony, and in times of crisis each would come to the aid of all.[25] "The commune is, at the same time, the property of all and of each."[26]

Capitalist production was seen as inevitably dividing people; it could not bring them together. "It is only through liberty that we achieve liberty," Reclus explained to Oscar Bertoia.[27] However, there was no turning back: "Whether we want to or not, we shall pass through the mill of [capitalist] large-scale industry." To know the future, however, was not to submit to it: "Alas, yes, but we shall rebel."[28] To submit was not only to prolong suffering, but to commit a kind of psychic suicide, for the capitalist process would destroy people morally and intellectually, making them unfit for liberated society. By attacking the social-economic system, however, people would hasten its fall while simultaneously keeping alive the spirit of revolt without which there could be no progress towards freedom.

> For if capital retains force on its side, we shall all be the slaves of its machinery, mere cartilages connecting iron cogs with steel and iron shafts. If new spoils, managed by partners only responsible to their cash books, are ceaselessly added to the savings already amassed in bankers' coffers, then it will be vain to cry for pity; no one will hear your complaints. The tiger may renounce his victim, but bankers' books pronounce judgments without appeal. From the terrible mechanism whose merciless work is recorded in the figures on its silent pages, men and nations come forth ground to powder. If capital carries the day, it will be time to weep for our golden age; in that hour we may look behind us and see like a dying light, love and joy and hope—all the earth had held of sweet and good. Humanity will have ceased to live.[29]

Whatever the outcome of the struggle between capital and labour, scientific method would be applied in industrial and agricultural production. And that method, by its nature, led inevitably to the disappearance of individual workers and the emergence of groups of workers. The question was whether they would come together under the cudgel of a master, or whether they would associate freely to produce a common work.[30]

The more deeply committed Reclus became to science and scientific method, the more closely he tied progress to scientific achievement. With his political interest in the peasants and his professional interest in geography, he was keen to explore the possibilities for the application of science to agriculture. In 1873, for example, he suggested that the combined efforts of scientists might work wonders on a river basin. The geographer and the meteorologist would provide information on probable temperatures and barometric pressures; the geologist and the chemist would together develop the most favourable mixture of soil; the hydrologist would suggest effective approaches to irrigation; the engineer would be responsible for building canals, bridges, and whatever

147

machines were thought necessary; and the agronomist would take care of the soil, the sowing and the planting. The services of statisticians, economists, and industrialists would be necessary in order to ensure that production and consumption patterns were in harmony and in the interests of society.[31] Reclus sounded like an updated version of Saint-Simon.

Unlike Proudhon, who lamented the demise of small proprietors and whose theories were designed to create a world in which they might avoid extinction, Reclus was confident that the small proprietor was doomed. Moreover, he declared that for certain types of production individual labour was absurd. It was as well to admit it: as harmonious as small craftsmanship might be, the lot of the worker could obviously only improve with help from the appropriate machine.[32] Through machines people would learn to interact with nature and solve the problem of scarce resources. "It is very pleasing to think that one man, using a machine, can provide enough products for a hundred other people."[33] It was in the social interest, said Reclus, "to develop indefinitely the power of humanity through machines, and thus to increase the resources that humanity possesses."[34]

Capitalism threatened to destroy society, but, ironically, it also provided the groundwork for the establishment of universal brotherhood. All potential victims would have to cooperate to survive, and would thereby develop resources within themselves to bring about change and hence alter the course of history. The destruction of capitalism and the success of communism would see bourgeois competition replaced by cooperation as the dominant social value. Reclus was silent on the details of future society. Such details, he believed, would be worked out by future generations.

Reclus never made it clear whether classes would be "abolished" in communist society, as Marx claimed, or whether, as Bakunin contended, they would be "equalised." The evidence suggests that he tended towards Bakunin's position. At the 1868 Congress of the League of Peace and Freedom, he and the Russian supported "as ideal 'the equalisation of classes and individuals,' understanding that equality is the point of departure for all, in order that each person might follow his career without hindrance."[35] For Reclus, revolution would abolish those classes deriving from capitalist society, but individuals of similar temperament and interests who performed certain social functions within communist society might come to be distinguished as a group. He was not explicit on this point, but his views allow for such an inference.

While Kropotkin (and to an extent Marx) was intrigued by the notion that the working day should be divided into so much physical and so much mental labour, Reclus advocated that people be free to decide the nature of their working day. So long as there was no prejudice in favour of particular tasks, and so long as each considered the well-being of all, there was no reason why individuals should not make their contributions how they pleased. Unlike Kropotkin, Reclus did not see any special virtue in manual labour. "Fundamentally," he wrote, "anarchy is nothing but perfect tolerance, absolute acknowledgement of the liberty of others."[36]

European anarchists at this time used the term "anarchist communism" to characterise the society which they advocated. It followed that a society based on communism in production and distribution would be anarchist—that is, "without masters." Reclus said that an anarchist was necessarily a communist[37]; he might also have said that a communist was necessarily an anarchist. Despite the awkwardness of the term "anarchist communism," Reclus and Kropotkin considered it important, for practical reasons, to approve of it. "Anarchist" avoided confusion with those varieties of communism that had developed authoritarian structures, and "communism" helped remind those who would pay heed that the people branded "anarchists" were out to destroy the capitalist social-economic system. Reclus and Kropotkin sought a society in which the social-economic system was communist, the dominant social value was cooperation, and government structures were controlled from below. The state, with its artificial boundaries and its capitalist social-economic and political relations, would have disappeared.

It is easy to see why Reclus never accepted Proudhon's mutualist position which advocated individual production and consumption and which, in a sense, would enhance rather than abolish private property. According to Proudhon's theories, mutualist society would develop out of a system of national credit set up to let small proprietors and workers free themselves from the shackles of debt and the wage system; they could then pursue their various careers as independent landowners and craftsmen. Mutualism never promised fundamental changes in the existing social-economic structure. It would, rather, re-order it, so that each individual would be given a "fair" share. But Proudhon's "anarchy" would not have abolished the market, merely the existing form of government.

Reclus, by contrast, aimed to destroy the market and private property, along with the government that policed the system. That is why he vehemently attacked the views of the mutualist Charles Beslay at a meeting at Vevey in 1875,[38] and why, in 1877, he insisted that the elimination of government would not necessarily destroy the capitalist system.[39] There is some justification for holding that Proudhon's ideas bear a relation to laissez-faire liberalism; the social-economic theory represented by Reclus and Kropotkin deviates substantially.

Like most socialists, Reclus seized upon private property as the basis of the capitalist system and insisted on the abolition of

149

both. In 1875 he said that private property had come about as the result of robbery and exploitation, that justice and liberty could be achieved only through the collectivisation of property.[40] His 1880 argument in support of communist distribution was based on the view that the products of labour were the result of collective effort in both the past and the present; no one had ever worked alone, nor was it possible to isolate parts of common work. It followed that all goods belonged to all people and that it was immoral for an individual or a group to appropriate common goods. Reclus agreed with Proudhon that property was theft, but, unlike Proudhon, he did not restrict the label to that part of the wealth claimed by the capitalist. All forms of property were considered theft; to be an owner of any amount of goods or money was to be a "thief." From this perspective, there was little difference between work in existing society and what the law termed "theft," because both resulted in unfair appropriation. Furthermore, Reclus insisted that it was perfectly just to recover the "stolen" goods extra-legally. To Kropotkin and Jean Grave this was an astonishing position, and for once there was no reconciling the differences. This became particularly clear in the late 1880s, in the discussion which arose over the question of *la reprise individuelle,* or individual recovery of the products of labour.

This question assumed importance in early 1887 when Clément Duval, a member of the anarchist group La Panthère des Batignolles, appeared before the Assize Court of the Seine on charges of stealing jewellery and injuring a policeman. In late October 1886, a few days after the robbery, Duval wrote to *Le Révolté* to explain the circumstances behind an earlier theft for which he had been sentenced to a year in prison. According to the letter and his statement at his trial in 1887, Duval considered theft to be no more than restitution of the products of labour produced by the collectivity and unjustly taken over by a few. He became a hero in many anarchist circles and went off bravely to serve his sentence of twenty years hard labour. There was some uneasiness, however, among *Le Révolté* anarchists. In 1885 the paper had claimed that there was little difference between a bourgeois and a thief who "is not a rebel, nor even a victim" but only "the product of society."[41] It published Duval's letter, but was careful to avoid compromising the paper. After Duval vehemently presented himself in court as an anarchist, though, *Le Révolté* was carried along with the enthusiasm in anarchist circles and gave its support, even if with a degree of ambiguity.[42]

Reclus, however, was decisively sympathetic. Because there was no reason to doubt the man's sincerity, as he saw it, there was no choice but to take Duval at his word. The facts were well known: an abandoned house had contained a fortune that could be used to feed the poor. Duval therefore took the money, even reproaching an accomplice who vandalised the property; when he was later attacked by a policeman, he defended himself. "Knowing, especially in a practical way," said Reclus, "that property is collective, he took his part of it, not for himself alone but for others, and he defended his right as a man when he was attacked." How, Reclus asked, did this action differ from the deeds of those beloved redressers of wrongs who supposedly took from the rich and gave to the poor? An individual who took property stolen from the people by the few did right, if the act was done in a spirit of justice and solidarity. By nature, habit, and personal inclination, he himself would never behave in this way; still, he had no right to expect others to follow his particular pattern.[43]

A few years later, Reclus would advise Jean Grave to revise his views concerning theft in a Le Révolté article which Grave had written under "the prejudice of the state." Otherwise, the article could not avoid attacking "our friends, the nihilists of Kharkof" and reducing to "smugglers" those who, according to Proudhon, acted not only out of right, but even out of duty.[44]

In 1889 the case of the militant anarchist Pini brought the discussion to a crisis in anarchist circles. An Italian who had founded the group Intransigenti in Paris two years earlier, Pini carried out a number of robberies there and in the countryside. La Révolte described him as a man of "very few needs, living simply and austerely, even in poverty," who stole "for propaganda."[45] Grave's misgivings were growing, however, and his position became hardened in relation to that of Reclus, who relentlessly pursued the anarchist right to "theft."

In a letter written in August 1889, almost certainly addressed to Grave, Reclus followed through on the logic of his theories.

1. Does the collectivity have the right to recover the products of its work? Yes, a thousand times yes. This recovery is the revolution and nothing can be done without it.

2. Does a proportion of the collectivity have the right to partial recovery of the collective products? Beyond question. When the revolution cannot be total, one makes it to the extent that one can.

3. Does the individual have the right to personal recovery of his part of the collective property? How can there be any doubt? Since the collective property is appropriated by a few, why would he acknowledge this property in detail, when he does not recognise it in toto? He has the absolute right, therefore, to take—to steal, in common language. The new morality must develop in this respect, it must enter into the spirit and into the mores.[46]

These were the truths that should guide anarchists. It was impossible to formulate rules for all cases, as religion and authority sought to do; the individual knew no law except his or her own conscience, and the morality of an act was determined by the extent to which the individual followed that guide. While it was true that the consequences led one to form opinions, Pini's case "does not prejudice anything, neither for nor against." If this "thief" was in effect a "redresser of wrongs," a man who sought justice, who rendered to labour that which belonged to it, who had rid himself of former prejudices to make his "little revolution" within the measure of his "little power... we ought sincerely to commend him and to understand the great example that he gives us." If, on the other hand, he was a simple "exploiter of the work of others," and if he merely pretended to defend the rights of work, he would be recognised for what he was; his boasting would never save him from the scorn of his comrades.

Reclus had settled in Switzerland as an exiled communard, but although he was granted amnesty in 1879 he did not return to France until the autumn of 1890. He stayed for a short while with his widowed daughter Jeannie at Nanterre, spent much of the following year travelling, and in the autumn of 1891 moved to Sevres.

It was at this time that Jean Grave, serving a six-month sentence at Sainte-Pélagie for press offences, left the management of *La Révolte* in the hands of Reclus's nephew Paul. A controversial article by Paul, "Travail et Vol" (Work and Theft), was published in the issue of 21-27 November. "I protest against this pretense that there is an honest means of earning a livelihood, work, and a dishonest one, theft or swindle," said the article. When Grave complained, Elisée replied that the article was one of two intended as food for thought. Although he understood Grave's agitation, he did not share it. It was not a bad thing, he said, to be reminded that "moralists and moralisers" like themselves also lived from "theft and pillage" and that "we all have to cleanse ourselves." He regarded these observations not as an insult, but as a subject for reflection. "In the society of injustice and caprice in which we live, we are, in spite of ourselves, supportive of all the evil which occurs..."[47] "We are all thieves," he wrote to the perplexed Grave, "and I am the worst, working for a publisher at a salary ten times, twenty times the ordinary pay of an honest man. Everything is theft."

To clarify his position, Reclus sent Grave a short article of his that he was asking Paul to publish in *La Révolte*.[48] The article expressed support for the author of "Travail et Vol." It was true, it said, that in current society everything was based on inequality and monopoly and only money could buy bread. All people were therefore obliged to live from thievery. "Like the raging wolves, we argue about the daily pittance at the expense of the weakest. Every crumb of bread we eat is snatched from other poor people and is stained with blood." Any attempt to end the corruption should be welcomed. It was true that there had always been "theft," said Reclus, but a new attitude now accompanied the act. Thieves saw that they had a right to the booty. This was one more step towards the creation of a society in which all robbery, "legal" and otherwise, would be no more, in which people would not be forced to degrade themselves in order to have their daily bread.

Grave was not alone in objecting to Paul's article. Kropotkin sent Elisée a letter with similar objections[49] and wrote an article, "Encore la morale," which appeared in three parts in December 1891.[50] The people, Kropotkin said, did not understand theft as bringing equality, deceit as realising liberty, nor the distribution of stolen money to the wretched as a form of solidarity. Such "jokes" might find an audience in anarchist groups, but ordinary people had too much good sense to follow these "digressions." Theft, deceit, and lies were characteristic of the existing order, and revolution would not be brought about by perpetuating such evils.

Kropotkin's advice was the well-known dictum preached in his pamphlet *Anarchist Morality*: "Treat others as you would like them to treat you under similar circumstances."[51] Accordingly, theft was wrong, whatever the individual motive. Under unusual circumstances, it was admitted, there might be strong arguments for abandoning the principle—for example, in the cases of Sophie Perovskaya and her comrades who had killed the Czar and those Russian terrorists who had to steal from the rich just to survive. However—and Kropotkin was most emphatic on this point—"if such an act is to produce a deep impression upon men's minds, *the right must be conquered*."[52] Those who practised retribution, this statement suggested, must be so pure of heart and be acting in circumstances so extreme as to leave no doubt about the morality of the deed.

Reclus, in contrast, would have responded by countering with something like: "Treat others as you would like them to treat you under similar circumstances, unless they are your enemies, whom you should always attack." He accepted the pre-Christian maxim "an eye for an eye, a tooth for a tooth" as a legitimate personal and collective defence. To the charge that such a perspective was primitive, Reclus would have said that the maxim was not, although it might be practised in a primitive way since very often a legitimate right of defence was allowed to degenerate to a mere act of vengeance.[53] When Reclus responded kindly to the hostility of such people as Paul Brousse and Kropotkin, he was not "turning the other cheek." Brousse and Kropotkin were not the enemy, in spite of how they might act; for Reclus the real enemy was the bourgeoisie.

Grave shared Kropotkin's views on theft; he never understood Reclus and saw him as an overly tolerant visionary who found plenty of excuses for thievery.[54] He also tended to blame the disagreements on Reclus's nephew Paul, about whom he expressed serious misgivings, in particular Paul's alleged adoption of the position "to understand is to pardon."[55] When Grave appealed from Sainte-Pélagie, Elisée replied that while such a position was naïve, Paul's article contributed to the ongoing discussion.[56] Grave refused to accept the full import of Reclus's interpretation of theft, for he pleaded with him to take over responsibility for the paper, an invitation which Reclus categorically refused: "With the comings and goings, the hitches, the shortage of money, that is to ask me to change my way of living and working completely. That seems unrealistic. I cannot do it."[57]

Unlike those anarchists who openly advocated theft,[58] Reclus thought Grave should open up *La Révolte* to a discussion of both sides of the question. For Grave, however, this would be tantamount to condoning the practice; he believed that the few thieves (property-owners) would be joined by an increasing number, making it more difficult to bring about a social transformation.[59] Reclus wrote to him that some of the so-called facts were based on "misunderstandings and misapprehensions," but that it was not worth the effort to linger over explanation.[60] He admitted that there was much to discuss, but insisted that propaganda be kept free of prejudice and quibbling.[61]

It may have been the question of theft that helped Reclus clarify his views on the logical distinction of ends and means. Here we can locate the root of the disagreements over *la reprise individuelle*. In a letter of late May 1893 Reclus stated that "the end justifies the means."[62] The letter dealt with Grave's new book, *La Société mourante et l'Anarchie*. Reclus pointed to what he saw as a contradiction between a chapter entitled "How Means are Derived from Principles" and Grave's disapproval of the Jesuit maxim "the end justifies the means." Whereas Grave assumed that the means determined the nature of the end, Reclus maintained that they were merely the tools. Just as hands could serve good or evil, means could be used to contribute to progress or regression. A person did well who lied to save a friend. The revolutionary who stole to serve his friends might "calmly and without regret allow himself to qualify as a thief." The man who killed to defend the weak was "a murderer with honourable intentions." Those who merely called themselves anarchists in order to justify lies and theft and murder did not employ the Jesuit principle; the principle which guided their actions was "the pretext justifies the means." It was the logical and moral worth of the means, not the means themselves, that was derived from the principle.[63]

154

His support of the anarchist "thief" never changed. Reclus could see no reason why an individual should not immediately reject the existing morality for a communist morality that derived from the needs of human beings rather than the social-economic system. How else could there be revolution? It was to be expected that changing social values would translate into new social practice. Thus, for Reclus those observers who reacted negatively to the anarchist redresser of wrongs had not distanced themselves from the prejudices of the state. As a man who had spent two decades lamenting the dangers of "circuitous" routes to social justice, he could also appreciate the boldness and directness of the individual recovery of property "stolen" from the people. Finally, every person possessed the right to interpret the dictates of the voice within and to act accordingly. The "thief" could not be condemned without destroying the basis of Reclus's social and political theory.

Ten

Party of Rebels

Anarchist intellectuals deliberately fostered an identification as *le parti des révoltés*—the party of the rebels—especially after they brought out *Le Révolté* in 1879. Significantly, this replaced earlier journals entitled *Le Travailleur* and *L'Avant-garde*, thus indicating a much more radical attitude. Propaganda by the deed, as it developed under the aegis of Reclus, was based on a number of convictions: all revolt against oppression was seen as in itself progressive, the transformation from blind, spontaneous reaction to injustice into "conscious," calculated acts was considered a step forward, and the decision to revolt rested with those who offered it. This amounted to an insistence that individuals had a right to act as they saw fit. Accordingly, some self-professed anarchists believed in the efficacy of violent acts, and these were to increase in number and intensity until they reached crisis proportions towards the end of the century. Reclus stood firm on the issue, even when others faltered in the face of the horror of the attentats which terrorised Europe in the 1890s.

The implications of the anarchist position on propaganda were evident as early as 1878, the year in which there occurred a number of sensational attacks on European authorities and heads of state. In February, Vera Zasúlitch took a shot at the St. Petersburg chief of police to protest his treatment of the "go to the people" movement; two attempts were made, in May and June, on the life of the German Kaiser; in October someone tried to assassinate Alfonso XII of Spain; and in November King Umberto of Italy was attacked. Accurately or not, these events were often linked to anarchists. The Swiss authorities suppressed *L'Avant-garde* for its views, arresting its editor, Paul Brousse, and bringing him to trial.

The anarchists' response to the events of 1878, however, was ambivalent. For example, *L'Avant-garde* made some effort to distinguish between the individual acts of assassins and the collective deeds of "conscious" anarchists. There also existed the view that assassination was of limited propaganda value, although a feeling persisted that under certain conditions it could lead to revolution.[1]

Anarchists were more decisive in interpretating the terrorism of the Russian "People's Will" that was struggling against impossible odds in Czarist Russia. Sophie Perovskaya, one of the five executed for their part in the assassination of Czar Alexander II in March 1881, became an inspiration. Wrote Peter Kropotkin:

> By the attitude of the crowd she understood that she had dealt a mortal blow to the autocracy. And she read in the sad looks which were directed sympathetically towards her that by her death she was dealing an even more terrible blow from which the autocracy will never recover.[2]

It is hardly surprising that Russian revolutionaries should receive such unqualified approval. In Western Europe there was an awareness of the extent of Czarist oppression, so that even liberals could extend their sympathies. Insofar as Russia provided specific lessons for the anarchists, it is clear that these largely consisted in a reaffirmation of the importance of spontaneous acts of revolt. In spite of anarchist enthusiasm, which might be expected in view of revolutionary events in Russia, lack of anxiety over what constituted legitimate acts of revolt there may be taken to indicate that the earlier ambivalence was gradually abating. Many anarchists must have been thinking of Russia in July 1881, four months after Alexander II's assassination, when the famous London International Congress advocated a study of how to use advances in science, particularly chemistry, for revolution.[3]

Propaganda by the deed demanded that anarchists be prepared to submit to the revolutionary course mapped out by "ordinary" people as they struggled, collectively and individually, to create a socialist society; and, moreover, that they make it their task to discover the revolutionary significance of all acts of social revolt, even to provide a sense of legitimacy for them.

Increasingly, there occurred incidents that were the work of individuals who had absorbed enough anarchist theory to translate specific grievances into hatred for the existing order. In 1881, for example, one Emile Florian went to Reims with the intention of killing Léon Gambetta, the noted radical supporter of the French Republic. Failing to do so, Florian decided to attack the first bourgeois he met, and shot (unsuccessfully) a Dr. Meymar. Brought to trial and found guilty, Florian greeted his sentence of twenty years hard labour with the cry, "Long live the social revolution!" *Le Révolté* referred to his act on a number of occasions and placed him in the tradition of propaganda by the deed. In late 1883, the seventeen-year-old Paul-Marie Curien travelled to Paris to kill Prime Minister Jules Ferry, but ended up pointing his gun at an usher in the Chamber of Deputies.

A more consciously "anarchist" act was that of Louis Chaves in 1884. Dismissed from his job as gardener for a convent near Marseilles, Chaves returned and killed the Mother Superior and injured the assistant director. He explained his behaviour in a letter to an anarchist paper: "It is not with words nor paper that we will change our condition."[4] Two years later, in March 1886, Charles Gallo threw a bottle of Prussic acid from a gallery of the Paris stock exchange and shot at panic-stricken brokers and employers. At his trial he provoked the court until the proceedings were adjourned and he was dragged out, screaming "Death to the bourgeois courts!" and "Long live anarchy!" Gallo later expressed his regret at not having succeeded in killing anyone and professed that he had wanted to commit an act of "propaganda by the deed of the anarchist doctrines."[5]

The Paris explosions of March 1892 initiated a period of terror which continued, principally in France, for more than two years. The first explosion of any consequence took place on 11 March, causing considerable damage to a property on boul. St- Germain. *La Révolte* commented that this incident had re-established the importance of dynamite—which had been somewhat devalued in the few minor explosions that had preceded it.[6] An explosion at the Lobau barracks followed within days, and the biggest bomb ever went off on 27 March in the apartment house inhabited by Bulot, a deputy who had demanded the death penalty for anarchists implicated in the disturbances of 1 May 1891.

A man known as Ravachol was arrested and condemned to twenty years hard labour for these explosions. He was then taken to Montbrison and charged with a number of crimes committed in

the period 1886-91. Ravachol admitted guilt to two of these: des-
ecration of the tomb of the Comtesse de la Rochetaillée at Terre-
noire on the night of 14-15 May, and the robbing and killing of
Jacques Brunel, the ninety-two-year-old hermit of Chambles, in
June 1891. The French establishment was startled when Ravachol
wanted to see himself not as a mere criminal but as an anarchist
redresser of wrongs. He claimed that he had killed and robbed
first to satisfy personal needs and then to aid the anarchist cause.
He greeted the verdict of death with "Long live anarchy!" and on
11 July 1892 marched to the guillotine singing an anti-clerical
song.

There was henceforth no shortage of aspiring terrorists, some
of whom could inject fame or infamy into an otherwise miserable
existence. The young shoemaker Léon-Jules Léauthier is remembered among anarchists for his words, "I shall not strike an innocent
if I strike the first bourgeois I meet." Léauthier earned a place
in history by seriously injuring the Serbian Minister Georgewitch
in November 1893 with his shoemaker's knife. In December Auguste Vaillant threw a bomb from the gallery of the Chamber of
Deputies, injuring several deputies, some of them seriously, as
well as a number of spectators, an usher, and himself. Although
no one was killed, Vaillant was condemned to death. He became
a martyr among the anarchists, having neither stolen nor killed,
but merely having attacked a "corrupt" Chamber severely dis-
credited by the recent Panama scandal. In February 1894, one
week after Vaillant's execution, Emile Henry blew up the Café
Terminus of the Saint-Lazare Station, injuring twenty people, one
of whom later died. The "Saint-Just of Anarchy," as Henry is
sometimes known, regretted not having more victims; his aim had
been to kill, not to injure. "There are no innocents," he cried. The
attentats reached a climax with the killing of President Sadi Carnot,
highest symbol of the bourgeois Republic, by the young Italian
Santo Caserio at Lyons on 24 June 1894.

It would be misleading to represent these attentats as simply
the story of a handful of individuals driven by wretched existence
and inspired by anarchist theory. The records show that there
was a considerable number of political activists whose explosions
were not serious enough to warrant lasting attention. Numerous
letters were also sent anonymously to property-owners, telling
them to expect an attack and sometimes warning them to vacate
the property by a certain time in order to escape injury. The Paris
Police Archives contain several boxes of "threatening letters"
passed on by their recipients to the police in the year 1892.[7] The
more sensational attentats were committed amid general excitement, panic in certain quarters, and approval, or at least tolerance,
in the anarchist press—even enthusiasm in some papers. Pictures
of Ravachol were distributed as would be images of a saint, and

his deeds were celebrated in song. For one anarchist, he was "a sort of violent Christ."[8]

Several years before these events, at least some observers considered the "anarchist party... a manifestation expressive of working-class spirit."[9] It is quite understandable that the attentats of the 1890s led the French to believe that just about every anarchist, from the theoretician to the bomber, was guilty of crimes against the state. In an 1895 analysis by a criminal lawyer named Garraud, the anarchists represented a division of labour whereby they contributed to the destruction of society according to character and ability. Some anarchists were "practitioners"—those who propagated the doctrine by means of the deed, that is, by theft, fire, and assassination. At their side were some gifted intellectuals who spread the anarchist idea through newspapers, pamphlets, songs, and pictures. Then there were the anarchist "door-to-door salesmen" who passed the word in working-class districts and in general incited rebellion in every corner of the land.[10] Garraud's analysis was oversimplified, but it grasped important elements of the underlying logic of anarchist theory.

It was a logic that some insiders were reluctant to admit. Approval was given for certain acts of violence in the 1880s, although the enormous scale of the terror of the 1890s caught some by surprise. It was not until after Ravachol's appearance in court that *La Révolte* gave a cautiously favourable appraisal, suggesting that a distinction be made between his earlier crimes and the Paris explosions.[11] Only after the death sentence was passed did the paper come out in open support.[12] It had been easier to applaud efforts of angry, unemployed persons seeking redress for immediate grievances than to sanction acts of bombers who professed to be practising what the intellectuals supposedly advocated in theory.

Kropotkin was genuinely troubled by the harm done to innocent people and wrote a letter intended for publication in *La Révolte* denouncing an explosion that had killed and maimed a large number of people in Spain. These initial waverings were met with arguments from Jean Grave that there was no basis on which to condemn the wretched as they struggled to overcome their misery.[13] There is reason to suspect that Kropotkin did some soul-searching in reaching his position on terrorism; we catch a glimpse of his agonising in comments to a friend about his regrets over the assassination of the Austrian Empress Elizabeth in 1898.[14]

Kropotkin's view of terrorism depicted the bombers as emotional cripples, victims of a vicious society, and it echoed significant elements of the sentiments of many non-anarchist intellectuals. He declared:

> In fact, *we* have not suffered from the persecutions as they, the workers, suffered; we who, in our houses, seclude ourselves

160

from the cry and sight of human sufferings, *we are no judges* of those who live in the midst of all this hell of suffering... Personally, I hate these explosions, but I cannot stand as a judge to condemn those who are driven to despair...[15]

This response is hardly consistent with his earlier (1880) eulogy of the "lonely sentinel" whose courage and integrity were crucial to the success of the revolutionary struggle.[16] Wrote Kropotkin in 1898:

So long as contempt for human life shall be taught to men, and so long as they will be told that it is good to kill for what one believes to be beneficial for mankind—new and newer victims will be added, even though the rulers should guillotine all those who take sides with the poor.[17]

Kropotkin's hesitancy (whether it was humanness or weakness, depending on one's view) was compensated for by Reclus's determination (whether it was commitment or fanaticism) to follow the logic of a theoretical position. Reclus, for one, refused to condemn acts that were the result of "horrible forces, the consequences of inevitable passions, the explosion of a rudimentary justice,"[18] and he insisted that anger had its "raison d'être... its day and its hour."[19] He saw Ravachol as a primitive lover of justice, striving for what he believed was right, an inevitable phenomenon in the progress towards justice. "I admire... his courage," wrote Reclus, "his kindness, his grandeur of soul, his generosity in pardoning his enemies, in truth his denunciators. I know few men who are more noble."[20] "It goes without saying that I regard every revolt against oppression as a just and good act."[21]

Reclus was not about to flinch at what he believed to be the verification of his theories. He had come to expect violence as a natural part of the process of social change, even as "a law of Nature, a consequence of the physical law of shock and countershock."[22] It was not difficult to see, he said, how a person could be brought to commit violence against another. It was easy to single out a name that symbolised the social order. There were too many daily acts of individual and collective cruelty for anyone to be astonished at the existence of hatred.[23] To side against the wretched would be tantamount to justifying the whole oppressive system.[24] There was no doubt that every person had the right to object to an evil society.[25] Reclus distinguished himself from those anarchists who advocated revolt for its own sake. To him, an act of revolt had to be of a "universal character"; it had to be committed for the good of the entire human race.[26] While the consequences of a particular act in terms of individual suffering might be lamentable, it was worthwhile if the consciousness of a common

161

humanity had been raised. It took a while for some of his friends to grasp the implications of this view.

The son of an English friend wrote to Reclus, in 1900, that his support of violence indicated that he was no longer Tolstoyan. Reclus replied that he was far from being Tolstoyan, and that he believed in the use of force to protect the weak. "I see a cat that is tortured, a child who is beaten, a woman who is mistreated, and if I am strong enough to prevent it, I prevent it."[27] He did not linger over such questions as who would make the decision to use force and who would decide when it should stop. As a conscious and rational being, he was prepared to resort to force when necessary and would stop at the point at which he judged that it was about to turn to vengeance.[28] "To be very strong and to use force, in the name of love, is normal behaviour for the anarchist."[29]

In 1896 Reclus attempted to clear up any lingering misunderstanding about where he stood on Tolstoy's Christian anarchism. In his foreword to the pamphlet *La Guerre et le Service obligatoire* he distinguished between his unreserved approval of Tolstoy's anarchist position on armies and governments and his equally strong disapproval of the Russian's pacifism. As Reclus explained it, Tolstoy drew on Matthew's gospel of the Sermon on the Mount for ideas which thoroughly incensed the anarchists around *Les Temps nouveaux* (the paper which replaced *La Révolte*). "'He who strikes you on the one cheek, offer him the other; he who steals your robe, give him your coat.' What is there left to say except: Deliver your soul to the Lord, give your head to the hangman!" Reclus saw these words, borrowed from the prophet of Nazareth, as "something abominable." Only slaves could allow themselves to be insulted like that. "Any man worthy of the name resists to the best of his ability, not only for his own sake, but for all human beings, whom he represents, degrading them through his cowardice and ennobling them through his courage." He saw more truth in the old Roman saying: "Against the enemy revolt is permanent."[30]

His position supported autonomy for each and every individual. It was the intention behind the act, and not the act itself, that was subject to moral scrutiny. Even then, there was no absolute moral standard to apply, for each individual could be assessed only in accordance with his or her own level of moral and intellectual development. Since one could never be certain that the facts were complete, one should never judge another person's conduct. Reclus summarised his thoughts in a letter to a friend:

1. Let us not judge—not, as the Bible says, "in order that we may not be judged," but because we do not know the motives and we may totally deceive ourselves.

162

2. Let us not moralise, because we do not have any right to substitute ourselves in this way for others... Each should follow his own evolution.

3. Let us not preach, all the more so because we do not have enough information to know, to see in advance.

4. Let us not interfere before the organism begins to grow of itself. Let us not force the flower to open up: it will open by itself if life penetrates it.[31]

Yet Reclus insisted on the superiority of "reasoned argument," even as he justified the use of violence. When he first heard of the March 1892 explosions, he maintained that they would never be attributed to "conscious" anarchists, those "who ponder their words and acts, who feel responsible to all humanity for their conduct." Bombs that went off haphazardly to destroy staircases were not arguments, nor even weapons used wittingly, since they could backfire. "Let us simply carry on with our propaganda; the bombings will not prevent us from being heard."[32]

The cynic might be inclined to view such insistence on the superiority of argument as evidence of ambivalence about violence, or, in Reclus's case, a sop to friends in the world of bourgeois scholarship. But this would misrepresent his views. Not once did Reclus say that violence was desirable, only that it was inevitable. To suggest that violence is inevitable, even to welcome it as indicative (or productive) of a higher degree of consciousness, is not to advocate its use (although the bombers might have so interpreted his position). For Reclus, the hope for the future lay in raising consciousness. The more aware people became the less instinctual their behaviour; and the more sensitive they became to the idea of a common human nature, the less they would resort to violence. In fact, "conscious" anarchists were expected to attempt the impossible, to live their lives as if the society of the future had already been established. Anarchists ought "to carry the torch, to make our cause shine as an actual revelation of justice."[33] Ravachol might call himself an anarchist and inspire hymns of praise, but he was still a "primitive rebel" wielding a crude weapon. This did not detract from his nobility, however, nor from the morality that guided his actions.

Even though Reclus placed his faith in a growing solidarity and was certain that reasoned argument would be recognised as the superior weapon, his theories did not preclude the use of violence by "conscious" anarchists. Means as such were neutral, so there could be no question as to whether the use of dynamite was immoral. If dynamite was to be condemned as a means, the decisive factor was its lack of accuracy. In recent bombings, said Reclus in 1892, passion and chance played a greater role than self-sacrifice and science. Moreover, while explosions might bring a greater degree of awareness and serve to further the cause among the uncommitted, there was also the risk of the inefficient use of energy in the event of wide-ranging repression. Indeed, the explosions of 1892 furnished the established order with advantages over the anarchists, although these were quickly lost (Reclus snickered and sighed with relief), as, driven to panic, it committed one stupidity after another.[34]

It is sometimes pointed out that Reclus wrote a letter condemning the explosions, and specifically Emile Henry's attentat at the Café Terminus. Such a letter signed "Elisée Reclus" appeared in Le Travail on 13 February 1894 and was reprinted in other papers.[35] However, Reclus publicly denied responsibility for the letter and claimed it was a forgery.[36] (It is likely that someone used his name in order to provide moral weight to an appeal to end the violence.) The refusal to condemn was interpreted as approval by the popular press and by the terrorists, so much so that some adherents of the theories of Reclus and Kropotkin became alarmed at the "wrong" impression being fostered on the question of terrorism.[37] In the analysis of one such social scientist of the time, the "true" anarchists were members of an exclusive club; they were rebels against injustice, lovers of liberty, altruistic, sensitive, and intelligent, while mere terrorists who acted in their name were a small minority with imperfectly formed brains.[38]

La Révolte continued to hold a central position in the anarchist movement, but it had to make room for the scurrilous Le Père Peinard which appeared in 1889. In the 1890s there emerged a whole flock of anarchist papers. In 1893, for example, there existed some seventeen in France, many appearing on the occasion of the attentats and lasting for only a few issues. Sneering at the timidity of La Révolte's rather insipid position, the more extreme openly advocated terrorism and provided information for would-be dynamiters.

While the French authorities might execute people like Ravachol, they were convinced that such a figure could not have been transformed from criminal into hero without the support of leading anarchists, and, furthermore, that the execution of one did not prevent the emergence of another. Certain that the only way to spare society another Ravachol was to cleanse it of the anarchists, and fired with a new enthusiasm following Vaillant's attentat (1893), the Chamber of Deputies passed a series of laws which became the infamous lois scélérates (wicked laws). Such legislation seemed necessary because anarchist activity could be subsumed only with the greatest difficulty under the relevant sections of the Penal Code. At the 1883 Lyons trial the anarchists had been charged with membership in an International Association; the nature of this International was anything but clear then, and in 1894 it was thoroughly bewildering. It was common knowledge that anarchists constituted "a sort of" association, and that it was their intention (*entente*) to destroy the existing order by every possible means. Also, it was widely assumed that those who carried out the attentats were inspired by anarchist theory, or what they understood of it. It was necessary, explained the criminal lawyer Garraud, "to expand the traditional notion of the term 'association' and to base criminal charges on 'intention'."[39]

Under the first of the new laws, it became a crime even to apologise for criminal acts; another was directed against "associations of malefactors," defining them by intention rather than by action; after President Carnot's death, a third law was passed forbidding acts of anarchist propaganda "by any means whatsoever." These laws have frequently been considered harsh, unreasonable, and also ridiculous. Certainly they reveal the helplessness of the French state when confronted with a determined effort to exploit its various "freedoms." French liberals of the period were anxious to justify restrictions on basic freedoms. As Garraud put it: "...the propaganda that the law condemns and punishes is not propaganda for the idea and by the idea—anarchy is not a crime—it is the application of anarchy, that is to say, violent solution to the social problem by theft, fire, murder."[40] The French legal system, even as it strived to preserve the status quo, revealed its Achilles Heel, its various liberal freedoms, as Reclus had perceived many years before. The "liberal" order could come to terms with the dynamiters only by becoming less liberal. Reclus must not have been surprised.

In December 1893 the police, armed with new powers, began large-scale searches and made numerous arrests. Most of the anarchist papers came to an end by early March 1894, *La Révolte* on the 10th. Many anarchist activists, including Reclus's nephew Paul, escaped arrest only by leaving France. Reclus himself was high on the list of suspects. On New Year's Day 1894 the police searched Bourg-la-Reine, where he was living, and uncovered a large cache of anarchist literature, collections of revolutionary and anarchist songs and poems, correspondence in French, English, Italian, and German, and various notes. The police report concluded that while Reclus had contact with individual anarchists, they could not link him directly with the "malefactors" since the search had failed to uncover any explosives.[41] Although the evidence against him was every bit as solid as that against many other anarchists indicted in this period, it was not compelling enough for the arrest of the scholar Reclus. The government was reluctant to weaken its case against the anarchists by causing a public (and international) outcry in defence of a man who less than two years previously had been awarded a gold medal by the Geographical Society of Paris.[42]

The fear that Reclus could command a large following was not unjustified. At a meeting of the Governing Council of the Free

165

University of Brussels on 16 July 1892, it had been decided, on the initiative of the Rector, to nominate Reclus as Fellow of the Faculty of Sciences and to authorise him to give a course in comparative geography at the university's School of Social Science.[43] Reclus accepted the nomination but asked that the course be postponed until early 1894 when *La Nouvelle Géographie universelle* would be completed.[44] In December 1893 he advised the Governing Council that he would commence at the beginning of the new term in early March. However, the Council members became uneasy over recent reports of events in France, especially the links being drawn between terrorism and the Reclus family. It was decided to postpone the course indefinitely, in order to avoid "demonstrations, sympathetic or hostile, inspired by excitable strangers" at the lectures.[45] This information was communicated to Reclus in a letter of 6 January 1894, but not before Belgian and French newspapers reported rumours of the Free University's reaction.

All kinds of student societies, convinced that the postponement effectively meant suppression, lobbied the Council and sent letters of sympathy to Reclus. This agitation won the support of politicians and scholars, as well as some faculty members. By 21 January a Protest Committee had been formed.[46] The agitation became violent and led to the expulsion of students and teachers, the resignation of the Rector, who sided with the students, and the closing down of the university for several weeks.[47]

With some amusement,[48] Reclus found himself a *cause célèbre*, and decided to act out the role which the fates had prepared for him. He accepted a request from the President of the University Circle of Brussels (a body of students and former students) to give the course on geography in spite of the administration's decision,[49] and on 2 March delivered his first lecture to an enthusiastic audience[50] in a large hall placed at his disposal by the Freemason Loge des amis philanthropes of Brussels. A witness recalled that first memorable lecture—the enthusiastic crowds, the tension, the excitement, and "the serenity of the professor in his triumph."[51] The disturbances over the postponement of the course brought to a climax a series of differences within the university, and at an assembly on 12 March the decision was taken to found a new university. Reclus continued his lectures in improvised surroundings until the opening of the New University of Brussels which offered a limited number of courses in the 1894-95 academic year. As if to confirm the fears of the French police concerning the support Reclus could muster among scholars, the Royal Geographical Society of London followed the example of their French counterpart by recognising his achievements with their 1894 gold medal.

The decision of the Geographical Society of Paris to award Reclus a gold medal had been taken, in February 1892, just before the period of the attentats. He anticipated the beating his vanity would take from his participation in the "absurd" ceremony, but Reclus was placed in an embarrassing position regarding the offer of this "large gold medal," for he had not returned the small medal the Society had sent him earlier. In the end, he was persuaded by the argument of the explorer Henri Duveyrier: "We wished to be fair to the geographer, and, without putting on airs, to treat ourselves to the pleasure of sympathising with the anarchist. Would it not be an injustice on your part to offend us?"[52] And once Reclus had accepted a gold medal from the French, it would be awkward to refuse one from the British.

His spirits were raised as the anarchists went about attacking social injustice, as the police attempted to rid society of anarchists, and as the popular press buzzed with the latest exploits. On 23 April 1892 Reclus wrote enthusiastically to his sister Louise: "It truly seems to me that the desire to learn and to know is becoming general; it is even seizing those filthy papers whose sole mission is to plead for the employer's coffer!" While avoiding reporters seeking interviews, he experienced "the joy of having to speak frequently with people passionately fond of the truth."[53]

Reclus handled much of the negotiations with Stock for the publication of Kropotkin's *La Conquête du pain*, read the proofs, and in April joyfully reported that after only a few months the book was going into the second edition. That morning he also entered into discussions with Stock concerning the publication of Bakunin's *Oeuvres choisies*.[54] On 27 April he wrote to his friend Félix Nadar that even though Jean Grave was in prison and there were not enough funds to run *La Révolte*, "we live from day to day, happy and confident, listening to the great blast of the revolution which is advancing."[55] The following month he was planning to bring out a collection of songs to be used as propaganda among the peasants. While the peasants did not care for erudite writings, he explained to Jacques Gross, they understood and loved the song.[56] It was in this period that he wrote the famous pamphlet *A mon Frère, le paysan.*

There was a side to Reclus which delighted in mocking authority. In his youth he composed an ode to the 1848ers who had toppled Louis-Philippe: "It was a beautiful day when the king paled at the approach of the people and looked for a dungeon in his splendid castle..."[57] In the 1870s he became uncharacteristically serious; this had much to do with the uncertainty following the repression of the Paris Commune, but Reclus was also preocuppied with his geographical projects. As the years passed, he became more optimistic as well as more openly defiant of authority. An example of his readiness to undermine the position of the "high and mighty" comes from late 1882, at the time of Kropotkin's arrest for having some connection with an international organisation forbidden by the Defaure Law of 1872.

In response to the arrest, Reclus wrote a provocative letter to the magistrate at Lyons on 24 December 1882.[58] He had read (in the *Lyon Républicain*), he stated, that according to the preliminary investigation, the two international anarchist leaders were Elisée Reclus and Prince Kropotkin, and that he did not share his friend's fate simply because French law did not allow for his apprehension outside the country. But, he declared, the magistrate was well aware that he had only recently spent two months in France. Moreover, he had attended the funeral of Kropotkin's brother-in-law the day after Kropotkin's arrest and had said a few words over the grave.[59] The officers, who were stationed immediately behind him, had had only to ask him to go with them. The letter closed by daring the court to make an arrest: "But it matters little whether I reside in France or in Switzerland... Let me know the place, the day, and the hour. At the appointed moment, I shall knock on the door of the designated prison."

Reclus wrote a similar letter to the Belgian paper *La Réforme* after arriving in Brussels in March 1894; here he remarked that on 19 March *La Réforme* had reported that the newspapers were demanding his arrest. If an order for his arrest were issued, he said, he would leave the "serious business" that had called him to Brussels.

> Abandoning my work as soon as possible, I shall present myself to the judges, not to satisfy the eager letter-writers, but out of a sense of duty and respect for my convictions. It is not that I am attracted to prison, but even in prison I can live a life that I know to be honourable.[60]

It was a game of "catch me if you can," and Reclus clearly felt he was on a winning streak. The jeers should be taken for what they were, mischievous delight in belittling the authority of a French state disillusioned by persecution beyond its comprehension, and, moreover, uncertain as to how to deal with the eccentric geographer. In July 1894 Reclus reported to a friend that he had been so overtly watched that he was forced to conclude that the exercise was a sham.[61] He had no intention of submitting to arrest, however, and when the pressure became too intense, he allowed himself to be whisked away to a country retreat where, for a few days, he worked away quietly. (The retreat, it is said, was the home of a man who happened to be the director of a Flanders prison.)[62]

While Reclus had written appropriately indignant letters to the university officials and mockingly signed himself "Fellow of the Free University,"[63] he obviously revelled in the excitement aroused on his behalf in Paris and Brussels. "I cannot feel offended; I have decided that it is very funny. I can say that I have had my share of experiences during my lifetime."[64] With a reputation in the world of science, and with the various manifestations of social progress around him, his 1870s uncertainty yielded to optimism. Anarchist ideas would continue to take hold, whatever steps might be taken by the authorities—whether they closed down the anarchist press or arrested the leaders.[65]

Reclus also acknowledged that, as a bourgeois, he was himself not immune to the anger of the oppressed. Early in the period of the attentats, he wrote that he was prepared to pardon in advance any wretch who might take him for an oppressor and strike him a mortal blow.[66] He did have the opportunity to respond to a lesser attack, the looting of his library. Félix Nadar recounted the story of how Reclus dealt with this "restitution" of common property. "My poor, dear friend! Your books..." "Well! What about my books? I have read all they have to say, and now they are going to be of use to others... Moreover, since I did not give them, they did well to take them." Reclus made these statements, so the story goes, while smiling and rubbing his hands briskly in the best of spirits.[67]

Had such good humour and renewed faith in the prospect of social justice been merely a response to immediate events Reclus would have been despondent when the anarchist movement came to an abrupt end with the Trial of the Thirty in 1894. As we shall see, though, his optimism continued in full force. At the turn of the century, Reclus the scholar of advanced years would become somewhat physically and emotionally detached from the European socialist movement. He would insist, however, that anarchism was not defeated, that, on the contrary, it was stronger than ever.

Eleven
Changing Times

The anarchists received surprisingly lenient sentences at their trial in 1894, and pardons were granted on the inauguration of President Faure in 1895. However, there was a general feeling among anarchists that times had changed, and the movement took a new direction and character. Individual anarchists, instead of reactivating the groups that had existed before 1894, began to infiltrate the syndicalist movement which had won recruits in the early 1890s and which was gaining momentum under the dynamic leadership of Fernand Pelloutier. The major development in the wider socialist movement was the Second International founded in 1889. Reclus remained decidedly distant from anarcho-syndicalism, and he openly condemned the Second International. Indeed, a curious thing happened. The more positive he became about social progress, the more negative he became in his critique of various forms of revolutionary strategy, and the man who was celebrated for his tolerance became ever more unyielding in his demands for perfection.

Reclus's apparent lack of interest in anarcho-syndicalism is on the surface rather puzzling, and since he said nothing explicitly we can only surmise what his views were. A central concern would have been the movement's perception of the trade union as the ideal unit of liberated society. In 1868, conforming to Bakuninist collectivism, he publicly endorsed a programme whereby future society would be based on producers' associations. However, Reclus had reformulated his position by 1880 when he defended the theory of anarchist communism at the Jura Federation Congress in La Chaux-de-Fonds. It was at his instigation that the Congress passed the resolution that the "natural" commune or community (as opposed to the existing administrative commune) would be the basic unit of "free" society.[1] Reclus could not help but view anarcho-syndicalism sympathetically, as part of the larger struggle against the existing order. Similarly, in the 1870s he had seen significant signs of progress in the varied efforts of the European working class—trade unionism in England, working-class parliamentary electioneering in Germany, Holland, and Denmark, and "revolutionism" in Spain, Italy, a part of Switzerland, and especially France.[2] James Guillaume, the noted revolutionary socialist who became a keen anarcho-syndicalist, said that, just before his death, Reclus expressed approval of the anarcho-syndicalist movement.[3] He was with the syndicalists in spirit, even though he could not agree with them on the fundamentals of their programme. He was far more critical in his attitude toward the Second International.

Anarchists attended the two rival socialist congresses which marked the birth of the Second International in 1889. Their admission became a major issue, however, when the socialists united at the Brussels Congress of 1891. At the Zurich Congress in 1893 anarchists claimed that they, too, were socialists, but were expelled amid noisy protests. After this experience, a resolution was passed to the effect that only socialists who agreed to the necessity of political action within the context of parliamentary politics should be admitted to future congresses.

It is likely that Reclus took an interest in these events, but it would be misleading to suggest that he was supportive of anarchist membership in the Second International, even though he was present for the final battle at the London Congress of 1896. His lack of enthusiasm towards the question of admission is indicated in letters to his sister Louise.[4] In one letter he spoke of the congress "in which, however, I did not take part" and went on to say that he had dropped by to meet the "anarchist elements."[5]

About two months earlier and in anticipation of their expulsion from the International, the anarchists had arranged for a meeting on 28 July in the Holborn town hall. This meeting happened to take place on the evening of the day the anarchists were expelled, and the timing won them much publicity, as well as sympathy from the more liberal-minded members of the congress—including such figures as Keir Hardie and Tom Mann. Reclus's address was to the point. Far from engaging in a battle with rival socialists, he welcomed all delegates to the congress, hastening to add that "as Anarchists and Communists we cannot agree with their belief in government and laws." It was a mistake, he said, for socialists to attempt to bring about revolution through the legal system because, as history showed, law did not promote social change, but rather put a brake on it. He saw the idea as the prime factor in human history: "When an idea grows, revolution must follow; it is impossible to stop it." As for the vindication of the anarchist position, he pointed out: "Throughout the world we arrive at the same conclusions and always cooperate. There is always a wonderful unity in thoughts, sentiments, and the desire and determination to be free."[6] If Reclus attended the "anarchist conference" at St. Martin's Hall, the birthplace of the First International back in 1864, he did not take an active part in the proceedings.[7]

It is clear that Reclus was in disagreement with those socialists who chose the parliamentary route to revolution, but only rarely did he focus on the differences between anarchists and other socialists. In the 1890s, however, European socialists were gaining increasing support at the polls and implicitly accepting the rules of the parliamentary system. Since, according to Reclus, socialists were thereby undermining the revolutionary struggle, he felt it was time to make his objections explicit.

If there were no revolutionary uprising in the immediate future, he wrote in 1898, parliamentary socialists would become enmeshed in the web of bourgeois politics and lose sight of the ultimate objective.[8] Even sincere socialists, who were conscious of the hazards of the parliamentary arena, were deluding themselves in their efforts to remain true to their ideals by means of a rigorous programme. In time, the sense of the words would change and each person would come to view the programme from a different perspective, until, finally, the most clearly stated declaration would take on no more than symbolic significance. Since socialists were faced with the necessity of winning votes, they would have to play to the prejudices of the unliberated crowd—they would have to flatter clericals, liberals, patriots, even employers. Socialist principles would be repeatedly compromised until socialists themselves became bourgeois.[9] This danger had to be made clear to those revolutionaries who unthinkingly entered the political mêlée.[10]

On the other hand, in the event of revolution there was another danger, establishment of a dictatorship. The revolutionary government advocated by some as the transition stage to the new society would, in all likelihood, give rise to despotism. This would occur if the revolution were premature—if it took place before

172

the people had passed through an evolutionary process that prepared them morally and intellectually for the revolutionary task. Despite the best of intentions, the socialists of the Second International would betray their own cause. The urgent question was how to channel social, economic, and political developments so that revolution would occur, but so that its fruits would go to the people, its rightful recipients.[11]

The anarchist way to socialism, according to Reclus, had to avoid the hazards of the parliamentary arena and the tragedy of despotism. Anarchists understood that historical phenomena could not be altered before the necessary transformations had taken place in the hearts and minds. Young people mistakenly believed that rapid change was possible, he told a student in 1895, whereas "transformations are made slowly, and therefore it is necessary to work with much more consciousness, patience, and devotion."[12] Reclus saw a growing divide between anarchists and other socialists, one for which he readily found historical comparisons. This divide shared features of a process which had earlier split the French republican party into opportunists and socialists. Now it was the socialists who were being split, "...one group, to sweeten their programme and render it acceptable to the conservatives; the other, to guard their spirit of free evolution and sincere revolution." The anarchists had their moments of discouragement and even scepticism. They were conscious, however, of the need to stop working within organisations—even ones like the Second International—which pursued a course that was dangerous, if not treasonous, to the revolutionary cause. Having allowed "the dead to bury the dead," anarchists would take their place "at the side of the living."[13] They were aware of the development of historical laws, Reclus wrote elsewhere, and seeing gradual changes in society, never despaired, however small their influence might seem to be.[14]

In the 1870s Reclus had felt it necessary to tolerate all approaches to socialism. By the 1890s, however, he believed the time had come to criticise "non-anarchist" socialism. We are used to tracing the Marxist-anarchist dispute back to the Marx-Bakunin quarrel, but the great cleavage was irrevocably established only by events connected with the Second International in the 1890s. The year 1896 marked the final parting of the ways. Those anarchists who were reluctant to turn to anarcho-syndicalism had to decide on the direction to take. Some thought they should carry on as before. On his release from prison in early 1895, Jean Grave was eager "to take up the propaganda where we left off," to republish *La Révolte*. When Reclus told him that "times had changed," Grave replied, "We are fifteen months older, that is all."[15] Nonetheless,

Reclus persuaded him to call the proposed paper *Les Temps nouveaux*, and the first issue appeared on 4 May 1895. Reclus's influence can be seen in the tone of the paper as well as its name. "We are entering a new phase of the struggle... Human emancipation cannot come from legislation; it must be the result of individual will... If [the people] wish to be free, they will find the means."[16] Reclus himself was but an infrequent contributor to the paper, but, according to Grave, he continued to provide financial assistance.[17]

His lack of enthusiasm for reviving the old anarchist movement was not based on a fading interest in the cause. It was rooted in a reassessment of propaganda. By early 1894 Reclus had come to the conclusion that newspaper propaganda no longer contributed—if it ever had—to the growth of anarchism, and that it might even be harmful. The newspaper, he claimed, expressed a "collective thought," and thus a somewhat "castrated" one; there was an unavoidable tendency to undermine the powerful springs of individual initiative.[18] "In a word," said Reclus in December 1895, "organisation is always unsound, regressive in proportion to the individual presumptuousness and authoritarian violence which it contains, always beautiful and good in proportion to the spirit of freedom which moves it."[19] He also warned that every "party" had its *esprit de corps* and that therefore it contained evil, as well as good. Each member could not help but share responsibility for the errors, lies, and ambitions of the others.[20] Even the New University was not immune to his vigorous denunciation of organisation. "Without doubt," he wrote to a friend in July 1895, "our University is an institution like any other—therefore bad—but for the moment it represents the struggle. We enter it anarchically and personally in order to take part in the combat."[21]

Reclus was disappointed that the students showed so little enthusiasm for the social question, but he believed that their attitude could be partly explained by their upbringing as "exploiters," a process in which even the New University participated.[22] Yet the fact that students and intellectuals, as a social group, were now playing a lesser role in the world of ideas and politics he welcomed as a sign of the times. He pointed to the increasingly active working class, from whom, he maintained, the students had much to learn.[23]

But Reclus still could not be precise about how to effect change. He was aware that, for many anarchists, old-style revolutionary agitation seemed extremely limiting in an age when socialists were participating as never before in the parliamentary system. Some of his friends, disillusioned at the prospects, believed that anarchist "colonies" could put beliefs into practice. As we have seen, Reclus sympathised with their motives, but utterly condemned these "backwoods utopias." Anarchists must not leave the scene of battle; they must stand their ground and continue to press for social change.

> At least [the anarchist] can work to free himself personally from all preconceived or imposed ideas, and gradually group around himself friends who live and act in the same fashion. It is step by step, through small, loving, and intelligent societies that the great fraternal society will be established.[24]

The small, loving societies which he advocated—really just groups of good friends—had to take root within the existing order, not in some monastery-like retreat.

Reclus could be understanding with regard to the mistaken assumptions underlying the attempt to establish anarchist colonies, but he was appalled at the move towards neo-Malthusianism which was propagated in the early 1900s by such prominent anarchists as Paul Robin and Sébastien Faure.

Robin accepted Malthus' proposition that the population of the world increased by geometric progression while the supply of food increased by arithmetic progression. However, he rejected the second part of the original theory which postulated that the population, because it tended to grow too large for the available food supply, would be reduced repeatedly by disasters as it searched for an equilibrium. To counteract this inevitability, Robin proposed that the birth rate be regulated by selective breeding under the best possible conditions, so that working people, having been reduced in number, would become healthier, better educated, and more socially valuable. The result would be better for everyone. A number of anarchists were recruited to this new creed, and neo-Malthusianism was proclaimed as the revolution—a pacific one.

It is hardly necessary to point out that this theory diverged in practically every respect from Reclus's anarchism. He was quick to see that the new movement would produce an elite and that it would work towards social integration rather than revolution.[25] Moreover, Reclus had always maintained that even the original Malthusian argument was untenable, that there would be "bread for all" once the private appropriation and waste associated with capitalism had been eliminated and industrial society was run on the principle of solidarity rather than profit for a few.[26] He considered it an urgent matter to reply to the neo-Malthusians, and, just before his death, attacked their main premise. He called for revolution as "the only means of winning bread."[27]

His intransigence on the question of revolutionary strategy in the post-1894 period followed upon his assessment of developments in the years just prior. The attentats had no doubt stirred his blood, but what gave him cause for hope was his view that the revolt expressed through terrorism was a manifestation of more widespread social progress. Reclus was confident and happy, however, even before the acts of terrorism broke out. He was especially thrilled by the example of the 1 May celebrations in 1890. "May 1st is a great historical date. For the first time there was conscious solidarity among all Internationalists, and the bourgeoisie instinctively trembled."[28]

There is a note of extreme optimism in his preface to Kropotkin's *La Conquête du pain*; the decade at hand, said Reclus in the preface—which was probably written in January 1892,[29] before the outbreak of the attentats—represented something quite different from what the doomsday talk of the "end of the century" would have one believe. It was true that people were seeing "the end of an epoch," but the old was giving way to the new. Science would form the basis of faith for all people seeking the truth, and this would surely lead them to see that this truth was anarchism. In ways too numerous to count, positive changes were afoot: "anarchical society has for a long time been in full bloom," in thought divorced from dogma, in independent research, in the refusal to submit to authority. "All this is anarchy, even when we are not conscious of it."[30] Into this pattern stepped the political terrorists who expressed their solidarity with humankind and nobly laid down their lives for the cause. It was their intentions which Reclus found to be progressive and so inspiring.

The political terrorists of the 1890s stood at the crossroads of instinct and consciousness. They represented both the instinctive grasping for justice characteristic of past revolutions and the "reasoned" revolution of the future. They also provided the clue to the failures of the past and suggested lessons for the future. Thus far, revolutionary forces had been unable to triumph completely, said Reclus in 1898, because no revolution had been fully rational. In 1848, too many peasants were unprepared.[31] In 1871, only half of Paris and the industrial areas were revolutionary, and the Commune ended in a deluge of blood.[32] It was not enough to repeat old formulae in the hope of raising revolutionary ardour, since success depended on the development of "conscious" forces.[33] "The transformation must be accomplished in the minds and hearts before the muscles are flexed."[34] The more thoroughly prejudices and fears were examined and destroyed, the weaker would be the forces of reaction and the less resistance there would be to revolutionary change. At some point in the future there would be no more than a few greedy capitalists facing the mighty hordes demanding retribution.[35] Science would explain the past and the present, and, most importantly, point to the possibilities for the future.

As Reclus saw it, "science and knowledge was not an abstract matter, to be pondered upon in the quiet study, but a *reality*, to be applied and utilised for the increase of the happiness of all."[36]

Science by its nature belonged to the people; using it for the benefit of the capitalists was a perversion. The dehumanising effects of applied science were readily seen in the factory where division of labour was used excessively for the maximisation of profits. At the university level, the oppressors of tomorrow were themselves the victims of a dehumanising process, as the educational system ensured its survival by emphasising career preparation and narrow vocationalism. Interest in justice and the social question were stifled; students were even denied the joy of learning.[37] Scientific specialisation in a capitalist society represented a waste of physical and intellectual effort.

This is not to say that Reclus objected to the principle of specialisation. As in the economy, division of labour in the sciences was seen as both inevitable and desirable. The physical, mathematical, and social sciences all contributed to knowledge about human existence. But science and its specialisations must be placed at the service of humankind rather than of the institutions of capitalism.

It is not difficult to imagine how Reclus's approach to geography would make him sensitive to the work of countless individuals, named and unnamed, in any project. His geography drew upon history, economics, anthropology, and especially sociology, as well as his own experience. As a synthesiser he was continually filling in the larger picture, and with such care and eloquence that he has been called an artist who painted in words and pictures[38] and elevated geography to literature[39] (which also won criticism from the more "scientific" geographers). This was a literature in which imagination was fused with careful study of the earth and its inhabitants. When Reclus could not observe directly, he sought contact with people upon whose personal experiences he could draw. He had a concrete knowledge of what he presented to the reader as a result, and it is this "feel" for his subject that he conveyed.

> For though Reclus could not rival the historic insight of Comte, the imagination of Michelet, the technical mastery and interpretation of Le Play, the psychology of Taine, the abstract power of Spencer, or the like, he had the advantage of knowing in his own way more of the concrete world than any of these, perhaps than all put together.[40]

His whole life may be seen as governed by an obsession with knowledge. A working man named Guérineau, who knew Reclus well, caught this spirit when he remembered him as "an indefatiguable worker of intellect,"[41] a man who would talk to him about the earth, the sky, the trees, the water, and the animals, and in turn ask Guérineau about the lives and attitudes of workers. "Always, one learns, he said, that the more one knows the less he believes he knows; in short the characteristic of the anarchist is never to pause and always to desire to know more."[42] His brother Elie, who had accepted an offer to teach Comparative Mythology at the New University, wrote in mid-November 1895 that Elisée spent every evening at the university, "not only to give courses, but also to take them."[43] Paul Reclus recorded that his uncle

> worked with remarkable regularity, only with great difficulty allowing himself to be diverted by the daily events; "every day its page" was his line of conduct, and he could write in pencil in the most unlikely places, when a train stopped, in the waiting-room of a rail-way station, on a corner of the table in a public house.[44]

Reclus's work was not accomplished without effort. Wrote one family friend: "He owned up to his daughter [Jeannie] that in the morning, when he set out to work, he felt as though before an abyss; yet every night the abyss was crossed, the daily task was done..."[45]

When he arrived in Brussels in 1894, Elisée was shocking the world as the anarchist theorist who showed sympathy for terrorism. The following description comes from a woman who left impressions of Reclus's encounter with the artist Verhaeren just after the triumphant arrival.

> I was living at Knocke when Elisée was called to Brussels; so I did not meet him there; but in the spring of that year he was on the Belgian coast and, knowing that Verhaeren was staying with me, he came to visit him. I do not think that Verhaeren had met him before; but when we saw him coming, as we sat in front of the house, we recognised him at once. He advanced, with his hands in the pockets of his every-day clothes, bare headed, with his hair and his loose tie floating in the breeze; and he looked, as he would have had everybody look, the type of a "free man." His salutation was simple and cordial, with a suggestion of youthful ardour; but his bearing had great nobility. Verhaeren and he greeted each other with the generous warmth of kindred spirits... I see him yet, on the beach, close to the waterside, making islands, capes and archipelagoes in the sand with his stick, to amuse some child, and saying: "This is the ideal place to teach geography."[46]

At this point in his life, Reclus liked to think of the theoretician and the primitive rebel as fellow workers, each involved in his or her own way in the great cause. He himself saw lecturing as a joyful way of communicating, and a friend recalled how he "loved to point out the collaboration of the listener to the speaker; 'the former,' he would say, 'holds up the mirror in which our thoughts take life before our eyes'."[47] Elisée Reclus had at last found the pulpit he had sought since his youth.

The rumours that the professors of the New University would preach the creed of anarchism were soon quashed.[48] It is important to see that for Reclus anarchism was not merely belief; it was the truth as revealed through science. If his arguments were valid—and he believed they were—they would be verified through the scientific method. If they were flawed—which they might be—then science would show how they might be improved.

It is worth noting that Kropotkin's science never carried him to this singular pursuit of freedom of thought. Shortly after his release from prison in 1886, he wrote to William Morris that "there is so much work to do for elaborating the principles of our Anarchist philosophy which, like each new system of thought, require so much labour."[49] Kropotkin was preparing to build a "new system"; Reclus was in revolt against all systems. Max Nettlau, who sensed this distinction, felt that Reclus lived in a "more distant epoch," one of anarchy where it was no longer necessary to become involved with dogmas; while Kropotkin was "closer to our epoch" and had elaborated a detailed system of dogmas and hypotheses.[50] Reclus's position did not preclude an unshakeable conviction in the essential correctness of the anarchist stance. "Not only was he a convinced anarchist, but he could hardly comprehend that an honest, well-meaning human being could fail to be one."[51]

The anarchist way to socialism was not the parliamentary system, nor was it anarcho-syndicalism; it took the form of persistent efforts to eliminate prejudices. Thus, it was with reawakened enthusiasm that Reclus immersed himself in scholarship and teaching in the last years of his life. As principal speaker at the opening ceremony of the New University in October 1895, he defined the "common purpose" of all those connected with it.

> Science, as we conceive it, and as we seek to interpret it, possesses that supreme bond of union which is found in a boundless respect for human thought. It [the University] will also have the bond which arises from community of method, the firm resolve to draw no conclusion that is not derived from observation and experiment, and to set aside scrupulously all preconceived ideas of merely traditional or mystic origin. Finally, we count on a third bond, that which our pupils and auditors will knit by their love of truth, and by the lofty spirit of sincere, disinterested study.[52]

Reclus was encouraging students to join him in the pursuit of truth through science. For him, that was also a call for revolution and the establishment of a society based on anarchist principles.

Twelve
The Battle for Truth

The anarchist movement is generally held to have reached an end with the trial of leading French anarchists in 1894. The groups were thrown into confusion, as their press was silenced and a number of activists were imprisoned or exiled. The movement appeared to have failed. The perpetrators of terrorist attacks, however, had not seen their acts as constituting "the revolution," but rather as propaganda, designed to inform, arouse, and prepare people for the "coming" battle. From this perspective, putting a handful of anarchists out of commission was hardly a clear indication of failure. Elisée Reclus spent his last years inspecting the "troops." Everywhere he found evidence that progress was on the side of those who revolted against injustice. A world was taking shape, he believed, whose resources were increasing and whose inhabitants were developing attitudes favourable to placing these resources at the disposal of all. The struggle was on to liberate people from centuries-old prejudices, to help them become conscious of what was rightfully theirs.

It was clear to Reclus that the arguments for communism must stand or fall on the essential equality or inequality of human beings. Undaunted by claims connected with the new racial theories which emerged in that era of nationalism and imperialism, he saw that battle had to be waged simultaneously against traditional prejudices and those conservative critics of democracy who abused science in the name of sanctifying and rationalising these same prejudices.

He vigorously opposed suggestions that the process of evolution and adaptation of the species had led to the development of specific racial characteristics and that this "racial soul," as Gustave LeBon described it, was a determining factor in the formation of national character. In this period, race theory was used to support claims that the more "advanced" nations had achieved superiority on the basis of natural selection and that the theory of survival of the fittest demanded imperialist policies for fear of losing advantage. It was also used to caution imperialist nations against assimilating subject peoples who, it was said, had their own peculiar racial makeup which should not be disturbed but allowed to develop at its own rate.

It was not difficult for Reclus to see that these were arguments conveniently designed to protect the established interests, even to assuage cries of conscience, so that the strong might rest easily in the exploitation of the weak. The same arguments were used to defend class and sex privilege. In the debate on race, Reclus followed the line which he had begun almost a half century earlier. As we have seen, unlike people such as Gobineau, he championed the fusion of races rather than racial purity. It now became important for him to show why it was that people who were fundamentally "equal" could manifest themselves so "unequally."

An underlying assumption of all Reclus's writings was that the elements making up "national character" were largely determined by environment, in particular that geographical location helped determine social and political institutions. In his preface to Léon Metchnikoff's *La Civilisation et les Grands Fleuves historiques* (1889) he drew attention to the chapter on the influence of the environment on races as "the part of the book which appears to me to have the most importance."[1] In the 1890s he maintained that the nature of all people, though frequently disguised or apparently distorted by the social and political conditions in which they lived, was essentially similar. All could be located somewhere on the spectrum of social evolution, and the highest existing level was that of Western Europe.

It seems remarkable today that Reclus, who fought so vehemently against the racial prejudices of conservatives, could, in the same breath, as it were, share their view of the superiority of European civilisation. It would hardly help matters to fault Reclus for a presupposition that remained unquestioned for the vast majority of his contemporaries. Like Kropotkin and Marx, he had no difficulty seeing Europe as the source of the standards against which to measure non-Europeans. Given his faith in the liberating effects of science, this perspective seemed to follow naturally. He clearly believed that in order to separate himself from advocates of European expansion, it was enough to argue that racial superiority was not the cause of European advances; rather, for various geographical and historical reasons, institutions favourable to human progress happened to have developed in Europe.[2]

The question for Reclus was whether the advantages enjoyed by Europeans were temporary or permanent. Since his anarchism could not tolerate the thesis that Europeans would maintain their lead forever, it became important to show why the factors that had supported their impressive leaps forward were no longer operable. It is in this spirit that he tried to demonstrate that the entire world was becoming "Europeanised." It is startling to us, in the latter part of the twentieth century, to learn that, in an effort to show the essential equality of all people, Reclus emphasised the "naturalness" of the spread of European culture. What we can now see is that, within the conceptual strategies available to him in the late nineteenth century, he, like other socialists, unwittingly lent support to Western imperialism. This assessment should in no way diminish the importance of his many insights, and it is wholly within the spirit of his anarchism (if we were to hold to such a thing) to make such a critique.

In October 1894 Reclus said that Western Europe was "the centre of equilibrium between the forces of the human race" and that from there radiated "not only all the roadways of commerce, but also the ideas and influences of social life, in its collective solidarity." While contrasts between East and West were still sharp, and at many points reconciliation appeared impossible, travel and commerce slowly contributed to a "mutual understanding between the races of men which points to their unification." In India, for example, England's homogenisation of the people was reducing contrasts and providing moral unity.[3] In 1898 he saw similar unifying forces at work with even more positive results. Japan had been transformed into a European power, "if not in language, history, and traditions, in the complete recasting of its administration, institutions, customs and theories, in its devotion to science, in its entire and unreserved acceptance of a policy based on observation and experience." This was the "great event of the century." There were unmistakeable signs that similar transformations were about to take place in China and in all those countries in which different races—yellow, red, or black—were being brought into close contact with people of the Aryan-Greco-Latin civilisation. "So vanishes that oft-repeated assertion that *race* is a final and irreducible fact, and that no possible progress in the perception of scientific or moral truths can ever prevail against it." Changes in China were not taking place at the governmental level, but where it really mattered, among the people. The steamboats on her rivers and the factories along their banks were "engines of revolution." Science had entered the schools, and its precepts had begun to compete with those of Confucian philosophy. Although the number of Europeans in China was extremely small, these foreigners, whatever their moral worth as individuals, were frequently "torch-bearers of learning and harbingers of ideas."[4]

It was becoming increasingly meaningless, Reclus believed, to speak of the history of a particular country. Europeanisation was dissolving the isolation between countries and creating an interrelated world. Henceforth history would be universal, the record of relations between the peoples of the entire world.[5] He remarked that the conventional boundaries between countries were gradually being eroded by the force of circumstances, and that the most ardent patriot was becoming a "citizen of the world."

> In spite of his aversion to the foreigner, in spite of the tariff which protects him from outside business, in spite of the cannon on both sides of the border, he eats bread from India, drinks coffee harvested by the Negroes or the Malaysians, dresses in material made from American fibre, uses devices that are the product of the combined work of a thousand inventors of every time and race, shares the sentiments and thoughts of millions of men from one end of the earth to the other.[6]

As many local histories became fused into a universal history, people were coming to recognise their common humanity. Despite the national hatreds which persisted, they understood the "same scientific laws formulated in a language of precision and consequently with a perfect identity"; they researched the same intellectual origins and the same historical figures; and they were concerned with the same political and social problems.[7]

> It is a fact of the first importance, showing as it does how the very shrinkage of the earth, brought about by the progress of science and by increased facilities of communication, has the effect of enlarging men's minds and of broadening every question. [Contemporary] history is far outstepping the narrow conceptions of the Monroe Doctrine.[8]

One wonders whether Reclus felt vaguely uneasy about this account of Europeanisation. In any event, he sought to widen the gulf between himself and advocates of European imperialism by adding that, in itself, this shrinkage of the world was not to be applauded, for it might indicate only that more of the world's people were becoming the unwitting victims of capitalist exploitation. But with the vision of universal brotherhood never far from his thoughts, Reclus was confident that, through the collective efforts of the oppressed, such capitalist exploitation would be only a temporary, if regrettable, stage in the course of human development. It was clearly advantageous to the revolutionary cause that, henceforth, relations between capital and labour would be played out on the world stage. All social questions would be exposed to public discussion, and the enemy would become aware that it had to deal with the disinherited of the world.

In the 1870s Reclus had expressed some anxiety about the exploitation of cheap, foreign labour by the highly industrialised countries.[9] By 1898 this fear was allayed by the speed with which the Chinese in New York and Boston had learned to bargain for the same wages as their white counterparts. The pattern of developments in the Far East—and he made particular reference to the role of the Americans—logically led back to the larger human question of "bread and justice" for all. Once again, he suggested that an evil situation could be made to yield good if the will were sufficiently strong. Not only would all people come to know each other as brothers and sisters, but they would hasten their emancipation through concerted action against the common enemy. The question of race should not be allowed to cloud the issue of relations between capital and labour.[10]

Reclus was on different ground when he drew attention to the ways in which race was used to mask bourgeois social-economic concerns. The Dreyfus affair led him to try to uncover the interests behind anti-Semitic outbursts. In a lecture given in early March 1898 he attempted to clear up certain misconceptions about the Jews. Tracing their history to earliest times, Reclus demonstrated that few Jews could call themselves Semites. Anti-Semitism was a response not to any set of racial characteristics, he said, because Jews were a mixture of many peoples, including Aryans. Another explanation was needed. For various historical reasons, he said, those who professed the Jewish religion had undergone repeated persecution. Victimisation had drawn them together in a spirit of solidarity, but this self-preservation had also ensured them a separate identity. As middlemen they had come into contact with many societies, but assimilation into these societies was impossible. However, the role of middlemen, assumed out of necessity in historical circumstances, explained Reclus, also provided the Jews with the skills to become keen businessmen. Having lived by their wits among foreign peoples for many generations, they had developed the desire to excel and could boast of accomplishments in the arts and sciences, as well as in business. The desire to excel, sometimes coupled with a need to display conspicuous consumption, had gradually elevated them to a highly visible, rich, and influential minority. Jews had become identified with "the monopolising of the commonweal"; it was the covetousness of this social position, real or imagined, which was at issue in the late-nineteenth-century attacks. The question of anti-Semitism could be reduced to the struggle between bourgeois Christians and bourgeois Jews. Both groups had an "identical desire egotistically to appropriate the goods of the earth to themselves." Hatred of the Jews was not a reflection of the antipathy of races: "As for the question of race, it becomes lost in the social question."[11]

When he was asked about the Dreyfus affair in France, Reclus replied that every social phenomenon had a complex origin and varied according to time and place. In the France of early 1898, anti-Semitism was a superficial movement, due almost entirely to "the envy of candidates outdistanced in the competition, of officials eliminated in the distribution of positions." It was understandable that wage-earners and the unemployed were not interested in the movement "because the holders of capital... all resemble each other, whether they be Jews or Christians." While recognising the viciousness of the attacks, he felt that the movement would produce no more than a transitory heat and that the Jewish question would only temporarily divert energies away from *la grande question* of bread and justice for all people—Jews, Christians, Muslims, or pagans.[12]

The question of race, as Reclus was well aware, is intimately connected with that of sex and gender. In June 1868 he showed some interest in the group La Société de la revendication des droits de la femme, in which Madame Champseix and Elie and Noémi Reclus were directly involved.[13] In July 1882 Elisée criticised a friend for alluding to Pierre-Joseph Proudhon's remarks on the position of women "since his words on women are still for all of us those which weigh most heavily."[14] In a letter on the subject of education in September 1894 he declared that "the question of sex... is the important one." Women had equal right to the fruits of liberation, he believed, such as a complete education. "Outside coeducation, there is no education."[15]

After 1894 we find Reclus probing into the origins of the relationship between men and women. He noted that there had been diverse marriage forms in primitive society, but pointed to two diametrically opposing fundamental facts: "The brutal sexual force of the man: the origin of patriarchy" and "the natural attachment of the child to the mother who suckles it: the origin of matriarchy." Throughout the ages the conflict between these two opposing forces produced the most "unequal" results. Even where matriarchy prevailed in principle, it was often patriarchy that existed in practice.[16] Reclus used these terms in the sense of influence by the man or by the woman, as the case might be. When he referred to the natural attachment of the child to the mother as the origin of matriarchy, he meant the development of woman's sphere of influence.

In *L'Homme et la Terre*, his final statement to the world of scholarship, Reclus objected to the view that the institution of patriarchy was the mature result of a slow evolutionary process from primitive forms of marriage. He insisted that the historical origins of patriarchy could be traced to the point when the man exerted force over the woman and claimed her as his private property.[17] The most barbarous society was that in which the man ruled simply because he wielded greater physical force, provided the food, and meted out blows to his enemies and the weak, while the woman was bearer of children, nurse, and servant to the master.[18] The introduction of elements of matriarchy, or the opening up of woman's influence, was based on a "natural fact," the birth of the child, rather than brute force. Matriarchy, he said, contrary to widespread belief, represented a higher stage in social evolution.[19] It is unfortunate that Reclus referred to the child's attachment to the mother as a "natural" phenomenon and failed to employ more thoroughly his own thesis on the influence of the environment.

Reclus was interested in getting to the root of inequality between the sexes. He was confident, as was Engels, that it could be traced to the rise of private property and that no lasting advances were possible without eliminating private property. Reclus had held this view for some time, since in 1882 we find him expressing support for Josephine Butler's work among the prostitutes in England yet maintaining that she was attacking a "simple consequence of the social regime." Like Marx and Engels, Reclus unhesitatingly subordinated the question of sex and gender to that of class. "As for us [anarchists]... we attack the regime itself, property, law."[20] He shared the view of other socialists that before the woman question could be successfully tackled, goods and services would have to be produced and enjoyed collectively: women would have to undergo double emancipation, since not only were they among the disinherited of the earth, but had themselves been reduced to private property.

Like most radical thinkers of the time, Reclus did not conclude that the family as an institution should be abolished. In free society, the family could be re-established on an entirely different basis, "solely on affection, on its free affinities." Every aspect of the family that rested on prejudice, the legal system, or the interests of capital ought to disappear: "Here, as in everything else, liberty and natural feeling are the elements of life."[21]

Reclus—belonging in no small measure as he did to the existing order he sought to overturn—retained a romantic notion that a man and a woman should be equals in a free union, working together to contribute individually and collectively to social development.[22] The year before his death he described the union of man and

186

woman as the joy "of feeling oneself absolutely one with another."[23] Such a relationship could not be "artifically" regulated, and he shocked his more conservative contemporaries in 1870 and again in 1875 by "marrying" with neither official nor religious recognition. In October 1882, his two daughters, as free and rational beings, according to their father, chose similar forms of marriage.[24]

Reclus was preoccupied with the question of progress. It was one thing to argue that progress was coincident with the movement of society towards anarchist communism. One must also isolate general (natural) laws of development in order to show how progress was achieved and to assess prospects for the future. *L'Homme et la Terre* lists three laws determining the development of the human race: "The 'class struggle,' the search for equilibrium, and the sovereignty of the individual."[25] The class struggle he saw as emerging from unequal individual and social development, resulting in human collectivities dividing into classes or castes with opposing and conflicting interests. The second law was a necessary consequence of these divisions. As the equilibrium was upset from individual to individual, from class to class, it constantly reestablished around the axis: "The violation of justice always demands vengeance." From that point of departure there were unending oscillations. While rulers attempted to keep their position, the ruled fought for liberty; but as soon as the oppressed won, they tried to reconstitute the power for their own benefit. Either there was submission to the new rulers, or the "demands of free men" prevailed. In the chaos it was possible to discern "real" revolutions—changes of a political, economic, and social nature resulting from heightened consciousness and individual initiative. Thus the third law, revealed through a study of human history, was that individual effort was essential to all change. It was the individual who felt the "impulsive shock" of the environment and whose responses led to the diffusion of ideas and social change. Social instability was a result of the constraints on free individual expression.[26]

Reclus located the key to progress in individual initiative, and it followed that this initiative could be promoted by removing all constraints. This would involve a struggle, he warned, since masters—religious or otherwise—always sought to retain their privilege through repression. Their most frequent means—and the most successful—was to divert anger over domestic affairs to hostility against foreigners.[27] Opposition to the state might be undermined by harmless or even attractive terms like "patriotism," "social peace," or "order." A natural and beautiful sentiment, love of one's country, said Reclus, was turned routinely into hatred for one's neighbours; patriotism became chauvinism. At the turn of the century, socialists everywhere had to defend themselves against the charge of disloyalty to their country.[28]

187

There were other ways, it was suggested, in which attention was diverted from the cause. Activities such as gambling, drinking, and debauchery created a depravity and demoralisation which, conveniently for the dominant class, tended to weaken the spirit of revolt and thus individual initiative.[29] Disappointed but not discouraged by such human frailty, Reclus insisted that the progress of history might be delayed but never brought to a halt.[30]

Nor was Reclus put off by the sheer number of social and political tendencies he observed. Within the evolutionary process, he said, there were groups at different levels of evolution, and thus many opposing movements. Progress did not take place in a straight line, but in complicated curves; thus it was all the more necessary to examine the record with care.[31] Even the ugliness and shame of the Dreyfus affair might be seen as progress, because it exposed to the world evils that might otherwise have remained hidden. Hastening the death of a society without justice was progress, even if it were not immediately followed by the society that anarchists aimed to create.[32]

In the larger scheme of things, Reclus charted alternating periods of action and reaction, and he believed reversals would be followed by progress: "The general thrust is accomplished by a sort of oscillation, by a series of comings and goings, comparable to the movement of waves in the flood-tide; there are always temporary reversals."[33] Sometimes regression was so extensive that one was tempted to believe in "irremediable decadence," to suffer the illusion that the present "iron age" had been preceded by a golden age and that it would be followed by a mud age. But even the darkness of the Middle Ages gave way to the light of science, announced Reclus with some satisfaction. And history made it clear, he insisted, that the periods of reaction were increasingly shorter. It was possible to see their rhythm—to forecast their length and even try to avert them.[34]

In the meantime, the battle continued: revolution was dependent on the liberation of the spirit from prejudices, which were essentially atavisms or remnants of a primitive age. Some of these remnants, such as modesty in dress,[35] were not of great importance, according to Reclus, and would disappear in time. Others should be tackled immediately. One of these was the fear of the foreigner which lay at the basis of racism. Another was religion.

In the 1870s, in an effort to establish the precise nature of the struggle between capital and labour, Reclus had resisted being diverted into a discussion of religion.[36] In 1884 he had said that religion had lost its power.[37] A few years later, however, he had come to see that religion was not going to disappear as easily as he had thought. Travelling in North America in 1889, he came into contact with several groups of Methodists, and recognised that religion, through such movements as spiritualism and neo-Buddhism, was able to accommodate itself to the milieu. The same was true of the Salvation Army in England. By means of joyous refrains, dances, and common outings, religion could feed on feelings of solidarity—to blend in with liberty, poetry, and love. Even Catholicism attempted to keep in step with the times, and was able, moreover, to persuade some socialists to practise their religion for fear of excommunication.[38]

Reclus was by 1894 seeking a scientific basis for religion's remarkable hold. In an address to the Ecole des Libres Etudes in Brussels, he placed religion within the context of universal evolution,[39] tracing it back to its earliest form, superstition and fear of the unknown. As time went on, superstitions passed into myths and symbols and crystallised into dogmas and theologies. (Note his critique of parliamentary socialism.) In its strict etymological sense, superstition designated those ideas and sentiments which survived the ages; they existed in the child because "every man develops as humanity develops."[40] However, contemporary society, Reclus insisted, was increasingly capable of ridding itself of remnants. The origins and development of religion had to be scientifically explained and its premises demolished; otherwise an attack on organised religion would be much less effective.[41]

Here we would be remiss if we failed to note the set of assumptions and organising principles that Reclus took over unquestioned from late-nineteenth-century sociological and anthropological research. At its root is the equation of ontogenesis and phylogenesis, the belief that stages in the maturation of the individual parallel stages of maturation of the human race. When this is coupled with the conviction that European civilisation and its science stands at the pinnacle of human development, it is easy to see how the experience of the European adult male becomes universalised as the norm against which the achievements of all societies are measured.

These are questions which we could not reasonably expect Reclus to have raised in the nineteenth century. It is from a later historical standpoint that one grasps the import of the unquestioned faith in science of Reclus and his contemporaries. It is worth noting that he arrived at the point where anarchism, religion, and science were barely distinguishable. "We profess a new faith," he said in 1892, "and as soon as this faith, which is also a science, becomes the faith of all those who seek the truth, it will take its place in the world of reality, for the first law of history is that society models itself after its ideals."[42]

The question of that religion represented by Christianity assumed some importance for Reclus as the dispute over clericalism gained momentum in France. In a letter to Jean Grave dated Christmas Day 1899 he criticised an article on religion that had appeared

189

in *Les Temps nouveaux* claiming that the battle against clericalism and Christianity was of secondary importance to the economic struggle—a view which Reclus himself had put forth some fifteen years previously but which he now questioned. From an historical point of view, he said, fear of the unknown preceded the regime of private property. "If a man finds it so difficult to rebel against injustice, it is because he always feels dominated by mystery."[43] To attack religion, the unknown, would be to undermine the system of private property, especially since, as he wrote elsewhere, the Church was actually in league with the defenders of property.[44] The faith of old was disappearing, but the Church continued to be a power, directly through its recruitment of the privileged and indirectly through the survival of religious superstition. The function of religion now was reinforcement of the authority of the bourgeois order.

As unequivocal as the attack on Christianity was, the religion of his youth continued to provide Reclus with inspiration for his social and political theories. One might suggest that the faith he had once had in Christianity had been transferred to science. There also remained more immediate connections, however, between Christianity and his anarchism. It hardly needs saying that the "brotherhood" central to the vision of a society based on anarchist principles represented the fulfillment of Christian promises. As a boy, he had imagined the Heavenly Father sending down the daily bread; several decades later he suggested *The Conquest of Bread* as the title for Kropotkin's book, which was published under that name in 1892. In 1894, Reclus summed up his view of the revolutionary struggle by insisting that anarchists had a triple ideal: bread for the body, since everybody had a right to eat; education, or "bread for the spirit," since everybody had a right to develop to his or her full potential; and brotherhood, or what he might have called "bread for the heart."[45] The daily bread had become nourishment for the whole person—physical, spiritual, and emotional.

As they marched into the future men and women had to overcome the remnants of primitive societies. This was not a simple matter, however. While some features lingered that would be better left behind, others were abandoned at a loss. For example, humans had become the poorer for developing attitudes that separated them from animals, which they then proceeded to debase and enslave. The noble wild boar became the filthy pig, the "intrepid" mouflon the "timid" sheep. The great preoccupation of flesh-eaters was "to augment certain four-footed masses of meat and fat... stores of walking flesh, moving with difficulty from the dung-heap to the slaughterhouse." Through thoughtlessness and cruelty whole species had become extinct. Most dogs were little more than "degraded beings trembling before the stick," some of them taught to be savage or vain or stupid. But ever searching for the ray of hope, Reclus believed that there had been some progress. The dog brought up in "generosity, gentleness, and nobility of feeling" might "realise a human or even superhuman ideal of devotion and moral greatness." Cats far surpassed dogs in learning to retain their "personal independence and originality of character," to become "companions rather than captives." Moreover, since their days in the wilderness, they had made miraculous moral and intellectual advances. "There is not a human sentiment which on occasion they do not understand or share, not an idea which they may not divine, not a desire but what they forestall it."[46] These are touching sentiments. They are also an argument for increased sensitivity to animals and to nature.

Although he was an enthusiastic proponent of technology, Reclus cringed at the havoc a "pack of engineers" could wreak upon a "charming valley."[47] One must be wary of placing this student of geography in the Western humanist tradition. The hero of Reclus's work was not a God-man whose greater glory the animals and trees existed to serve. In many ways, "man" is the villain of the piece, as for example when he needlessly slaughters would-be companions for food. While the inspiration for Reclus's work was hope for the future, he retained a romantic longing to re-establish a certain closeness to nature that he associated with the "primitive." Here we can also detect that spirit which led him to elevate a Ravachol. Once the bankruptcy of the present was declared, he said, and wealth was forsaken for friendship, people would remember the animals left behind and seek their companionship anew.[48] There was much to be learned. "The study of primitive man has greatly contributed to our understanding of the 'law and order' man of our own day. Animal behaviour will help us penetrate deeper into the science of life, to increase both our knowledge of the world and our capacity to love."[49]

Reclus's vegetarianism was not based solely on convictions formed from his study of nature. He himself tells us that he was a "potential vegetarian while still a small boy wearing babyfrocks."

I have a distinct remembrance of horror at the sight of blood. One of the family sent me, plate in hand, to the village butcher, with the injunction to bring back some gory fragment or other. In all innocence I set out cheerfully to do as I was bid, and entered the yard where the slaughtermen were. I still remember this gloomy yard where terrifying men went to and fro with great knives, which they wiped on blood-besprinkled smocks. Hanging from a porch an enormous carcass seemed to me to occupy an extraordinary amount of space; from its white flesh a reddish liquid was trickling into the gutters. Trembling and silent I stood in this blood-stained yard incapable of going forward and too much terrified to run away. I do not know

191

what happened to me; it has passed from my memory. I seem to have heard that I fainted, and that the kind-hearted butcher carried me into his own house; I did not weigh more than one of those lambs he slaughtered every morning.

Other pictures cast their shadows over my childish [sic!] years and, like the glimpse of the slaughterhouse, mark so many epochs in my life. I can see the sow belonging to some peasants, amateur butchers, and therefore all the more cruel. I remember one of them bleeding the animal slowly, so that blood fell drop by drop; for, in order to make really good black puddings, it appears essential that the victim should have suffered proportionately. She cried without ceasing, now and then uttering groans and sounds of despair almost human; it seemed like listening to a child.

...One of the strongest impressions of my childhood is that of having witnessed one of those rural dramas, the forcible killing of a pig by a party of villagers in revolt against a dear old woman who would not consent to the murder of her fat friend. The village crowd burst into the pigsty and dragged the beast to the slaughter place where all the apparatus for the deed stood waiting, whilst the unhappy dame sank down upon a stool weeping quiet tears. I stood beside her and saw those tears without knowing whether I should sympathise with her grief, or think with the crowd that the killing of the pig was just, legitimate, decreed by common sense as well as by destiny.[50]

These recollections at the age of seventy-one demonstrate an early sensitivity and suggest that childhood experiences fused with scholarly investigation. Along with emotional revulsion at the sight of the slaughterhouse and the learned arguments which together produced his vegetarianism, we might also include the influence of Reclus's early encounter with Christianity. "Do we understand the meaning of the traditions which place the first man in a garden of beauty, where he walks freely with all the animals, and which tell us that the 'Son of Man' was born on a bed of straw, between the ass and the ox, the two companions of the field-worker?"[51]

Reclus not only preached the ideals he saw entrenched in Christianity; he sought to live by them. His "revolutionary" strategy was to treat everyone as an equal; he resisted the pressure to rise above his "brothers" by reminding himself that "nothing depraves like success."[52] "For shame," he wrote in 1882 to a young woman who called herself his disciple. "Is it right for some to be subordinated to others? I do not call myself 'your disciple'."[53] He explained in 1887:

As for my definition of equality, I can give it only from my point of view, which is that of the Revolution. But, as usual,

192

> I restrict myself to indicating the effects: equality is the en-
> semble of social facts that permits a man to look another man
> in the eye and to extend his hand to him without thinking
> twice. [54]

A story has been passed down about a faculty meeting at which it was decided that lectures should not be read. Reclus, who had thus far been silent, said quietly, "Gentlemen, I have been in the habit of reading my lectures; I shall have need of indulgence." His colleagues made an exception for the Institute of Advanced Studies where Reclus taught, but, according to the story, he never read another lecture. [55] As might be expected, he approached his students not as disciples, but as equals. From his first lecture in March 1894, he invited them to challenge his conclusions. [56] The programme of his Geography Institute [57] stated that "as much time as possible is to be reserved for individual initiative in organising the courses, or rather the informal discussions." [58]

The eminent biologist Alfred Russell Wallace described his first meeting with Reclus in 1895:

> He was a rather small and very delicate-looking man. highly
> intellectual, but very quiet in speech and manner. I really did
> not know that it was *he* with whose name I had been familiar
> for twenty years as the greatest of geographers, thinking it
> must have been his father or elder brother; and I was surprised
> when, on asking him, he said that it was he himself. [59]

The anarchist Johann Most met Reclus in the late 1800s in New York:

> I was sitting in my poor editorial chair in William Street, where
> at the time the *Freiheit* was published. Suddenly someone
> tapped me on my back, while I was writing. Turning angrily
> around, I saw before me a small-sized personality of advanced
> age, but with striking features whose eyes streamed kindness
> and fraternity.
>
> "I am Reclus," says he, with absolutely no air of pride or
> affection, as though he would be the most commonplace visitor.
>
> "Excuse me for disturbing you," he added modestly. I must
> say, I was happy to be thus disturbed. I embraced Elisée Reclus,
> and the hours which I enjoyed in his company belong to the
> brightest and happiest in my life. His whole personality is
> invigorating. His eyes penetrate the universe and give one the
> feeling that one is, in the struggle for the emancipation of the
> workers, in unity and harmony with cosmic forces. Elisée Reclus
> I count as one of the greatest inspirers, since I became an
> anarchist. [60]

The tales of Reclus's uncommon goodness are legion. A friend of his daughter Jeannie remembered:

> Never shall I forget the perfect courtesy of his manner as he bowed to the slip of a girl I was then [1880]. Towards the old and feeble, this courtesy remained the same. I can see him, advancing gaily towards his aged mother-in-law [Ermance's mother], helping her up, and slipping her arm through his, as he led her, with cheerful words, in to dinner.[61]

"He did not encase himself in the superiority which a great many savants believe they possess," said a person of humble origins. "He inclined toward simple men, toward workingmen before all others."[62] Reported a lifelong friend: "While to those who claimed superiority of any kind he could be terrible in the scathing contempt or mocking bitterness with which he spoke, to the unhappy—the moral failures—he was gentle and much enduring."[63]

Reclus was generous with his time and money. "One could come and find him at any hour, and he interrupted himself in the midst of his work to discuss with people whose conversation must frequently have been without any interest to him."[64] He was forever contributing to worthy causes and at least on one occasion was reduced to near poverty.[65] He had a "naïve confidence,"[66] according to some observers, and was thus "easy prey."[67]

It is not difficult to see that Reclus's approach to life could be seen as evidence of goodness. "In another age, Reclus would have been considered a saint; he had all the characteristics."[68] "One of the most truly religious spirits of this age, he was of the race from which springs saints and martyrs... He practiced all the virtues, simply and naturally... He saw the future as a dawn rising over a world of men, good, simple, and brotherly—made in his own image."[69] Elisée Reclus "belonged to the greater order of men: he was a man sui generis—one whom the pagans would have made a demigod or hero."[70] Though the pictures are clearly overdrawn, and we need not take them literally, it is worth pointing out that such a canonisation represented a kind of defeat for Reclus. He would hardly have relished being remembered with such sentimentality and with what he would have seen as a lack of understanding of the great cause for which he worked.

There is also evidence that some people resented his saintliness and insinuated that he was setting himself up as a model.[71] This was to some extent true, since Reclus saw the individual as a microcosm of society; to change the individual was therefore to contribute to the establishment of a new society. He apparently reacted to the criticism by blaming himself and consciously working at self-improvement. In 1904 he confided to a friend: "I still have my faults and weaknesses, but I also have my sincere kindnesses,

my high desires, my interior ideal. I am always working at the...
hero which I dream of and which is the better me."[72] The more
Reclus struggled for perfection the more elusive it became. Toward
the end of his life he grew increasingly disgruntled with the limitations of the capitalist system of production and distribution
within which he had to write his geography.[73] Shortly before his
death, he wrote to a friend: "Are not even revolutionaries bourgeois
in spirit?"[74]

Reclus's fanatical insistence on perfection was to some degree
a response to the limited political options following upon his rejection of all party-political activity after the Paris Commune. It
might be helpful to reflect a little on his views of the use of franchise.
His break with the parliamentary system came swiftly and in
painful circumstances, and it was a partial reversal of his earlier
position. We also know that Reclus could never again be joyful
about Paris. Consider, for example, his reply in 1882 to the ac-
cusation that he did not visit Paris because he did not love it. "I
love Paris very much," he insisted, "and it is precisely because I
love it so much that I would like to find myself there again in
conditions similar to those which I have known"—that is, those
which existed in the early days of the Commune.[75] In late 1895
or early 1896 Jean Grave asked Reclus to give an address in Paris
in order to help *Les Temps nouveaux* out of financial difficulty. A
reasonable request, one would think, but it was refused. Grave
believed that Reclus held a "sort of hatred for the people of Paris."[76]

In the 1870s Reclus rarely went into detail or spoke with clarity
on electoral abstention, although to those around him it was obvious
that he was utterly opposed to participation in the parliamentary
system. Even so, it was not out of the question that he might in
time modify his position. There were others, such as Paul Brousse,
who had been intransigent anarchists but who relented when the
Jura movement went into decline. Apparently, the depth of Reclus's
antagonism to party politics was not comprehended even by
Brousse, who in late 1879 was planning a newspaper project for
which he was hoping to gain the collaboration of such a varied
lot as Reclus and Peter Kropotkin, Andreas Costa, Benoît Malon,
Jules Guesde, and Xavier de Ricard.[77]

Reclus offered little in defence of his position on party politics
other than to say that power corrupts. In 1884 he declared:

> It is now a matter of common knowledge that power, whether
> its nature be monarchic, aristocratic, or democratic, whether
> it be based on the right of the sword, or inheritance, or of
> election, is wielded by men neither better nor worse than their
> fellows, but whose position exposes them to greater temptations
> to do evil. Raised above the crowd, whom they soon learn to

195

despise, they end by considering themselves essentially superior beings; solicited by ambition in a thousand forms, by vanity, greed and caprice, they are all the more easily corrupted that a rabble of interested flatterers is ever on the watch to profit by their vices. And possessing as they do a preponderant influence in all things, holding the powerful lever whereby is moved the immense mechanism of the State—functionaries, soldiers, and police—every one of their oversights, their faults, or their crimes repeats itself to infinity and magnifies as it grows.[78]

It is surprising that as late as 1885 his position on party politics was so unclear to some radicals that his name was placed on the electoral list of Lissagaray's *La Bataille*. Reclus, Kropotkin, and several others who were being sponsored without their permission in the October 1885 general elections vehemently objected and declared that they did not intend to stand as candidates under any circumstances.[79]

This notice was not enough for Reclus, and he wrote to Jean Grave on the matter in a letter dated 26 September. The letter was subsequently reproduced as an electoral poster and published in *Le Révolté*.[80] To vote, it declared, was to abdicate one's sovereignty, to be duped into believing that representatives were wise enough to legislate on everything, to invite treachery because power corrupted even the most sincere and honest. It called on people to defend their interests and to accept responsibility for their actions. The statement was enthusiastically received by the anarchist groups in late 1885 and early 1886. According to a February 1886 police report, it "was peddled in the meetings and greeted with unanimous approval."[81]

From an early age Reclus had sensed the delusions associated with the ballot box. By mid-century he had balked at the notion that democracy (read brotherhood) consisted in the "sham" of universal suffrage.[82] Following repression of the Commune, he must have felt that he had himself been deluded into believing that social change could be effected in this way. He could hardly argue that use of the franchise stopped progress; it merely slowed down the revolutionary process—it was another of those "circuitous" routes.

And yet the logic of his own theories also led him to condemn any "outside" constraint on behaviour, so that any particular anarchist might be directed to the ballot box by the "interior voice." Moreover, from his position that the end justifies the means, it followed that the franchise could be a neutral means. Reclus recognised the validity of such arguments when he wrote in 1897:

On the question of voting, I would comment on this act as I would on any other, that is it is neutral in itself and should be

196

studied in its dynamics and its relations with circumstances and men. In such and such a circumstance, the conscience of so and so, among the anarchists, might justify, even approve it.[83]

In view of the moral and intellectual progress which Reclus saw all around him at the turn of the century, he might have conceded that the use of the franchise was less hazardous to the cause than it had been in former years. But he had no interest in addressing the question, nor did he feel there was a need to do so, especially in his last days when he was able to participate in the enthusiasm over the news from Russia.

When the revolutionary events broke out in January 1905 Reclus was an old man suffering acute spells of angina pectoris and still shaken by Elie's death the year before. But the unrest following "Bloody Sunday" roused his spirits, and he set out for Paris—"revolutionary" Paris, where he had been reluctant to address gatherings ever since the suppression of the Commune. "Alas!" he wrote to Kropotkin, "I should speak to them in words of fire, and I have only an asthmatic puff to give them. Nonetheless, I shall do it with my whole spirit. It is no mistake to repeat: 'The Revolution has begun'."[84] At the meeting he began to speak, but, too ill to withstand the excitement, asked a friend to read his prepared address.[85]

The audience was reminded of the terrible end of the Paris Commune, and links were drawn to the bloody events around the Winter Palace on 9 January. St. Petersburg had become, like Paris, a revolutionary city. The great question was the magnitude which the revolution in Russia would ultimately assume, since all revolutions, although similar in movement and rhythm, differed in detail and scope. He was convinced that it would rank with the French Revolution among the great historical events. Moreover, this time the issue was not simply the entrance of the Third Estate into the social body. The workers, as well as the intellectuals and the bourgeoisie, were demanding their share of liberty; the peasants too would take part. Furthermore, the Russians would be forced to consider the question of the cultural and linguistic groups confined in the Russian Empire. All peoples would be first emancipated and then joined in a free association.

[A] federal tie will unite them, assuring each human being, of whatever race, complete liberty. The French Revolution proclaimed the "right of man"; we demand that the Slavic Revolution make this a living reality. We prophesy for it the joy of achieving the greatest accomplishment of history, the conciliation of races in a federation of equity.

197

Finally, the historical development of Russia, its vast domains enveloping many peoples and its extensive contacts with East and West, held out the promise that the revolution would have a universal character:

> Here is the promise of a national revolution, which, by the force of circumstances, will evolve in the "global" sense, that is to say, a real liberty which will no longer be the prerogative of some whites, but the right of all men, whether they be white, yellow, or even black, whether they be Arab or Turkish, or even belong to the category of "hereditary enemies," such as the English or the Germans.

The events of 1905 were a dream come true, the theory of the old International Working Men's Association in practice, proof that "emancipation of the Workers will be made by the Workers themselves."

In the latter part of June 1905 Reclus's physical condition rapidly deteriorated. His last days were spent at Thourout in the countryside west of Brussels at the home of his close friend Florence de Brouckère. Shortly before he died, he completed the preface to the Russian edition of *L'Homme et la Terre*, and a few hours before his death on 4 July listened to his daughter read a telegram carrying the glad tidings of the revolt of the sailors on the battleship *Potemkin* in the Black Sea. "Elisée Reclus was luminously smiling... He had no more strength to speak. After a few hours he died peacefully."[86] Two days later his nephew Paul accompanied the body to the cemetery at Ixelles where it would be interred with that of Elie. In keeping with his wishes, there was no procession.[87]

Endnotes

Author's Introduction

1. Max Nettlau, *Elisée Reclus: Anarchist und Gelehrter* (Berlin, 1928); a revised edition appeared in Spanish also in 1928.
2. Gary S. Dunbar, *Elisée Reclus: Historian of Nature* (Hamden, Conn., 1978).
3. Marie Fleming, *The Anarchist Way to Socialism: Elisée Reclus and Nineteenth-Century European Anarchism* (London, 1979). Dunbar and I had decided independently to pursue our studies of Reclus, and his work appeared too late for me to consult.
4. H. Roorda van Eysinga, "Avant tout anarchiste" in *Elisée Reclus (1830-1905): Savant et Anarchiste* (Paris-Brussels, 1956).
5. Peter Kropotkin, "Elisée Reclus" in *Les Temps nouveaux*, July 1905.
6. Nettlau to Jacques Gross, 17 July 1905, Fonds Jacques Gross, IISG.
7. Quoted in Pierre Ramus, "In Commemoration of Elisée Reclus" in Joseph Ishill, *Elisée and Elie Reclus: In Memoriam* (Berkeley Heights, 1927), p. 125.
8. Peter Kropotkin, "Must We Occupy Ourselves With the Examination of the Ideal of a Future System?" in P.A. Kropotkin, *Selected Writings on Anarchism and Revolution*, ed. Martin A. Miller (Cambridge, Mass., 1970), p. 47.
9. *Le Révolté*, 21 Jan. 1882. See also the proceedings of the Jura Federation Congress of 1880 in which the theory of anarchist communism was adopted: *Le Révolté*, 17 Oct. 1880.
10. Elisée Reclus's preface to Peter Kropotkin, *La Conquête du pain* (Paris, 1892).

199

11. Reclus to Bakunin, 17 Apr. 1875, *Corr.* II, p. 170. See Bakunin to Reclus, 15 Feb. 1875, in Max Nettlau, "Elisée Reclus and Michael Bakunin" in Ishill, *Elisée and Elie Reclus,* p. 203ff.
12. Frank Harrison, *The Modern State: An Anarchist Analysis* (Montréal, 1983), p.118. Cf. his review of my book in *Our Generation,* Vol. 14, No. 2, pp. 46-48.
13. Harrison, *The Modern State,* p. 118.
14. Ernest Alfred Vizetelly, *The Anarchists* (New York, 1972; originally 1911), p. 10.
15. See Paul Eltzbacher, *Anarchism* (London, 1960; originally 1900).
16. J. Garin, *L'Anarchie et les Anarchistes* (Paris, 1885), pp. 167, 185.
17. Eltzbacher, *Anarchism.*
18. *The New Leader,* 28 July 1980, p. 22-23; see also 28 Jan. 1980, pp. 21-22.

Chapter 1

1. For a copy of Reclus's birth certificate, see Papiers ER NAF 22909. His godfather was Jacques Drilholle, Protestant pastor and president of the Consistoire of Sainte-Foy. The most important sources for Reclus's early years are Elisée Reclus, *Correspondance,* 3 vols. (Paris, 1911-25), esp. Vol. I; Paul Reclus, *Les Frères Elie et Elisée Reclus* (Paris, 1964); Elisée Reclus, *Elie Reclus, 1827-1904* (Paris, 1905), also as "Vie d'Elie Reclus" in Paul Reclus, *Les Frères*; Max Nettlau, *Elisée Reclus: Anarchist und Gelehrter* (Berlin, 1928).
2. Elisée Reclus, *La Terre,* 2 vols. (Paris, 1868-69), Vol. 2, p. 757.
3. Reclus, *Elie Reclus,* p. 9. Although the word "son" refers to Elie, the passage is also a description of Elisée's impressions.
4. *Corr.* I, p. 9.
5. *Ibid.,* p. 8.
6. *Ibid.*
7. Reclus, *Elie Reclus,* p. 9.
8. *Ibid.*
9. Elisée Reclus, "An Anarchist on Anarchy" in *Contemporary Review,* May 1884, as pamphlet *An Anarchist on Anarchy* (Boston, 1884).
10. See esp. *ibid.*
11. Reclus, *Elie Reclus,* p. 11.
12. *Ibid.,* p. 13.
13. Paul Reclus, "Biographie d'Elisée Reclus," p. 19. Elisée's "Diplôme de Bachelier ès Lettres" was awarded 5 Aug. 1848 by the "faculté des Lettres, Académie de Bordeaux." For the document, see Papiers ER, NAF 22909.
14. Paul Reclus, "Biographie," p. 19.
15. Reclus, *Elie Reclus,* p. 16.
16. *Corr.* I, pp. 15-16; Paul Reclus, "A Few Recollections on the Brothers Elie and Elisée Reclus" in Ishill, *Elisée and Elie Reclus,* p. 8.
17. Reclus, *Elie Reclus,* p. 16.
18. Reclus to his mother, Apr. 1851, *Corr.* III, p. 2.
19. Reclus, *Elie Reclus,* p. 18.
20. Richard Heath, "Elisée Reclus" in *Humane Review,* Oct. 1905.
21. Elisée Reclus, "Développement de la liberté dans le monde," an essay written very likely in 1851. The manuscript was discovered by Louise in Brussels in the late 1890s or early 1900s and passed on to Clara Mesnil. When Reclus was approached, he commented: "Oh! That silly thing!" (See account by Clara Mesnil in NA, IISG.) Jacques Mesnil quoted parts of the essay in 1906 (*Les Temps nouveaux,* 29 Sept.-1 Dec. 1906) and *Le Libertaire* published the entire essay in 1925 (28 Aug.-2 Oct.). The manuscript was not initially dated, and it was at the end of his life that Reclus wrote "1851 Montauban" at the head of it. *Le Libertaire* changed the date to 1850 because "in 1851 Elisée Reclus was no longer at Montauban" and because the manuscript seemed "to have

been conceived after the revolutionary period of 1848." While some parts of the essay appear to have been written in 1849, there are also similarities between the essay and a letter that Reclus wrote to his mother from Berlin in April 1851 (*Corr.* III, p. 1ff.). It is possible that the essay was composed sometime during the period 1849-51 and completed in the few days of Reclus's stay in Montauban in the autumn of 1851. Cf. Nettlau, *Elisée Reclus*, pp. 8-9. For the original manuscript, see Archief ER, IISG.

22. Reclus, "Développement."
23. *Ibid.*
24. Quoted in Boris Nicolaevsky and Otto Maenchen-Helfen, *Karl Marx: Man and Fighter* (London, 1973), p. 148.
25. Reclus, *Elie Reclus*, p. 18.
26. *Ibid.*, p. 20.
27. *Ibid.*, p. 19.
28. For Elisée's excitement on seeing the Mediterranean for the first time, see Paul Reclus, "A Few Recollections," pp. 24-25.
29. Elisée recorded: "He [the doyen] sent for the three youths, and, not without chagrin, officially transmitted the consilium abeundi...", *Elie Reclus*, p. 20.
30. *Ibid.*, pp. 20-21.
31. Reclus to his mother, n.d. (1850), *Corr.* I, p. 29.
32. On 1 Feb. 1851, Dr. A. Twesten, Rector at the university, signed Reclus's certificate of acceptance. For the original document, see Papiers ER, NAF 22909.
33. Reclus to his mother, 11 Feb. 1851, *Corr.* I, p. 37. In the introduction to his translation of an essay by Carl Ritter in 1859, Reclus recalled Ritter's courses: "De la configuration des continents sur la surface du globe, et de leurs fonctions dans l'histoire" in *La Revue germanique*, Nov. 1859.
34. Reclus to his mother, Apr. 1851, *Corr.* III, p. 2.
35. *Ibid.*, p. 1.
36. For the original manuscript, see Archief ER, IISG. A published (unedited) copy can be found in *Le Libertaire*, 28 Aug.-2 Oct. 1925. See above, n. 21.
37. Elisée Reclus, "On Vegetarianism" in *Humane Review*, Jan. 1901 (reprinted as a pamphlet by the Humanitarian League, London, 1901).
38. Pierre-Joseph Proudhon, *Qu'est-ce que la propriété?* (Paris reprint, 1873), p. 212ff.
39. Reclus to Elie, n.d. (1855), *Corr.* I, pp. 95-96.
40. Reclus, *Elie Reclus*, p. 21. The title of Elie's thesis was "Le Principe d'autorité." Elisée described it as "a beautifully original work for which he would have been burned at the stake or hanged three or four centuries earlier" (*ibid.*).
41. *Ibid.*, pp. 22-23.
42. *Ibid.*, p. 23.
43. *Ibid.*, Paul Reclus, "Biographie," p. 23.
44. Reclus, *Elie Reclus*, pp. 23-24.
45. Reclus, "An Anarchist on Anarchy."
46. Reclus to Pastor Roth (Orthez), n.d. (1904), *Corr.* III, p. 285.
47. Richard Heath, "Elisée Reclus" in *Humane Review*, Oct. 1905.

Chapter 2

1. Elisée Reclus, *Elie Reclus*, p. 24.
2. Richard Heath, "Elisée Reclus."
3. The few letters of 1852 which have survived suggest that Elisée and Elie shared what money was available. See Reclus to Elie, n.d., *Corr.* I, pp. 54-55. Cf. Paul Reclus, "Biographie," p. 25.
4. Reclus, *Elie Reclus*, p. 24. Cf. Leroux's impressions of life in London in the early 1850s in his *Quelques pages de vérité* (Paris, 1859), p. 47ff.
5. Reclus to Elie, 2 Mar. 1852, *Corr.* I, pp. 50-51.

6. Elie Reclus, *La Commune de Paris au jour le jour 1871 (19 mars-28 mai)* (Paris, 1908), pp. 134-38. Elisée was acquainted with the ideas of Leroux by 1849; Reclus, *Elie Reclus*, p. 19. See references to Leroux: Reclus to Elie, n.d., *Corr.* I, p. 125, and 1 Feb. 1857, *ibid.*, p. 153.
7. In conversation with Max Nettlau in 1895, Elie said that he remembered Coeurderoy very well; Max Nettlau, *Elisée Reclus*, p. 54.
8. By 1855 Elie had come into contact with Herzen and Elisée had some appreciation of Herzen's ideas. Reclus to Elie, n.d., *Corr.* I, p. 94.
9. See David McLellan, *Karl Marx: His Life and Thought* (London, 1973), pp. 252-62. Cf. Reclus to Elie, 8 Mar. 1852, *Corr.* I, p. 53.
10. Reclus to Elie, 8 Mar. 1852, *Corr.* I, p. 53.
11. Reclus to Elie, n.d. (1852), *Corr.* I, p. 55.
12. See *Corr.* I, p. 71ff.
13. Reclus, *Elie Reclus*, p. 26.
14. Paul Reclus, "A Few Recollections," pp. 24-25.
15. Reclus to Elie, n.d. (1852), *Corr.* I, p. 65.
16. Reclus, *La Terre* I, preface.
17. Reclus to his mother, 13 Nov. 1855, *Corr.* I, p. 109.
18. Reclus to Elie, n.d. (1855), *Corr.* I, p. 106.
19. See Elisée Reclus's articles in *La Revue des deux mondes*: "De l'esclavage aux Etats-Unis," 15 Dec. 1860, pp. 868-901, and 1 Jan. 1861, pp. 118-54; "Les Noirs américains depuis la guerre," 15 Mar. 1863, pp. 364-94; "Un écrit américain sur l'esclavage," 15 Mar. 1864, pp. 507-10; "Deux années de la grande lutte américaine," 1 Oct. 1864, pp. 555-624; "Le Coton et la crise américaine," 1 Jan. 1862, pp. 176-208. See also "John Brown" in *La Coopération*, 14 July 1867.
20. Reclus to Elie, n.d. (1855), *Corr.* I, pp. 104-5.
21. Reclus to Clara Mesnil, 25 Oct. 1904, Fonds ER, IFHS. He had earlier indicated that the Fortier children, and especially the eldest, a girl of 14, were fond of him (Reclus to Elie, n.d. (1855), *Corr.* I, p. 102). In his 1904 letter to Clara Mesnil, he explained that the girl had been in love with him, but that he had felt only a brotherly affection for her.
22. Count Joseph-Arthur Gobineau published his *Essay on the Inequality of Human Races* in 1853. While it is not known what, if anything, Reclus knew of Gobineau's theories at that time, he subsequently studied them with a great deal of scrutiny. Reclus to De Gérando, 24 June 1883, *Corr.* II, p. 307.
23. Reclus, "Développement."
24. Reclus to Elie, n.d. (1855), *Corr.* I, p. 97.
25. *Ibid.*, p. 96.
26. *Ibid.*, p. 92.
27. *Ibid.*
28. *Ibid.*, p. 97 (original emphasis).
29. *Ibid.*, p. 96.
30. *Ibid.*, p. 92.
31. *Ibid.*, p. 91.
32. *Ibid.*, pp. 92-93.
33. *Ibid.*, p. 93.
34. Reclus to his mother, 28 June 1855, *Corr.* I, p. 87.
35. Reclus to Elie, n.d. (1855), *Corr.* I, p. 105.
36. Reclus to Elie, 5 May 1856, *Corr.* I, p. 117.
37. For Reclus's experiences in Colombia, see his *Voyage à la Sierra-Nevada de Sainte-Marthe* (Paris, 1861); *Corr.* I, esp. pp. 112-67; "La Nouvelle-Grenade: Paysages de la nature tropicale" in *La Revue des deux mondes*, 1 Dec. 1859, pp. 624-62; 1 Feb. 1860, pp. 609-35; 15 Mar. 1860, pp. 419-52; 1 May 1860, pp. 50-83. See also Reclus to "Société anonyme de colonisation de la Sierra-Nevada," 20 Feb. 1884, and Reclus to P. Gérance, 6 Mar. 1885, in Papiers ER, NAF 22917.

38. Reclus to Elie, 1 June 1857, *Corr.* I, p. 164.
39. Reclus to Elie, 1 Feb. 1857, *Corr.* I, p. 155, and 1 June 1857, *ibid.*, p. 164.
40. Reclus to Elie, 1 Feb. 1857, *Corr.* I, p. 153.
41. *Ibid.*, pp. 154-55.
42. Reclus to his mother, 14 Oct. 1856, *Corr.* I, pp. 146-47.
43. *Ibid.*, p. 147.
44. Reclus to Elie, 10 Mar. 1857, *Corr.* I, p. 161.
45. Reclus to Elie, n.d. (1855), *Corr.* I, p. 105.
46. See the copy of a circular put out by the Société anonyme de colonisation de la Sierra-Nevada, dated Paris, 1 Feb. 1884, and quoting from Reclus's book, in Papiers ER, NAF 22917.
47. Reclus to Société anonyme de colonisation de la Sierra-Nevada, 20 Feb. 1884, Papiers ER, NAF 22917. Cf. Reclus to Gérance, 6 Mar. 1885, Papiers ER, NAF 22917.
48. Reclus, "An Anarchist on Anarchy."
49. *Ibid.*
50. Elisée Reclus, "Les Colonies anarchistes" in *Les Temps nouveaux*, 7-13 July 1900.
51. *Ibid.*

Chapter 3

1. Reclus to his mother, n.d. (1857?), *Corr.* I, p. 172.
2. Paul Reclus, "Biographie," pp. 43-44.
3. Reclus, *Voyage à la Sierra-Nevada.*
4. *Ibid.*, pp. 58-59.
5. Elisée Reclus, *Elie Reclus*, p. 26.
6. Paul Reclus, "Biographie," p. 43.
7. Proudhon exclaimed: "What can he [Napoleon] do? Nothing, nothing, nothing." Quoted in George Woodcock, *Pierre-Joseph Proudhon: A Biography* (Montréal, 1987), p. 224.
8. Elisée to Noémi and Clarisse, 12 or 13 Aug. 1860, *Corr.* III, p. 22.
9. See Elisée Reclus, *Londres illustré: Guide spécial pour l'Exposition de 1862* (Paris, 1862), abridged edition of his *Guide du voyageur à Londres et aux environs* (Paris 1860).
10. "Well done, workers of London!" exclaimed Reclus. Letter to Noémi, n.d. (1863), *Corr.* I, p. 231.
11. It is difficult to establish the date of Reclus's membership in the IWMA. See police report of 27 Aug. 1874, P.Po. B a/1237; another of 2 Feb. 1879, AN BB24 732. Cf. Kropotkin, "Elisée Reclus," and E. Vaughan, "The Criminal Record of Elisée Reclus," in Reclus, *An Anarchist on Anarchy*, p. 18.
12. Cf. Reclus's correspondence for the period, esp. letter to Elie, 11 June 1868 (see below, n. 15).
13. See the letter of 10 Feb. 1865 from Tolain to Lelubez in which Tolain attacks Elie: I. Tchernoff, *Le Parti Républicain au coup d'état et sous le Second Empire* (Paris, 1906), pp. 455-56.
14. *L'Association*, Apr. 1865.
15. Reclus to Elie, 11 June 1868, Papiers ER, NAF 22910. The letter is undated; however, the day it was written Elie continued writing on the piece of paper on which Elisée had written his letter and dated it 11 June 1868. The published version of Elisée's letter (*Corr.* I, p. 289ff.) has been misdated 11 Oct. 1868.
16. Reclus to Elie, n.d. (Oct. 1868), *Corr.* I. p. 294.
17. Malon and his companion Madame Champseix were among the handful of relatives and friends who witnessed Reclus's second marriage held at Vascoeuil on 26 June 1870. See Papiers ER, NAF 22909.
18. Note Reclus's involvement with *La Republique des travailleurs*, organ of the Batignolles section, in early 1871. According to Jacques Rougerie, "L'A.I.T.

et le mouvement ouvrier à Paris pendant les événements de 1870-1871" in *International Review of Social History*, 1972, 1-2, pp. 84-5n, Reclus was a member of the Batignolles section.

19. *Documents of the First International*, 5 vols. (Moscow) III, pp. 122, 143-46.
20. Karl Marx, *Chronik seines Lebens* (Frankfurt, 1971), p. 448.
21. Max Nettlau, *Elisée Reclus*, p. 95.
22. Marx to Ludwig Büchner, 1 May 1867, *Marx Engels Werke* (Berlin, 1956ff.) 31, pp. 544-45. As early as Dec. 1862, Marx had been looking for a French translator. On 2 Jan. 1863 he wrote to Engels that Jenny Marx (who had been in Paris in late Dec. 1862) had met a "certain Reclus" who wanted to undertake the work; Marx to Engels, 2 Jan. 1863, *MEW* 30, p. 306. According to the notes there and those in *Chronik*, p. 223, Jenny met Elie. Nettlau was aware of some talk that Marx considered Elie a possible translator of "an economic composition" in the early 1860s; Nettlau, *Elisée Reclus*, p. 95n.
23. *MEW* 31, p. 676, n. 443. Cf. *Chronik*, p. 264. The *MEW* and the *Chronik* contain notes about the letters from Schily, not their contents. The letters from Marx and Engels concerning the translation of *Das Kapital* in *MEW* mention only the family name Reclus. According to the *Chronik*, originally put together in 1933 by the Marx-Engels-Lenin Institute in Moscow, Elie was supposed to be the translator. However, the much later *MEW* of the Institute for Marxism Leninism (which developed out of the earlier Marx-Engels-Lenin Institute) names Elisée as the translator. It can be established that it was Elisée whom Marx met the summer of 1869.
24. Marx to Victor Schily, 30 Nov. 1867, *MEW* 31, p. 573.
25. Jan. 1868: *MEW* 31, p. 727, n. 46.
26. Engels to Marx, 2 Feb. 1868, *MEW* 32, p. 28. Cf. Marx to Engels, 1 Feb. 1868, *MEW* 32, p. 26.
27. The discussion probably continued for another year. In October 1869 Charles Keller, a member of the Paris section of the IWMA, undertook the task, but did not complete it, and in late 1871 Marx began to make arrangements with Joseph Roy. See Marx to Laura and Paul Lafargue, 11 Apr. 1868, *MEW* 32, p. 544, and p. 733, n. 109. Cf. *Chronik*, p. 267. See also Marx to Engels, 4 Aug. 1868, *MEW* 32, p. 131.
28. Marx to Engels, 18 Nov. 1869, *MEW* 32, p. 394.
29. Marx to Engels, 1 Aug. 1877, *MEW* 34, p. 65 and Marx to Wilhelm Bracke, 20 Nov. 1876, *MEW* 34, p. 225.
30. Engels to Wilhelm Liebknecht, 31 July 1877, *MEW* 34, p. 285.
31. Marx to Engels, 1 Aug.1877, *MEW* 34, p. 65.
32. Preface by Elisée Reclus to F. Domela Nieuwenhuis, *Le Socialisme en danger* (Paris, 1897), p. viii. Cf. Nieuwenhuis, pp. 46, 166-67.
33. Reclus to his mother, n.d. (1862), *Corr.* I, p. 217, and to Noémi, n.d. (1863), *ibid.*, p. 230.
34. *L'Association*, 17 June 1866.
35. Reclus, *Elie Reclus*, p. 28.
36. Jean Gaumont, *Histoire générale de la coopération en France*, 2 vols. (Paris, 1924) I, p. 465. Cf. Guillaume de Greef, *Elogie d'Elie Reclus: Discours prononcé le 31 octobre à la séance de rentrée* (Brussels, 1904), p. 23.
37. Reclus, *Elie Reclus*, pp. 27-28.
38. Reclus to Elie, 11 June 1868, Papiers ER, NAF 22910 (see above, n. 15).
39. Cf. Reclus to Alfred Dumesnil, n.d. (1868), *Corr.* I, p. 300.
40. See Boris I. Nicolaevsky, "Secret Societies and the First International" in Milorad M. Drachkovitch (ed.), *The Revolutionary Internationals 1864-1943* (Stanford, 1966), p. 36ff.
41. Jean Bossu, *Elisée Reclus* (S. et O. Herblay, n.d.), p. 18n.
42. Reclus to Mlle. Rachel Goron, 17 Dec. 1894, Autographes XIXème-XXème Siècles, NAF 25101.

43. Elisée Reclus, *L'Anarchie* (Publications des *Temps nouveaux*, No. 2, Paris, 1896), "Notice préliminaire."

44. Bossu, *Elisée Reclus*, p. 18n. Léo Campion, *Les Anarchistes dans la F.M.* (Marseilles, 1969), pp. 87-91.

45. Campion, *Les Anarchistes*, p. 91. The account is incorrect insofar as it implies that Elisée and Elie (and their brother Paul) were lifelong Freemasons.

46. Reclus to Rachel Goron, 17 Dec. 1894, NAF 25101.

47. Reclus, *L'Anarchie* (address delivered to the Loge des amis philanthropes at Brussels in 1894) (Paris, 1896).

48. Reclus to Elie, n.d. (1868), *Corr.* I, p. 314.

49. Quoted in Bossu, *Elisée Reclus*, p. 17.

50. Reclus to Noémi, n.d. (1869), *Corr.* I, pp. 294-95.

51. For example, see Reclus to Elie, n.d. (Oct. 1868), *Corr.* I, pp. 294-95.

52. Quoted in George Woodcock, *Anarchism* (London, 1963), p. 147.

53. Marx to Engels, 4 Nov. 1864, *MEW* 31, p. 16.

54. Elie and Elisée provided Nettlau with information about their meeting with Bakunin in Paris. Nettlau, *Elisée Reclus*, p. 109.

55. *Ibid.*, p. 108ff., and Nettlau, "Elisée Reclus and Michael Bakunin" in Ishill, *Elisée and Elie Reclus*, p. 197ff. Woodcock, *Anarchism*, p. 149, says Elisée "later claimed that as early as the autumn of 1864 he and Bakunin were making plans for an International Brotherhood."

56. Elisée is named as member of the Alliance of Social Democracy in Guillaume, *L'Internationale* I, p. 77. Cf. Jean Maitron (ed.), *Dictionnaire biographique du mouvement ouvrier français* VIII (Paris, 1970), pp. 299-300.

57. See Elisée Reclus, "La Sicile et l'éruption de l'Etna en 1865: Recit de voyage" in *Le Tour du monde* VIII, 1865, pp. 353-416, and *La Revue des deux mondes*, 1 July 1865, pp. 110-38.

58. See the comments of Angelo de Gubernatis, *Fibra, Pagine di Ricordi* (Rome, 1900), p. 238ff.

59. Reclus to Elie, n.d. (Oct. 1868), *Corr.* I, p. 293.

60. Such mystery surrounds the secret societies of Bakunin that there exists much controversy concerning their activities, and even their existence. Cf. Max Nomad, "The Anarchist Tradition" in Drachkovitch, *The Revolutionary Internationals*, pp. 65-66.

61. G.D.H. Cole, *A Study of Socialist Thought*, 5 vols. (London, 1958ff.) II, p. 114. For Marx's comments, see *Documents of the First International* II, pp. 152-53.

62. Bakunin had suggested at the Central Committee meeting of 20 Oct. 1867 in Berne that Elie be asked to become the French editor of the proposed journal. See Reclus to Elie, n.d. (Oct. 1867), *Corr.* I, pp. 262-64, which includes a copy of the letter from Gustave Vogt asking Elie to take up the position. Cf. Reclus to Elie, n.d. (Nov. 1867), *ibid.*, pp. 265-66, and n.d. (1867), *ibid.*, pp. 267-68.

63. Guillaume, *L'Internationale* I, p. 78.

64. Reclus to Elie, n.d. (Oct. 1867), *Corr.* I, p. 264.

65. Elisée was not present at the 1867 Geneva meeting of the League of Peace and Freedom as claimed in Tchernoff, *Le Parti Républicain*, p. 468.

66. Jacques Freymond (ed.), *La Première Internationale: Recueil de documents*, 4 vols. (Geneva, 1962-71) I, p. 388ff.

67. Reclus to Elie, n.d. (Oct. 1868), *Corr.* I, p. 280.

68. *Ibid.*, p. 281.

69. *Ibid.*, p. 282.

70. *Ibid.*, p. 284.

71. *Ibid.*, p. 279.

72. For Reclus's speech, see *Bulletin sténographique du deuxième Congrès de la paix et de la liberté. Stenographisches Bulletin des zweiten Friedens-und Freiheits-Kongresses* (Berne, 1868), pp. 235-38. See also Reclus to Elie, n.d. (Oct. 1868), *Corr.* I, p. 285.
73. For Gambuzzi's speech, see *Deuxième Congrès de la paix et de la liberté*, pp. 197-202.
74. Reclus to Elie, n.d. (Nov. 1867), *Corr.* I, p. 272.
75. Cf. Bakunin's 1866 *Revolutionary Catechism* and his *Organisation* which he prepared for the International Brotherhood: Michael Bakunin, *Gesammelte Werke*, III (Berlin, 1924), pp. 7ff. and 29ff. Cf. also *Deuxième Congrès de la paix et de la liberté*, pp. 214-35, and Guillaume, *L'Internationale* I, p. 78. See Bakunin's statement, which was read out at the 1868 Brussels Congress of the IWMA in *Supplément au journal le peuple belge*, 22 Sept. 1868, and in Freymond, *La Première Internationale* I, p. 391. See also Bakunin's 10 May 1872 letter to Lorenzo in Arthur Lehning (ed.), *Archives Bakounine* II (Leiden, 1965), pp. xxviii-xxx, esp. p.xxix where Bakunin states: "Since 1868... I have carried on at Geneva a crusade against the principle itself of authority and preached the abolition of States..."
76. For the statement and a more complete list of signatories, see Guillaume, *L'Internationale* I, pp. 75-76.
77. Nettlau, *Elisée Reclus*, p. 121ff.
78. Nettlau's opinion that Reclus left almost immediately for Paris is based on a letter written by Reclus in Paris and dated 11 Oct. 1868. However, this letter has been misdated in the published correspondence. See above n. 15.
79. *Documents of the First International* III, pp. 300-1.
80. Freymond, *La Première Internationale* I, p. 454.
81. Marx to Bracke, 20 Nov. 1876, *MEW* 34, p. 225; Engels to Liebknecht, 31 July 1877, *MEW* 34, p. 285. Guillaume, *L'Internationale* II, p. 344, says that the Alliance was founded by Bakunin, Reclus, and "their friends." For the programme and rules of the Alliance (and Marx's comments), see *Documents of the First International* III, p. 273ff. and 379ff. For an official list of "Les Membres du groupe initiateur de Genève" (which does not include Reclus), see *Documents of the First International* III, pp. 276-77 and 382-83. Cf. Jacques Freymond, *Etudes et Documents sur la Première Internationale en Suisse* (Geneva, 1964), appendix; Max Nettlau, *Michael Bakunin, Eine Biographie*, 3 vols. (London, 1898ff.) II, p. 262ff.
82. Marx to Bracke, 20 Nov. 1876, *MEW* 34, p. 225; Engels to Liebknecht, 31 July 1877, *MEW* 34, p. 285; *Documents of the First International* III, p. 463ff.
83. Reclus to Elie, n.d. (Oct. 1868), *Corr.* I, p. 294. Cf.Reclus to Elie, n.d. (Oct. 1868), *Corr.* I, p. 281.
84. Tchernoff, *Le Parti Républicain*, p. 479.
85. Gerald Brenan, *The Spanish Labyrinth* (Cambridge, 1962), p. 138.
86. Reclus to Elie, n.d. (Oct. 1868), *Corr.* I, p. 294.
87. Reclus wrote to Elie that if he went to Spain, Carlo Gambuzzi would be one of his "mandators": *Corr.* I, p. 293.
88. Nettlau, *Elisée Reclus*, p. 130.
89. Letter of 17 Feb. 1869 in *L'Egalité*, 20 Feb. 1869.
90. Letter of 21 Feb. 1869 in *L'Egalité*, 27 Feb. 1869.
91. Letter of 10 Mar. 1869 in *L'Egalité*, 20 Mar. 1869.
92. *Corr.* I, p. 323; Reclus to Noémi, 24 Mar. 1869, *ibid.*, pp. 324-25.
93. Letter of 2 Mar. 1869 in *L'Egalité*, 13 Mar. 1869.
94. *L'Egalité*, 27 Mar. 1869.
95. *Ibid.*
96. Quoted in Nettlau, "Elisée Reclus and Michael Bakunin," p. 201.
97. Reclus to Elie, n.d. (Oct. 1868), *Corr.* I, pp. 292-93, and n.d. (Oct. 1868), *Corr.* I, pp. 294-95.
98. Reclus to Elie, n.d. (autumn 1868), *Corr.* I, pp. 315-16.

99. Reclus to Elie, n.d. (autumn 1867), *Corr.* I, p. 267.
100. *Ibid.*, p. 262.
101. Reclus to Faure, n.d. (1869), *Corr.* III, pp. 62-63.
102. Reclus to De Gérando, 24 June 1883, *Corr.* II, p. 308.
103. Reclus to Faure, n.d. (1869), *Corr.* III, pp. 62-63.
104. Cf. Reclus's letter to the Congress of the Jura Federation of 1878 in *L'Avant-garde*, 12 Aug. 1878; his *Evolution et Révolution* (Geneva, 1880); and his *L'Evolution, la Révolution et l'Idéal anarchique* (Paris, 1898).
105. Reclus to Faure, n.d. (1869), *Corr.* III, p. 64.
106. *Ibid.*
107. See his well-known letter on electoral abstentionism in *Le Révolté*, 11 Oct. 1885.
108. Reclus to Faure, n.d. (June 1869), *Corr.* III, p. 61.
109. Reclus to "Mes biens chers amis" (Elie and Noémi?), n.d. (1869?), Papiers ER, NAF 22910.

Chapter 4

1. Han Ryner, Elisée Reclus (1830-1905) (Paris, 1928), pp. 12-13. Cf., however, the observation in Paul Reclus, "Biographie," p. 65; "...it is not as a patriot, it is as a revolutionary that Elisée took part in the war of 1870." Cf. Max Nettlau, *Elisée Reclus*), p. 138ff.
2. Reclus, *Elie Reclus*, p. 28.
3. Paul Reclus, "A Few Recollections," p. 12. See the couple's wedding address in Papiers ER, NAF 22919.
4. Reclus was in Paris on 23 Aug. 1870. See the document "Mon testament" in Papiers ER, NAF 22919. However, on 29 Aug. he was at Sainte-Foy-la-Grande where he made arrangements for the care of Fanny and his two daughters in the event of his death. For the document, see *ibid.* According to a police report, Reclus (and his brothers Elie and Paul) took part in the "invasion of the legislature... he broke windows and furniture." The report contains inaccuracies and is not reliable in this kind of detail. Police report of 27 Aug. 1874, P.Po. B a/1237.
5. Cf. the reports of 16 Jan. 1872, AN BB24 732; P.Po. B a/1237.
6. Reclus to Fanny, 25 Oct. 1870, *Corr.* II, p. 8.
7. Reclus to Fanny, 6 Nov. 1870, *Corr.* II, p. 13.
8. The police report of 9 Jan. 1874, P.Po. B a/1237, states that Reclus "did duty on the ramparts." See references in *Corr.* II, and in Fonds ER, 14 AS 232, IFHS.
9. Balloons left Paris, but did not return. Reclus was still in Paris in Feb. 1871 when he left the city with a *laissez-passer*. Reclus to his sister Louise, 8 Feb. 1871, *Corr.* II, p. 14.
10. See Tchernoff, *Le Parti Républicain*, p. 455-56. See also Henri Lefort's announcement in *L'Association*, Apr. 1865.
11. Jacques Rougerie, "L'A.I.T. et le Mouvement ouvrier à Paris pendant les événements de 1870-1871," *International Review of Social History*, 1972, p. 35.
12. According to *ibid.*, pp. 84-85n, Reclus was a member of the Batignolles section.
13. *Ibid.*, p. 29ff.
14. For a copy of the IWMA address, "Au peuple allemand, à la démocratie socialiste de la nation allemande," see *Les Murailles politiques françaises* (Paris, 1873), p. 6. Cf. Reclus to Faure, n.d. (Sept. 1870), *Corr.* II, p. 4-5.
15. Reclus to Faure, n.d. (Sept. 1870), *Corr.* II, p. 4.
16. *Ibid.*, pp. 4-5. On 15 Oct. Reclus's confidence in a military victory was raised by his view (and that of many others, including the Germans) that bombardment was becoming less likely. Reclus to Fanny, 15 Oct. 1870, *Corr.* II, p. 7.
17. He was thinking of journals such as *Le Réveil* and *La Marseillaise*. Reclus to Faure, n.d. (1870), *Corr.* II, p. 10.

18. *Ibid.*, pp. 10-11.
19. *Ibid.*, p. 11.
20. Cf. the similarity of views in the "Second Address of the General Council of the International on the Franco-Prussian War," written by Marx and endorsed on 9 Sept. 1870. Karl Marx and Friedrich Engels, *Selected Works* (London, 1970), p. 269.
21. On 27 July 1869, during a visit to London, Reclus was presented with a personally signed copy of the "Achtzehnten Brumaire" by Marx. *Chronik*, p. 448.
22. Karl Marx, "The Eighteenth Brumaire of Louis Napoleon" in *Selected Works*, p. 154.
23. See Serraillier's report to the General Council meeting of 28 Feb. 1871 in *Documents of the First International* IV, p. 140.
24. Reclus to Fanny, 6 Nov. 1870, *Corr.* II, pp. 12-13.
25. Cf. Reclus's comments on Elie's residence in "beautiful" Zurich. One of the advantages of living in Zurich was the "contact of two races." Reclus to Alfred and Louise Dumesnil, 7 Sept. 1871, *Corr.* II, p. 65.
26. Reclus described *La République des travailleurs* as "a new organ of militant socialist democracy... founded by the Batignolles section of the 'International'." *Le Combat*, 11 Jan. 1871; clipping in P.Po. B a/1237.
27. See Reclus's contributions to *La République des travailleurs*, 10 and 13-22 Jan. 1871.
28. *La République des travailleurs*, 3 Feb. 1871.
29. *Le Vengeur*, 3 Feb. 1871; *La République des travailleurs*, 4 Feb. 1871.
30. L. Dautry and L. Scheler, *Le Comité central républicain des vingt arrondissements de Paris* (Paris, 1960), p. 160ff.; *Documents of the First International* IV, pp. 141-42; Rougerie, "A.I.T.," p. 41.
31. *Le Mot d'ordre*, 6 Feb. 1871. Before 4 Feb. there were already sharp differences of opinion, of which Reclus must have been aware, concerning the appropriate IWMA attitudes towards the election. See *Documents of the First International* IV, pp. 141-42.
32. Reclus to Louise, 9 Feb. 1871, *Corr.* II, p. 14.
33. For a copy of the electoral poster, see *Murailles politiques*, p. 873.
34. Nettlau, *Elisée Reclus*, p. 145.
35. Elie Reclus to Charton, 18 Apr. 1871, Papiers Nadar, NAF 25016.
36. Reclus to Louise, 9 Feb. 1871, *Corr.* II, p. 14.
37. *Ibid.*, p. 15.
38. Reclus to Elie, n.d. (Feb. 1871), *Corr.* II, p. 18.
39. *Ibid.*, pp. 18-19.
40. Reclus to Nadar, Feb. 1871, *Corr.* II, p. 16.
41. The earliest surviving letter written by Reclus after his return to Paris, but before the Commune, is undated; Reclus to Noémi, *Corr.* II, p. 20.
42. Paul Ghio, *Etudes italiennes et sociales* (Paris, 1929), p. 200, attributes to Reclus a statement of 26 Feb. (Ghio mistakenly wrote 25 Feb.) in *Le Cri du peuple*. The statement expressed wonder at the "human sea" of demonstrators who would willingly die for their beliefs.
43. Rougerie, "A.I.T.," pp. 52-53.
44. Firmin Maillard, *Affiches, professions de foi, documents officiels, clubs et comités pendant la Commune* (Paris, 1871), pp. 101-2; reprinted in *Le Cri du peuple*, 26 Mar. 1871. Cf. Elie's diary, published as *Commune de Paris*.
45. For a copy of the statement, see Maillard, pp. 99-100, and Louise Michel, *La Commune* (Paris, 1898), p. 181.
46. For a copy of the electoral poster, see Maillard, pp. 186-88. Cf. police report of 27 Aug. 1874, P.Po. B a/1237.
47. Reclus to Dumesnil, 27 Mar. 1871, *Corr.* II, p. 23.
48. *Ibid.*

49. According to *Le Cri du peuple*, 7 Apr. 1871, there were 500 men present at Châtillon.

50. For a description of the events of 4 Apr. see Reclus's *Evolution et Révolution* (1891), pp. 58-59; his letter concerning the death of Emile Victor Duval in P. Cattelain, *Memoires inédits du chef de la Sûreté sous la Commune* (Paris n.d., 1900), pp. 108-9, and *Corr.* II, pp. 27-28; his account as related to Kropotkin in *Les Temps nouveaux*, 15 July 1905.

51. Elie to Charton, 18 Apr. 1871, Papiers Nadar, NAF 25016.

52. Mary Putnam was a close friend of the Reclus and stayed with them for a while; for the impressions recorded in her letters, see Ruth Putnam (ed.), *Life and Letters of Mary Putnam Jacobi* (New York, 1925). See also Paul Reclus, "A Few Recollections," pp. 18-20; according to this account, Washburne had taken a particular interest in Reclus's articles on behalf of the North in the American Civil War. Cf. Charles Delfosse, *Elisée Reclus: Géographe* in the series *Hommes du jour* (Brussels, n.d.).

53. Dossier ER, AHG, 7e Conseil de Guerre Permanent, dossier no. 46. For the impressions of Nadar, who spoke in Reclus's defence at the trial, see his "Elisée Reclus" in Ishill, *Elisée and Elie Reclus*, pp. 109-10; *Les Temps nouveaux, Supplément* No. 33, Dec. 1950. For the text of Elie's letter of 17 Nov. 1871 to Elisée, see Guillaume de Greef, *Eloges d'Elisée Reclus et de De Kellès-Krauz, Discours* (Ghent, 1906), pp. 54-55.

54. See the letter from F.D. Leblanc and a French translation of the petition, including the signatories, in *Le Courrier de l'Europe, Supplément*, 20 Jan. 1872, and a supplementary list of signatories in *ibid.*, 23 Mar. 1872; as newspaper clippings in Papiers ER, NAF 22909. See also the letter from Eugene Oswald to the President of the French Republic on behalf of Reclus, London, 27 Dec. 1871, in Papiers ER, NAF 22909. Reclus expressed gratitude to Oswald on 21 Mar. 1872; *Corr.* II, pp. 92-93.

55. See Dossier ER, AHG; official report from the Ministry of War to the Ministry of Justice, 8 Feb. 1872, AN BB24 732; Paris police report of 27 Oct. 1903, "Bulletin de vérification aux Sommiers judiciaries," P.Po. B a/1237. The commutation of penalty was granted on 3 Feb. and not on 15 Feb. as sometimes reported.

56. Reclus to Heath, 8 Jan. 1872, *Corr.* II, pp. 86-87.

57. Reclus to Fanny, July 1871, *Corr.* II, p. 53.

58. Reclus to Fanny, 20 Oct. 1871, quoted in Fanny to "soeur aimée" (Louise?), 25 Oct. 1871, Papiers ER, NAF 22913. Reclus's letter was written in English; for a French translation, see *Corr.* II, pp. 68-69.

59. *Corr.* II, p. 40ff.

60. Reclus to Dumesnil, 20 Aug. 1871, *Corr.* II, p. 61.

61. *La Liberté*, Apr. 1871; for a copy of the letter, see Michel, *La Commune*, pp. 467-70.

62. Reclus to Fanny, 8 June 1871, *Corr.* II, pp. 40-1; cf. letter to Alfred and Louise Dumesnil, 15 June 1871, p. 44. See Reclus to his sister Loïs, 17 May 1871, and to his mother, 20 May 1871, both in Fonds ER, 14 AS 232, IFHS.

63. Reclus was optimistic about the possibility of release. In August he learned that more than 900 of the 12,000-13,000 prisoners at Brest had been freed and that the only charge against him was that of having marched against the regular army. Reclus to Fanny, 3 Aug. 1871, *Corr.* II, pp. 55-56.

64. AN BB24 732.

65. Cf. Reclus to Kahn, n.d. (1878), Archief ER, IISG; Reclus to Buurmans, 20 Oct. 1871, *Corr.* II, p. 71.

66. Reclus to Fanny, 3 Aug. 1871, Papiers ER, NAF 22913; letter in English, French translation in *Corr.* II, pp. 55-56.

67. *Ibid.*

209

68. See police report of 27 Aug. 1874, P.Po. B a/1237, which holds up in substance in spite of exaggerations. Cf. Reclus to Fanny, 3 Aug. 1871; Nettlau, *Elisée Reclus*, p. 165.
69. Reclus to Clara Mesnil, 23 July 1904, *Corr.* III, pp. 277-78.

Chapter 5

1. Marx called Elisée and Elie the "souls" of *Le Travailleur*; Marx to Engels, 1 Aug. 1877, *MEW* 34, p. 65.
2. David Stafford, *From Anarchism to Reformism: A Study of the Political Activities of Paul Brousse 1870-1890* (London, 1971), p. 302.
3. The proposed article was intended for *La Commune: Almanach socialiste pour 1877*.
4. Reclus to Joukowsky, n.d. (1877), Fonds ER, 14 AS 232, IFHS.
5. Reclus to Kahn, n.d. (1878), Archief ER, IISG.
6. Reclus to Galleani, 15 May 1905, in *Corr.* III, pp. 318-19.
7. Reclus to Joukowsky, n.d. (1877), Fonds ER, 14 AS 232, IFHS.
8. Reclus to Noémi, 8 June 1872, *Corr.* II, p. 109.
9. Reclus to De Gérando, Oct. 1873, Fonds ER, 14 AS 232, IFHS.
10. Reclus to De Gérando, 4 July 1874, *Corr.* II, p. 156.
11. Reclus to Elie, 29 Apr. 1872, *Corr.* II, pp. 101-2.
12. See Reclus to Elie, n.d. (Oct. 1868), *Corr.* I, p. 279ff.; *Deuxième Congrès de la paix et de la liberté*, p. 235ff.
13. Reclus to Elie, 23 Sept. 1872, *Corr.* II, p. 113ff.
14. In 1897 Reclus admitted that under unusual circumstances an anarchist might be able to justify or even to approve use of the vote. Reclus to B.P. Van der Voo, Apr. 1897, *Corr.* III, p. 201.
15. Notes written by Reclus on 14 Mar. 1872, Papiers ER, NAF 22913.
16. See Reclus to Louise, n.d. (Dec. 1875), *Corr.* II, pp. 175-76; Reclus to Nadar, 15 Sept. 1880, *Corr.* II, pp. 225-26; Séance du 3 aôut 1874, Procès-verbaux des séances du Comité fédéral jurassien, AEN; Jura Federation circular of 13 Aug. 1874, AFJ, IISG; police report of 2 Feb. 1879, P.Po. B a/1237; Guillaume, *L'Internationale* III, p. 289.
17. Reclus to his sister Julie, 12 May 1876, Papiers ER, NAF 22909.
18. A copy can be found in Archief ER, IISG. The letter is reproduced in *Corr.* II, p. 209.
19. Police report of 20 Dec. 1885, P.Po. B a/1502.
20. *1871: Enquête sur la Commune de Paris* (Paris, 1897).
21. Elisée Reclus, *L'Homme et la Terre*, 6 vols. (Paris, 1905-8) V, p. 246ff. A few chapters appeared before Reclus's death.
22. *Ibid.*, pp. 246-47.
23. *Ibid.*, p. 247.
24. *Ibid.*, pp. 247-48.
25. Elisée Reclus, "Quelques mots sur la propriété" in *Almanach du peuple pour 1873* (St-Imier, 1873), p. 326.
26. *Le Révolté*, 17 Oct. 1880.
27. Reclus, *L'Homme et la Terre* V, p. 247.
28. *Ibid.*
29. *La République des travailleurs*, 29 Jan.-5 Feb. 1871.
30. There is little doubt that the "friend" is Reclus, who was a close friend at the time of writing. Peter Kropotkin, "Revolutionary Government" in Roger N. Baldwin (ed.), *Kropotkin's Revolutionary Pamphlets* (New York, 1970), pp. 239-40. For the original essay, see "Le Gouvernement pendant la Révolution" in *Le Révolté*, 2 Sept.-14 Oct. 1882, republished in *Paroles d'un révolté* (Paris 1885), pp. 245-65. Cf. the statement of 21 Mar. in *Le Cri du peuple* which Ghio attributes to Reclus.

31. Kropotkin, "Revolutionary Government," p. 240. A passage of a letter written by Reclus the same year records similar impressions; Reclus to Heath, 18 Feb. 1882, *Corr.* II, pp. 242-43.
32. Reclus to Clara Mesnil, 23 July 1904, *Corr.* III, p. 277.
33. Reclus to Fanny, 28 Aug. 1871, Papiers ER, NAF 22913.
34. Reclus to Nadar, 8 May 1872, Autographes Félix et Paul Nadar, NAF 24282.
35. *Ibid.*
36. Reclus to Kahn, n.d. (1878), Archief ER, IISG.
37. *Enquête*, p. 53.

Chapter 6

1. See esp. Stafford, *From Anarchism to Reformism*, p. 12ff.
2. Reclus initially hoped to find "a calm and orderly life of work" (Reclus to his mother, 15 Mar. 1872, in *Corr.* II, p. 90) and was determined to "create a new existence, to enter into a new life" (Reclus to Eugene Oswald, 21 Mar. 1872, *Corr.* II, p. 93). See also Reclus to Buurmans, 19 May 1872, *Corr.* II, pp. 107-8.
3. Report of 9 Jan. 1874, P.Po. B a/1237.
4. Nettlau, *Michael Bakunin* III, p. 739; *Elisée Reclus*, pp. 172-73; "Elisée Reclus and Michael Bakunin," p. 202. Reclus and Bakunin visited each other several times in 1872-73 and were on good terms. See also Guillaume, *L'Internationale* II, p. 279; Elisée to Elie, 29 Apr. 1872, *Corr.* II, p. 102.
5. Reclus to Buurmans, 2 June 1873, *Corr.* II, pp. 129-30.
6. Reclus to Buurmans, 17 Feb. 1878, *Corr.* II, p. 199. Cf. Paul Reclus, "A Few Recollections," p. 12.
7. See correspondence in *Corr.* II, Fonds ER, 14 AS 232, IFHS, Papiers ER, NAF 22913. See document dated 10 Oct. 1875, which appears to be the address given by Reclus at his marriage to Ermance; Papiers ER, NAF 22911.
8. Reclus to Heath, 30 Jan. 1880, *Corr.* II, p. 223.
9. AFJ, IISG. Cf. Guillaume, *L'Internationale* III, p. 196.
10. Reclus to Bakunin, 17 Apr. 1875, *Corr.* II, p. 170. The Vevey section had originally been attached to the Fédération Romande, but was reconstituted under the name of La Rénovation des bords du Leman and affiliated to the Jura Federation in Aug. 1874. See Séance du 13 août 1874, PV du CFJ, AEN; circular dated 28 Sept. 1874, of the propaganda section of the federal committee announcing the formation of the new section at Vevey in AFJ, IISG. The name was changed to the Section de Vevey; see report of May 1878 from the section to the Federal Committee of the Jura sections in AFJ, IISG.
11. See report in AFJ, IISG. The report was in response to a circular of 14 Apr. 1878 requesting information about membership and policies.
12. Reports of 9 Jan. 1874 and 8 Feb. 1874 in P.Po. B a/1237.
13. AN BB24 732.
14. P.Po. B a/1237.
15. Report of 2 Feb.1879, P.Po. B a/1237.
16. *Documents of the First International* V, p. 407.
17. For the proceedings of the St-Imier Congress of 15-16 Sept. 1872, see Freymond, *Première Internationale* III, p. 3ff. Cf. *Mémoire de la Fédération jurassienne* (Sonvilier, 1873).
18. See *Supplément au journal le peuple belge*, 22 Sept. 1868, and Freymond, *La Première Internationale* I, p. 391.
19. Elisée Reclus, "L'Evolution légale et l'Anarchie" in *Le Travailleur*, Jan.-Feb. 1878.
20. See esp. Karl Marx, *Economic and Philosophic Manuscripts of 1844*, ed. Dirk J. Struik (London, 1970), and Michael Bakunin, *God and the State* (Dover, 1970).

21. For the proceedings of the Brussels Congress of 7-13 Sept. 1874, see Freymond, *La Première Internationale* IV, p. 251.
22. Guillaume, *L'Internationale* IV, p. 202.
23. Joseph Favre and Benoît Malon adopted the terms in a "lettre addressée au meeting de l'Internationale, réuni à Lausanne, le 18 Mars 1876." See Guillaume's comments in BFJ, 30 Apr., 7 May 1876. The Lausanne section wrote a letter protesting Guillaume's criticism of Malon and Favre which the *Bulletin* did not wish to publish. There arose the question of the right of the editorial committee to suppress members' views. An enquiry among the sections found that eight were against publication of the letter, two were in favour, and four did not reply. Vevey was of the opinion that the *Bulletin* did not have the right to suppress the publication of any articles, letters, or remarks. *BFJ*, 25 May and 29 June 1876; Nettlau, *Elisée Reclus*, p. 189.
24. See above, Chapter 1.
25. Cf. Nettlau, *Elisée Reclus*, p. 189; *Histoire de l'Anarchie* (Paris, 1971), p. 140; Paul Reclus, "Biographie," p. 57; Ryner, *Elisée Reclus*, p. 16; Bossu, *Elisée Reclus*, p. 42; note in *Corr.* II, p. 171.
26. *BFJ*, 11 Mar. 1877.
27. *Le Travailleur*, Jan.-Feb. 1878.
28. *Le Travailleur*, Jan.-Feb. and Feb.-Mar. 1878.
29. *BFJ*, 11 Mar. 1877.
30. The programme of *Le Travailleur* appeared as a leaflet at the end of April and was reprinted in the first issue in May 1877.
31. *BFJ*, 11 Mar. 1877.
32. *Le Travailleur*, May 1877.
33. *BFJ*, 11 Mar. 1877.
34. *Le Travailleur*, Jan.-Feb. 1878.
35. *Ibid.*
36. *Ibid.*
37. *BFJ*, 8 Aug. 1875.
38. *Le Travailleur*, Jan.-Feb. 1878.
39. See below, Chapter 10.
40. Reclus to De Gérando, 25 May 1877, *Corr.* II, p. 188.
41. *Le Révolté*, 21 Jan. 1882.
42. *Le Travailleur*, May 1877.
43. Kropotkin to Robin, 16 Feb. 1877, NA, IISG.
44. Brousse to Kropotkin, 6 Apr. 1877, Guillaume, *L'Internationale* IV, p. 180.
45. Kropotkin to Robin, 29 Apr. 1877, NA, IISG.
46. Kropotkin to Emile Darnaud, 6 June 1891, as mentioned in Darnaud to Gross, 20 Jan. 1891, Fonds Jacques Gross, IISG.
47. See Stafford, *From Anarchism to Reformism.*
48. Kropotkin to Robin, 29 Apr. 1877, NA, IISG.
49. Bakunin to Reclus, 15 Feb. 1875, in Nettlau, "Elisée Reclus and Michael Bakunin," p. 203ff.; Reclus to Bakunin, 17 Apr. 1875, *Corr.* II, p. 170.
50. Champseix to Reclus, 2 Apr. 1877, Papiers ER, NAF 22914.
51. Reclus to Kahn, n.d. (1877?), Archief ER, IISG.
52. De Paepe to Malon, 6 Nov. 1877, *La Revue socialiste*, July 1913.
53. Malon to De Paepe, 3 Dec. 1877, *La Revue socialiste*, Nov. 1908.
54. *Le Travailleur*, Jan.-Feb. 1878.
55. *Le Travailleur*, May 1877. *Le Travailleur*, which appeared monthly from May 1877 to April 1878, had an editorial committee of four—Reclus, Oelsnitz, Perron, and Joukowsky. As of Nov. 1877, on Reclus's initiative, the names of the members of the editorial committee were replaced by a list of collaborators, which included Arthur Arnould, Klementz, Metchnikoff, Ralli, and Elie Reclus, as well as those formerly listed as editors. Although Rodolphe Kahn's name did not appear on the list, he played an important part in managing

the affairs of the journal. (See correspondence Reclus to Kahn in Archief ER, IISG.)

56. *L'Avant-garde*, 2 June 1877.
57. For the proceedings of the Verviers Congress, see Freymond, *La Première Internationale* IV, p. 515ff.
58. For the proceedings of the International Socialist Congress at Ghent, see *ibid.*, p. 555ff.
59. Séance du 12 juin 1878, PV du CFJ, AEN; *L'Avant-garde*, 29 July 1878.
60. *L'Avant-garde*, 12 Aug. 1878.
61. Reclus to Elie, 10 June (1878), Papiers ER, NAF 22911.
62. For an account of Brousse's arrest and trial, see Stafford, *From Anarchism to Reformism*, p. 126ff.
63. "Reclus is taking an active part in the Brousse affair," wrote Kropotkin to Robin, 18 Jan. 1879, NA, IISG.
64. See the reference to the trips in Reclus's account book, Fonds ER, 14 AS 232, IFHS.
65. Reclus to Fauquiez, 4 May 1879, Fonds ER, 14 AS 232, IFHS; reprinted in *Grütlin* (Lausanne) 13 Sept. 1912. The letter was written from Stromstadt in Sweden.
66. Stafford, *From Anarchism to Reformism*, p. 144.
67. Kropotkin to Robin, 18 Jan. 1879, NA, IISG.
68. Peter Kropotkin, *Memoirs of a Revolutionist* (New York, 1971; new edition, Montréal, 1988), p. 418.
69. According to *ibid.*, 600 had been the most copies sold of any edition of any paper. The first number of *Le Révolté* printed 2,000 copies, which were all sold in a few days. Elsewhere Kropotkin said that 3,000 were printed and 2,000 sold; Kropotkin to Darnaud, 6 June 1891, as mentioned in Darnaud to Gross, 20 Jan. 1891, Fonds Jacques Gross, IISG.
70. See Reclus's account book in Fonds ER, 14 AS 232, IFHS. From May 1879 Reclus began to contribute to *Le Révolté* on a more or less regular basis. It is likely that he was asked to help set up *Le Révolté*, and that he refused. In early 1879 he did not show much enthusiasm for any newspaper project. In January he told Kropotkin that he would consider bringing out *Le Travailleur* again if he could raise 1,000 or 2,000 francs in advance. There was also some question of who would edit such a newspaper. Reclus was of the opinion that Lefrançais was the only man for the job, but found him to be "an obstinate fellow." (Kropotkin to Robin, 18 Jan. 1879, NA, IISG.) Under these circumstances he was not likely to find Kropotkin's proposal to launch a paper on 23 francs a very exciting prospect.
71. Elisée Reclus, *La Peine de mort: Conférence faite à une réunion convoquée par l'association ouvrière à Lausanne* (Geneva, 1879). After the printer had approached Kropotkin (in about April) to say that he could not print any more issues of *Le Révolté* for fear of losing government contracts, it was decided to take up Dumartheray's suggestion that they start their own printing press. See Kropotkin, *Memoirs*, pp. 420-21.
72. For the proceedings of the meeting, see *Le Révolté*, 17 Oct. 1880.
73. Nettlau, *Elisée Reclus*, p. 189.
74. George Woodcock and Ivan Avakumović, *The Anarchist Prince: Peter Kropotkin* (New York, 1971), p. 317; Clara E. Lida, *Anarquismo y Revolución en la España del XIX* (Madrid, 1972), p. 243.
75. *BFJ*, 3 Dec. 1876.
76. *Le Révolté*, 18 Oct. 1879.
77. *Le Révolté*, 17 Oct. 1880.
78. *Procès des anarchistes devant la police correctionnelle et la Cour d'Appel de Lyon* (Lyons, 1883), p. 10.

Chapter 7

1. Reclus to Dumesnil, 23 July 1871, *Corr.* II, p. 51.
2. Elisée Reclus, "Du Sentiment de la nature dans les sociétés modernes" in *La Revue des deux mondes*, 15 May 1866, p. 379.
3. Elisée Reclus, "De l'action humaine sur la géographie physique" in *La Revue des deux mondes*, 1 Dec. 1864, p. 763.
4. Gary S Dunbar, *Elisée Reclus: Historian of Nature* (Hamden, Conn., 1978), p. 112. This is a superb portrait of Reclus the geographer, and I am indebted to its insights in my analysis of the relationship between Reclus's anarchism and his geography.
5. *Nouvelle Géographie universelle* I (Paris, 1876), Avertissement.
6. Dunbar, *Elisée Reclus*, p. 112, makes this point nicely.
7. Carl Ritter, "De la configuration des continents sur la surface du globe," translated and with an introduction by Elisée Reclus, *La Revue germanique*, Nov. 1859, p. 242.
8. Reclus to De Gérando, 1 Aug. 1877, Fonds ER, 14 AS 232, IFHS. Further evidence of this line of thought can be found in 1876. On 2 Sept. 1876 Reclus participated alongside Schwitzguébel and Brousse at a meeting in Berne organised to protest attempts to arrange a German celebration of the anniversary of the French capitulation at Sedan. Reclus's address concentrated on the "free formation" of nationalities. See *BFJ*, 10 Sept. 1876; Guillaume, *L'Internationale* IV, p. 79.
9. Reclus to Fanny, 28 Aug. 1871, Papiers ER, NAF 22913.
10. *BFJ*, 15 Oct. 1876.
11. *BFJ*, 4 Feb. and 11 Mar. 1877.
12. *Le Travailleur*, Feb.-Mar. 1878.
13. Reclus to De Gérando, 25 May 1877, *Corr.* II, pp. 187-88.
14. *Le Travailleur*, Feb.-Mar. 1878.
15. *Ibid.*
16. Reclus to De Gérando, 25 May 1877, *Corr.* II, p. 188.
17. Reclus to Buurmans, 17 Feb. 1878, *Corr.* II, p. 196ff.
18. Reclus to Bakunin, 17 Apr. 1875, *Corr.* II, p. 170. See Bakunin to Reclus, 15 Feb. 1875, in Nettlau, "Elisée Reclus and Michael Bakunin," p. 203ff.
19. Elisée Reclus, preface to Léon Metchnikoff, *La Civilisation et les Grands Fleuves historiques* (Paris, 1889), p. xxvii.
20. See esp. Reclus, *L'Idéal anarchique*, p. 44ff.
21. Reclus to unnamed person, 18 July 1892, *Corr.* III, p. 122.
22. Reclus, *Evolution et Révolution* (1884), p. 24ff.
23. *Ibid.*, pp. 25-26.
24. Reclus to Heath, n.d. (1884), *Corr.* II, p. 324.
25. Reclus, *Evolution et Révolution* (1884), p. 26.
26. See esp. Reclus's remarks in his "Pages de sociologie préhistorique" in *L'Humanité nouvelle*, Feb. 1898. Cf. his *L'Homme et la Terre* V, p. 134ff.
27. See, for example, Reclus to Faure, n.d. (1869), *Corr.* III, pp. 62-63; his letter of 1878 to the Congress of the Jura Federation in *L'Avant-garde*, 12 Aug. 1878; his *Evolution et Révolution* (Geneva, 1880).
28. Reclus, *Evolution et Révolution* (1884), pp. 26-27.
29. Reclus, *Evolution et Révolution* (1880), p. 10.
30. Elisée Reclus, "L'Avenir de nos enfants" in *La Commune: Almanach socialiste pour 1877* (Geneva, 1877).
31. Reclus's preface to Peter Kropotkin, *La Conquête du pain* (Paris, 1892); English from *The Conquest of Bread* (London, 1972).
32. Reclus to Heath, 14 Aug. 1903, *Corr.* III, p. 263.
33. Reclus to Darnaud, 21 Jan. 1891, mentioned in Darnaud to Gross, 6 Feb. 1891, Fonds Jacques Gross, IISG.
34. Reclus to Georges Renard, 2 June 1888, *Corr.* II, pp. 441-42.

35. *Ibid.*, p. 442.
36. See Pierre Ramus's recollections on Johann Most's enthusiastic reception of Reclus in the late 1880s; Ramus, "Recollections of Elisée Reclus" in Ishill, *Elisée and Elie Reclus*, pp. 124-25.
37. Reclus to Renard, 27 Dec. 1895, *Corr.* III, p. 192.
38. See Elisée Reclus, "La Grève d'Amérique" in *Le Travailleur*, Sept. 1877; reprinted in *BFJ*, 20 and 28 Oct. and 4 Nov. 1877.
39. Reclus to Buurmans, 25 Apr. 1878, *Corr.* II, pp. 202-3.
40. Reclus to Fauquiez, 4 May 1879, Fonds ER, 14 AS 232, IFHS.
41. Reclus to Buurmans, 25 Apr. 1878, *Corr.* II, p. 203.
42. Cf. Marie Fleming, "Life, Liberty and the Pursuit of a Natural Order: The Anarchism of Elisée Reclus" in *Social Anarchism*, Vol. 2, No. 1, 1981, pp. 19-35.
43. See, for example, *Le Travailleur*, Jan.-Feb. 1878; Reclus to Auguste Rouveyrolles, 9 July 1890, *Corr.* III, p. 82.
44. Reclus to unnamed person, 18 July 1892, *Corr.* III, p. 122.
45. *Le Travailleur*, Feb.-Mar. 1878.
46. Reclus to Bakunin, 17 Apr. 1875, *Corr.* II, p. 170.
47. *Le Travailleur*, Feb.-Mar. 1878.
48. *Ibid.*
49. Reclus to unnamed person, 18 July 1892, *Corr.* III, p. 122.
50. Reclus to Gross, 12 Jan. 1887, Papiers Gross, Dépôt du CIRA, 1964, BPU, Geneva. The greater part of this letter has been reproduced, but without date, in *Corr.* II, pp. 410-11.
51. Report of 8 Dec. 1887, P.Po. B a/75. Reclus was closely identified with the anti-militarist point of view, and at a meeting in 1892 the anarchist Denéchère is supposed to have said that Reclus would give 100 francs to any conscript desiring to escape across the border to avoid the exigencies of the military law. See police report of 13 Nov. 1892, P.Po. B a/77.
52. Reclus to Gross, 12 Jan. 1887, Papiers Gross, Dépôt du CIRA.
53. George Bernard Shaw said of Kropotkin: "His only weakness was a habit of prophesying war within the next fortnight. And it came true in the end." Quoted in Woodcock and Avakumović, *The Anarchist Prince*, p. 225.
54. *Le Révolté*, 1-7 and 8-14 Jan. 1887; Woodcock and Avakumović, *The Anarchist Prince*, p. 225.
55. Reclus to Gross, 12 Jan. 1887, Papiers Gross, Dépôt du CIRA.
56. Reclus, *L'Idéal anarchique*.
57. Reclus to the Congress of the Jura Federation, *L'Avant-garde*, 12 Aug. 1878.
58. Reclus to Bakunin, 8 Feb. 1875, *Corr.* II, p. 169.
59. Bakunin to Reclus, 15 Feb. 1875, in Nettlau, "Elisée Reclus and Michael Bakunin," p. 203ff.
60. See reference in Reclus to Bakunin, 8 Feb. 1875, *Corr.* II, p. 169.
61. *BFJ*, 9 July 1876. Graveside speeches were also delivered by Schwitzguébel, Joukowsky, Guillaume, Carlo Salvioni, Brousse, and a German workman called Betsien. After the Geneva Congress of 1873 Bakunin had decided to retire from the Jura Federation and to devote his attention to his memoirs. Reclus had encouraged him to write and had replied favourably to Bakunin's request to help polish up his literary style; see Reclus to Bakunin, 8 Feb. 1875, *Corr.* II, p. 168.
62. Reclus to the Congress of the Jura Federation, *L'Avant-garde*, 12 Aug. 1878; cf. *Le Travailleur*, Jan.-Feb. 1878.
63. Reclus to the Congress of the Jura Federation, *L'Avant garde*, 12 Aug. 1878.
64. *Encyclopaedia Britannica*, 1905.

Chapter 8

1. *Le Travailleur*, Jan.-Feb.1878.
2. Reclus, *Evolution et Révolution* (1880), p. 25.
3. *Le Révolté*, 10 June 1882.
4. *BFJ*, 10 Dec. 1876.
5. See below, Chapter 12.
6. Kropotkin to Robin, 11 Feb. 1877, NA, IISG.
7. Kropotkin to Robin, 27 Feb. 1877, NA, IISG.
8. *BFJ*, 4 Mar. 1877; the letter is addressed, according to the *BFJ*, to the "Fédération ouvrière du district de Courtelary." See *BFJ*, 11 Mar. 1877, where this error is acknowledged.
9. Guillaume expressed his thanks in the *Bulletin* on 11 Mar. 1877. Cf. Guillaume, *L'Internationale* IV, pp. 148-49.
10. Kropotkin to Robin, 29 Mar. 1877, NA, IISG.
11. *Ibid.*
12. For example, Reclus's experience with *Le Travailleur* seems to have been at least partly responsible for his initial lack of enthusiasm for *Le Révolté*. He thought that Lefrançais was a good person to edit a paper, but found him to be an "obstinate fellow." Kropotkin to Robin, 18 Jan. 1879, NA, IISG.
13. Elisée Reclus, "L'Avenir de nos enfants."
14. Reclus to Bakunin, 17 Apr. 1875, *Corr.* II, p. 170.
15. For Reclus's attitudes during this period, see *Corr.* II, pp. 202-23.
16. *Le Révolté*, 10 June 1882.
17. *Ibid.*, 24 June 1882.
18. *Ibid.*, 8 July 1882.
19. *Ibid.*, 24 June 1882.
20. *Ibid.*
21. Throughout the 1870s Reclus did not attend any congresses of the International. At the 1875 Vevey Congress, the Vevey section was represented by two minor members, while Reclus stayed "among the people" and participated in the "popular assembly" arranged to coincide with the Congress. He was proposed as a delegate to the 1876 Berne Congress, but replied that "pressing business" prevented him from undertaking the task and requested that his name be withdrawn (*BFJ*, 15 Oct. 1876). Although he had withdrawn his name, two sections voted for him; Séance du 19 octobre 1876, *PV du CFJ*, AEN.
22. *Le Révolté*, 10 June 1882.
23. Among the French there were twelve delegates from Lyons, three from Saint-Etienne, three from Vienne, one from Villefranche, one from Bordeaux, one from Cette, and two from Paris. Herzig to Kropotkin, 21 Aug. 1882, cited in *Procès des anarchistes*, p. 129.
24. *Le Révolté*, 19 Aug. 1882. The last international congress of the anarchists for many years enthusiastically applauded the delegate from Cette who made the intriguing statement: "We are united because we are divided."
25. The statement was made by Jules Trenta on 9 Jan. 1883. *Le Temps*, 10 Jan. 1883; newspaper clippings in P.Po. B a/394.
26. Tscherkesoff claimed that Reclus had composed the draft and that others (among them Dumartheray) had edited it. Nettlau, *Elisée Reclus*, p. 221.
27. Quoted in James Joll, *The Anarchists* (London, 1964), p. 121.
28. "La propagande par le fait" in *BFJ*, 5 Aug. 1877.
29. *Le Révolté*, 1 Nov. 1879.
30. Reclus to Mlle. De Gérando, 7 Dec. 1878, *Corr.* II, pp. 210-11.
31. Reclus to Elie, 20 July 1878, *Corr.* II, p. 214.
32. Kropotkin met Vera Zasúlitch in Geneva in the autumn of 1878. Woodcock and Avakumović, *The Anarchist Prince*, p. 167.
33. Reclus to the Congress of the Jura Federation, *L'Avant-garde*, 12 Aug. 1878.

34. At the London Congress there were 31 delegates representing 56 federations and 46 sections or groups without ties to federations. According to *La Révolution sociale*, 24 July 1881, delegates came from Germany, America, England, Belgium, Egypt, Spain, France, Holland, Italy, Russia, Serbia, Switzerland, and Turkey. For the proceedings of the Congress, see *Le Révolté*, 23 July 1881.
35. AN F7 12504.
36. The statement was signed by C. Thomachot, Dumartheray, Reclus, and Charles Perron. Nettlau, *Elisée Reclus*, p. 218.
37. *Le Révolté*, 8 July 1882.
38. In Reclus's view, even enemies of the anarchists were engaged in making incessant propaganda on their behalf. See his *An Anarchist on Anarchy*.
39. *Le Révolté*, 1 Apr. 1882.
40. *Ibid.*, 2 Sept. 1882.
41. See *Procès des anarchistes*.
42. *Ibid.*, p. 29. For an account of anarchist theory and practice as it relates to propaganda by the deed, see Marie Fleming, "Propaganda by the Deed: Terrorism and Anarchist Theory in Late Nineteenth-Century Europe" in *Terrorism: An International Journal*, Vol. 4, Nos. 1-4, 1980, pp. 1-23.
43. Police reports of 28 Jan. and 17 Feb. 1883, P.Po. B a/1502, contain copies of the poster. On 28 Oct. 1882, *Le Révolté* had published the poster of the Justiciers du peuple which advocated burning the furniture of property-owners known for their harshness.
44. Reclus to Heath, 18 Feb. 1883, *Corr.* II, p. 279.
45. *Ibid.*
46. Reclus to Heath, 10 Jan. 1885, Fonds ER, 14 AS 232, IFHS.
47. Reclus, *An Anarchist on Anarchy*, p. 9.
48. *Ibid.*, p. 14.
49. *Ibid.*
50. *Ibid.*
51. Reclus to De Gérando, 24 June 1883, *Corr.* II, p. 307.
52. Reclus, *Evolution et Révolution* (1884), pp. 9-10 (English from London 1885 edition). Cf. Reclus, *An Anarchist on Anarchy*, p. 14.
53. *Le Révolté*, 21 Jan. 1882.
54. Reclus to De Gérando, 24 June 1883, *Corr.* II, p. 308.
55. Reclus to Rigot, 24 Dec. 1882, *Corr.* II, pp. 266-67. Cf. police report of 28 Dec. 1882, P.Po. B a/1237. The letter was reproduced in *La Justice* and *L'Intransigeant* on 28 Dec. 1882.
56. For example, excerpts of letters from Reclus to Jean Ricard were read out in court. See the report of the proceedings of the trial on 9 Jan. in *Le Temps*, 10 Jan. 1883.
57. *Procès des anarchistes*, p. 84.
58. See, for example, Jean Grave, *Quarante ans de propagande anarchiste* (Paris, 1973; originally 1930), p. 223. Cf. A. Hamon, *Psychologie de l'anarchiste-socialiste* (Paris, 1895); Félix Dubois, *Le Péril anarchiste* (Paris, 1894); Cesare Lombroso, *Les Anarchistes* (Paris, 1896; Italian, 1894).
59. Kropotkin to Robin, 11 Feb. 1877, NA, IISG.
60. Marc Vuilleumier, "Elisée Reclus et Genève" in *Musée de Genève*, Apr. 1971, p. 11.
61. In 1879 the Ukrainian Michael Dragomanoff, whom Reclus had met through the Geneva exiles, helped prepare the sections on Russia. *Nouvelle Géographie universelle* V, p. 919.
62. Kropotkin, *Memoirs*, p. 424; *Nouvelle Géographie universelle* VI, p. 918.
63. Kropotkin, *Memoirs*, p. 424.
64. *Ibid.*, p. 450.
65. *Ibid.* See also correspondence Reclus to Kropotkin, in *Corr.* II, and Fonds ER, 14 AS 232, IFHS. Kropotkin was sentenced to five years, but served three.

66. Grave, *Quarante ans*, pp. 194-95.
67. Kropotkin, *Memoirs*, p. 423.
68. Grave, *Quarante ans*, p. 194.
69. *Ibid.*, pp. 195, 197.
70. Fonds ER, 14 AS 232, IFHS. There was a decrease in contributions to the "movement" from the late 1880s, and funds were directed instead to Reclus's daughter Jeannie, who was left with three children on the death of her husband Louis Cuisinier in 1887. Reclus also helped his daughter Magali and her husband Paul Régnier.
71. Kropotkin, *Memoirs*, pp. 406-7.
72. Kropotkin to Morris, 11 Apr. 1886, Morris Papers VIII, BM Add. MS. 45, 345.
73. For an account of the searches ordered by the government authorities, see J. Langhard, *Die Anarchistische Bewegung in der Schweiz* (Berlin, 1903), p. 148ff.
74. Police report of 8 Dec. 1887, P.Po. B a/75 and B a/1237.
75. Reclus to Gross, 17 Sept. 1888, Fonds ER, 14 AS 232, IFHS.
76. Police report of 12 Oct. 1892, P.Po. B a/77.
77. Peter Kropotkin, *La Conquête du pain* (Paris, 1892).
78. See the correspondence Reclus to Louise in Papiers ER, NAF 22912.
79. Reclus to Grave, 2 Nov. 1891, Fonds ER, 14 AS 232, IFHS.
80. Grave, *Quarante ans*, p. 223.
81. Richard Heath, "Elisée Reclus," *Humane Review*, Oct. 1905.

Chapter 9

1. Reclus to Bakunin, 8 Feb. 1875, *Corr.* II, p. 169.
2. Reclus to Bakunin, 17 Apr. 1875, *Corr.* II, p. 170.
3. *Ibid.*
4. *BFJ*, 7 Mar. 1875.
5. In Archief ER, IISG, there are two letters in one envelope. One is Bertoia to Reclus, 20 Oct. 1887; the other is not dated and contains no greeting, but according to the internal evidence of both letters is from Reclus to Bertoia, 15 Oct. 1887. The envelope which contains the two letters is addressed to Max Nettlau and postmarked 19 June 1897, and the sender indicated is Jacques Gross.
6. Elisée Reclus, *Ouvrier, prends la machine! Prends la terre, paysan!* (Geneva, 1880), p. 7; as article in *Le Révolté*, 24 Jan. 1880.
7. Elisée Reclus, "Sur la propriété," p. 327; *Ouvrier*, pp. 7-8.
8. Reclus, *Ouvrier*, p. 4.
9. *Ibid.*, p. 7.
10. *Ibid.*, pp. 7-8.
11. Elisée Reclus, *A mon Frère, le paysan* (Geneva, 1893), p. 10.
12. *Ibid.*, p. 14.
13. Reclus, *An Anarchist on Anarchy*, p. 4.
14. *Ibid.*, p. 9.
15. See "Tous les démocrates," extract from *L'Agriculteur*, n.d. (1886), at BN.
16. General Council meeting of 13 July 1869; *Documents of the First International* III, p. 122.
17. See above, Chapter 4.
18. Reclus, "Sur la Propriété," p. 325.
19. Reclus, *Ouvrier*, p. 3.
20. *Ibid.*, pp. 2-3.
21. *Ibid.*
22. Reclus, "Sur la propriété," p. 325.
23. *Le Révolté*, 24 June 1882. The statement was made at the Lausanne Congress of the Jura Federation. When Reclus mentioned that there already existed brochures for country people, Klementz replied that the articles and brochures

were too theoretical and difficult to appeal to peasants. Reclus later made an effort to reach them through his *A mon Frère, le paysan*. In 1892 he was planning to bring out a collection of songs to be used as propaganda among the peasants.

24. Reclus, *A mon Frère*, p. 6.
25. *Ibid.*, pp. 7-9.
26. *Ibid.*, p. 9.
27. Reclus to Bertoia, n.d., 15 Oct. 1887, Archief ER, IISG.
28. *Ibid.*
29. Reclus, *Evolution et Révolution* (1884), pp. 27-8 (English from London, 1885 edition).
30. Reclus, "Sur la propriété," p. 327.
31. *Ibid.*, p. 328.
32. Reclus to Bertoia, n.d., 15 Oct. 1887, Archief ER, IISG. Cf. his *Evolution et Révolution* (1880), p. 13ff.
33. Reclus, *Ouvrier*, p. 7.
34. Reclus to the editor of *La Vie naturelle*, 6 Feb. 1897, *Corr.* III, pp. 197-98 (*La Vie naturelle*, Dec. 1911).
35. Elisée to Elie, n.d. (Oct. 1868), *Corr.* I, p. 282.
36. Reclus to Renard, 2 June 1888, *Corr.* II, p. 445.
37. Reclus to Heath, 4 Nov. 1887, *Corr.* II, p. 428.
38. *BFJ*, 8 Aug. 1875.
39. *Ibid.*, 11 Mar. 1877.
40. *Ibid.*, 8 Aug. 1875.
41. *Le Révolté*, 21 June-4 July and 2-15 Aug. 1885.
42. *Ibid.*, 5-11 Feb. 1887.
43. Reclus to Heath, n.d. (1887), *Corr.* II, pp. 414-15.
44. Reclus to Grave, 2 Nov. 1891, Fonds ER, 14 AS 232, IFHS.
45. *La Révolte*, 22-29 Nov. 1889.
46. The original can be found in P.Po. B a/1237.
47. Reclus to Grave, 29 Nov. 1891, *Corr.* III, pp. 96-97.
48. *La Révolte*, 28 Nov.-4 Dec. 1891; *Corr.* III, pp. 97-98.
49. Reclus to Grave, 29 Nov. 1891; *Corr.* III, p. 98.
50. *La Révolte*, 5-11, 12-18, and 19-25 Dec. 1891.
51. Peter Kropotkin, *Anarchist Morality* (*Freedom* Pamphlet, 1892) in *Revolutionary Pamphlets*, p. 80ff., esp. 97.
52. Kropotkin, *Anarchist Morality*, p. 101.
53. Reclus to Pastor Roth, n.d. (1904), *Corr.* III, pp. 285-86.
54. Jean Grave, *Quarante ans*, p. 223.
55. Cf. *ibid.*, p. 247.
56. Reclus to Grave, 2 Nov. 1891, Fonds ER, 14 AS 232, IFHS; cf. Reclus to Grave, 21 Nov. 1891, *ibid.*, and Grave, *Quarante ans*, p. 222.
57. Reclus to Grave, 21 Nov. 1891, Fonds ER, 14 AS 232, IFHS.
58. In response to *Ça Ira*, which extolled the virtues of thievery, Reclus wrote to Gross that he had shown his chagrin to Constant Martin by refusing to contribute a sou to the paper. Reclus to Gross, 2 Nov. 1888, Papiers Gross, Depôt du CIRA 1964, BPU, Geneva. An edited copy of the letter exists in Fonds ER, 14 AS 232, IFHS.
59. Grave, *Quarante ans*, p. 223.
60. Reclus to Grave, 21 Nov. 1891, Fonds ER, 14 AS 232, IFHS.
61. Reclus to Grave, 22 Nov. 1891, Fonds ER, 14 AS 232, IFHS.
62. Reclus to Grave, 21 May 1893, *Corr.* III, pp. 139-40.
63. Cf. Octave Mirbeau's opinion: "What I find unique in your book is that it is impossible to find fault in the logic; it is full of clarity." Grave, *Quarante ans*, p. 253.

Chapter 10

1. For Brousse's position, see Stafford, *From Anarchism to Reformism*, p. 122ff.
2. Quoted in Woodcock and Avakumović, *The Anarchist Prince*, p. 343.
3. For the proceedings of the congress, see *Le Révolté*, 23 July 1881.
4. *L'Hydre anarchiste*, 9 Mar. 1884. Chaves fired at the police who came to arrest him, but was killed by one of them. *Le Droit social* (16-23 May 1885) opened up a subscription to purchase a revolver to avenge him.
5. Jean Maitron, *Le Mouvement anarchiste en France*, 2 vols. (Paris, 1975) I, p. 212.
6. *La Révolte*, 19-25 Mar. 1892.
7. For documents collected under the heading *Explosions*, see B a/66, B a/67, B a/136, B a/139, B a/140, B a/141, B a/142, B a/143; see also B a/508, B a/509, B a/510 entitled *Lettres de menaces*, 1892.
8. Victor Barrucand in *L'En Dehors*, 24 July 1892; quoted in Maitron, *Mouvement anarchiste* I, p. 224.
9. J. Garin, *L'Anarchie et les Anarchistes* (Paris, 1885), p. 1.
10. R. Garraud, *L'Anarchie et la Répression* (Paris, 1895), pp. 17-18. Cf. P. Fabrequettes, *De la complicité intellectuelle et des délits d'opinion. De la provocation et de l'opologie criminelles. De la propagande anarchiste* (Paris, 1894-1895).
11. *La Révolte*, 23-30 Apr. 1892.
12. See *La Révolte*, 7-14 May 1892, for an article by Octave Mirbeau, and 1-7 July 1892 for "Déclarations de Ravachol."
13. Grave, *Quarante ans*, pp. 296-97.
14. Kropotkin to Brandes, *Freedom*, Oct. 1898; Martin A. Miller, *Kropotkin* (Chicago, 1976), p. 174.
15. Quoted in Woodcock and Avakumović, *The Anarchist Prince*, p. 248.
16. Peter Kropotkin, "The Spirit of Revolt" in *Revolutionary Pamphlets*, p. 39.
17. Kropotkin to Brandes, *Freedom*, Oct. 1898.
18. Reclus to Heath, n.d., *Corr.* II, p. 425.
19. Reclus to Zibelin-Wilmerding, 7 June 1892, *Corr.* III, p. 118.
20. Reclus to Sempre Avanti, 28 June 1892, *Corr.* III, p. 120.
21. Reclus to Zibelin-Wilmerding, 7 June 1892, *Corr.* III, p. 118.
22. Reclus, *An Anarchist on Anarchy*, p. 14.
23. Reclus to Roorda van Eysinga, 25 Mar. 1892, *Corr.* III, p. 108.
24. Reclus to Heath, n.d., *Corr.* II, p. 425.
25. Reclus to Roorda van Eysinga, 5 May 1894, *Corr.* III, p. 164.
26. *Ibid.*
27. Reclus to Karl Heath, 31 Mar. 1900, *Corr.* III, p. 218.
28. *Ibid.*, p. 218-19.
29. *Ibid.*, p. 219.
30. Quoted in Max Nettlau, *Anarchisten und Syndicalisten*, Teil 1, Vol. 5, of *Geschichte der Anarchie*, herausgegeben in Zusammenarbeit mit dem Internationaal Instituut voor Sociale Geschiedenis, Amsterdam (Vaduz, 1981), pp. 435-36.
31. Reclus to Roorda van Eysinga, June 1892, *Corr.* III, pp. 119-20.
32. Reclus to Roorda van Eysinga, 25 Mar. 1892, *Corr.* III, pp. 108-9.
33. Reclus to Roorda van Eysinga, 9 Apr. 1892, *Corr.* III, p. 111.
34. *Ibid.*, p. 112.
35. See, for example, *Le Radical*, 30 Mar. 1894; *L'Eclair*, 28 Apr. 1894; also, Dubois, *Le Péril anarchiste*, p. 181.
36. Reclus to *L'Eclair*, 2 May 1894; *Corr.* III, p. 163. See also Reclus to Gross, 3 Sept. 1896, Papiers Gross, Dépôt du CIRA 1964, BPU, Geneva, in which Reclus mentions in passing that he had "an extremely precious letter from Emile Henry setting forth his ideas in response to a letter from Malatesta."
37. See, for example, Hamon, Dubois, Lombroso. The reports on Reclus's reactions to terrorism in Jehan-Préval, *Anarchie et Nihilisme* (Paris, 1892) are fabrications; cf. pp. 89, 95-96, and 235.
38. Hamon, *Psychologie*.

39. Garraud, L'Anarchie, p. 38. Cf. Robert Jousseaume, *Etude sur les lois contre les menées anarchistes et sur les modifications que ces lois ont apportées à la législation pénale* (Paris, 1895).

40. Garraud, L'Anarchie, p. 78.

41. See the police report of the search in P.Po. B a/1237. Another was carried out at Reclus's home in Sevres on 10 Jan. 1894; see account in *L'Intransigeant*, 12 Jan. 1894. Searches were also made at the homes of Reclus's relatives in Algeria, and reports were filed on the Reclus family and newspaper clippings collected; see esp. P.Po. B a/1237.

42. Reclus to Louise, n.d. (Feb. 1892), *Corr.* III, p. 103.

43. Governing Council to Reclus, 28 July 1892, Papiers ER, NAF 22915.

44. Reclus to Governing Council, 1 Aug. 1892, *Corr.* III, p. 125.

45. Governing Council to Reclus, 6 Jan. 1894, Papiers ER, NAF 22915. See Reclus's letter of 5 Jan. to the Governing Council; *Corr.* III, pp. 152-53.

46. University Circle to Reclus, 21 Jan. 1894, Papiers ER, NAF 22915.

47. See "Notes et documents relatifs à l'Université Nouvelle de Bruxelles," Papiers ER, NAF 22915; newspaper clippings in P.Po. B a/1237; Hem Day, *Elisée Reclus en Belgique: Sa vie, son activité, 1894-1905* (Paris-Brussels, 1956); Bernard Lazare, "A School of Liberty" in *Liberty*, 30 Nov. 1895; De Greef, *Eloges d'Elisée Reclus*, p. 34ff.

48. Reclus to Perron, 6 Jan. 1894, *Corr.* III, p. 154.

49. Reclus to President of the University Circle, n.d. (Jan. 1894?), *Corr.* III, pp. 154-55.

50. See Reclus's comments to Joukowsky, 4 Mar. 1894, *Corr.* III, pp. 159-60.

51. Edmond Picard, quoted in Thérèse Dejongh, "The Brothers Reclus at the New University" in Ishill, *Elisée and Elie Reclus*, p. 225.

52. Reclus to Louise, n.d. (Feb. 1892), *Corr.* III, p. 103. See announcement of the British award in *Geographical Journal* (London), May 1894.

53. Reclus to Louise, 23 Apr. 1892, *Corr.* III, p. 114. Cf. report in *Le Temps*, Apr. 1892; clipping in AN F7 12504.

54. Reclus to Zibelin-Wilmerding, *Corr.* III, p. 113. See also correspondence Reclus to Louise in Papiers ER, NAF 22912.

55. Reclus to Nadar, 27 Apr. 1892, *Corr.* III, p. 115.

56. Reclus to Gross, 10 May 1892, *Corr.* III, pp. 116-17.

57. Reclus, "Développement."

58. Reclus to Rigot, 24 Dec. 1883, *Corr.* II, pp. 266-67. Cf. police report of 28 Dec. 1882, P.Po. B a/1237.

59. According to Kropotkin, *Memoirs*, p. 450, his brother-in-law Ananieff died late on 21 Dec. and the arrest took place in the early hours of 22 Dec. Reclus's letter to Nadar of 19 Dec. (*Corr.* II, p. 263ff.), which mentions the death of Ananieff, is misdated; it must have been written on 22 or 23 Dec. Reclus was notified by telegraph of Ananieff's death and Kropotkin's arrest, and left Clarens for Thonon immediately (Kropotkin, *Memoirs*, p. 450). The funeral took place on 23 Dec. and Reclus was back in Clarens on 24 Dec.

60. Reclus to *La Réforme*, Mar. 1894, *Corr.* III, p. 161.

61. Reclus to Roorda van Eysinga, 17 July 1894, *Corr.* III, p. 169.

62. Paul Reclus, "Biographie," p. 145.

63. Reclus to Governing Council, 13 Jan. 1894, *Corr.* III, pp. 155-56.

64. Reclus to Perron, 6 Jan. 1894, *Corr.* III, p. 154.

65. Reclus to Gross, n.d. (Mar. 1894), Fonds ER, 14 AS 232, IFHS.

66. Reclus to Roorda van Eysinga, 25 Mar. 1892, *Corr.* III, p. 108.

67. Félix Nadar, "Elisée Reclus," in *Les Temps nouveaux*, Dec. 1905.

Chapter 11

1. For the proceedings of the meeting see *Le Révolté*, 17 Oct. 1880.
2. *Le Travailleur*, May 1877.
3. Guillaume, *L'Internationale* II, p. 279. Reclus was enthusiastic about Guillaume's plans to write a book of commentary and documentation on the anti-authoritarian and anarchist trends within the First International.
4. Letters of Reclus to Louise in the summer of 1896, Papiers ER, NAF 22912.
5. Reclus to Louise, Aug. 1896, Papiers ER, NAF 22912. Reclus made short trips to England in 1894 and at least two trips in 1895. See Reclus to Grave, 19 Sept. 1894, Fonds ER, 14 AS 232, IFHS; Anne Cobden-Sanderson, "Elie and Elisée Reclus" in Ishill, *Elisée and Elie Reclus*, p. 45; Reclus to Louise, July 1895, *Corr.* III, p. 187. Reclus delivered an address on anarchy in London on 26 July 1895. See report, P.Po. B a/1237. The Paris police continued their interest in his activities, especially when he visited Paris.
6. *Freedom*, Aug.-Sept. 1896. At the reunion on Tuesday, 28 July, the speakers included Kropotkin, Reclus, Louise Michel, V. Gori, Keir Hardie, Tom Mann, Domela Nieuwenhuis, Bernard Lazare, and Gustave Landauer. The decision was taken that the anarchists assemble every evening as long as the London Congress was in session, and that, moreover, those anarchists who were excluded (some had been admitted as trade unionists) meet every day in St. Martin's Hall—the same hall, Tcherkesoff reminded them, in which the First International had been founded 32 years previously. The anarchists held meetings until Friday, 31 July. See *Les Temps nouveaux*, 22 Aug. 1896.
7. Reclus is not mentioned in the report of the proceedings in *Freedom*.
8. Reclus, *L'Idéal anarchique*, p. 171ff.
9. *Ibid.*, pp. 176-77.
10. *Ibid.*, p. 177.
11. *Ibid.*, p. 43ff.
12. Reclus to Clara Koettlitz, 12 Apr. 1895, *Corr.* III, p. 182.
13. Reclus, *L'Idéal anarchique*, pp. 177-78.
14. Reclus to Clara Koettlitz, 12 Apr. 1895, *Corr.* III, p. 182. Cf. Reclus to Buurmans, 17 Feb. 1878, *Corr.* II, p. 198.
15. Grave, *Quarante ans*, p. 338ff.
16. *Les Temps nouveaux*, 4 May 1895.
17. Grave, *Quarante ans*, p. 339. Since Reclus's financial position deteriorated after 1894, his contributions must have been small.
18. Reclus to Gross, n.d. (Mar. 1894), Fonds ER, 14 AS 232, IFHS.
19. Reclus to Renard, 27 Dec. 1895, *Corr.* III, pp. 192-93.
20. Reclus, *L'Idéal anarchique*, pp. 178-79.
21. Reclus to Roorda van Eysinga, 1 July 1895, *Corr.* III, p. 186.
22. Reclus to Grave, 6 Oct. 1894, *Corr.* III, p. 172.
23. Elisée Reclus, *L'Idéal et la Jeunesse* (Brussels, 1894). Cf. his address at the official opening of the New University in 1895: *Université Nouvelle de Bruxelles: Séance solennelle du rentrée du 22 octobre 1895, Discours de M. Elisée Reclus* (Brussels, 1895).
24. Reclus to Clara Koettlitz, 12 Apr. 1895, *Corr.* III, p. 182.
25. Reclus to Henri Russ, n.d. (1904), *Corr.* III, pp. 295-96. Cf. Reclus to Fuss, n.d., *Corr.* III, p. 299.
26. Cf. Reclus's remarks at the 1880 Congress of the Jura Federation in *Le Révolté*, 17 Oct. 1880; Reclus to Heath, n.d. (1884), *Corr.* II, p. 325. See also Reclus, *L'Idéal anarchique*, p. 128ff., and his "Quelques mots d'histoire" in *La Société nouvelle*, Nov. 1894.
27. Elisée Reclus, "A grande mistificaçao" in *Aurora* (Brazil), Apr. 1905. Reclus reserved the right to expand upon these views elsewhere and to bring out a pamphlet. See Reclus to Neno Vasco, 3 Mar. 1905, *Corr.* III, pp. 310-11. Cf. a response to Reclus by a neo-Malthusian: G. Giroud, "La Grande Erreur" in *La*

Régénération, Dec. 1905 (journal founded by Paul Robin). Reclus maintained a continuing interest in the problem of population and food supply. He made some contribution to the pamphlets *Les Produits de la terre* (Geneva, 1885), *Les Produits de l'industrie* (Paris, 1887), and *La Richesse et la Misère* (Paris, 1888). These were published in several forms, usually anonymously, but occasionally under Reclus's name. According to Max Nettlau, *Bibliographie de l'anarchie* (Brussels, 1897), pp. 70-71, Reclus collaborated in the writing of the pamphlets. Reclus, who wrote the preface to Nettlau's book, may have provided this information. In 1901 he wrote to Grave that *Les Produits de la terre* was not his work, but had been republished under his name, he thought, by some of his friends in Geneva. (The same was probably true for *Les Produits de l'industrie*.) In any case, he was not satisfied with the work, and expressed a desire to revise it. Reclus to Grave, 19 Dec. 1901, Fonds Jean Grave, 14 AS 184b, IFHS. Cf. Reclus to Roorda van Eysinga, 16 Mar. 1891, *Corr.* III, p. 91. Grave, *Quarante ans*, p. 557, claimed that the three pamphlets were written by Reclus.
28. Reclus to Paul Régnier, 6 May 1890, *Corr.* III, pp. 81-82.
29. Reclus to Louise, 15 and 20 Dec. 1891, Papiers ER, NAF 22912.
30. Peter Kropotkin, *La Conquête du pain* (Paris, 1892), preface by Reclus, pp. ix-xi.
31. Reclus, *L'Idéal anarchique*, p. 61.
32. *Ibid.*, p. 62.
33. *Ibid.*, p. 44.
34. *Ibid.*, p. 63.
35. *Ibid.*, pp. 63-64.
36. Quoted in Pierre Ramus, "In Commemoration of Elisée Reclus" in Ishill, *Elisée and Elie Reclus*, p. 124.
37. Reclus, *La Jeunesse*. Cf. his address at the official opening of the New University in 1895.
38. See, for example, N. Roubakine, "Elisée Reclus and the Russian Readers" in Ishill, *Elisée and Elie Reclus*, p. 166.
39. Patrick Geddes, "A Great Geographer: Elisée Reclus" in Ishill, *Elisée and Elie Reclus*, p. 155.
40. *Ibid.*, p. 158.
41. L. Guérineau, "Recollections of Elisée Reclus" in Ishill, *Elisée and Elie Reclus*, p. 119.
42. *Ibid.*
43. Elie Reclus to Daniel Baud-Bovy, 14 Nov. 1895, Archives Baud-Bovy 36, BPU, Geneva.
44. Paul Reclus, "A Few Recollections," pp. 3-4.
45. Lilly Zibelin-Wilmerding, "Elisée Reclus" in Ishill, *Elisée and Elie Reclus*, p. 103.
46. Madam Theo van Rysselberghe, quoted in Dejongh, "The Brothers Reclus," p. 238.
47. Zibelin-Wilmerding, "Elisée Reclus," p. 102.
48. See the discussion in Lazare.
49. Kropotkin to Morris, 11 Apr. 1886, Morris Papers VIII, Brit. Mus. Add. Ms. 45,345.
50. Nettlau to Gross, 17 July 1905, Fonds Jacques Gross, IISG.
51. Zibelin-Wilmerding, "Elisée Reclus," p. 102.
52. Reclus's address at the official opening of the New University in 1895, p. 6; English from Thérèse Dejongh, "The Brothers Reclus at the New University" in Ishill, *Elisée and Elie Reclus*, p. 228.

Chapter 12

1. Léon Metchnikoff, *La Civilisation et les Grands Fleuves historiques* (Paris, 1889), Preface, pp. xiv-xv.
2. Cf. for example, Elisée Reclus, *Hégémonie de l'Europe* (Paris, 1894).
3. Elisée Reclus, "East and West" in *Contemporary Review*, Oct. 1894.
4. Elisée Reclus, "The Vivisection of China" in *Atlantic Monthly*, Sept. 1898.

5. Reclus, "D'Histoire," p. 489.
6. *Ibid.*, pp. 489-90.
7. *Ibid.*, p. 490.
8. Reclus, "Vivisection."
9. Elisée Reclus, "L'Internationale et les Chinois" in *Almanach du people pour 1874* (revised in *Le Travailleur*, Mar.-Apr. 1878).
10. Cf. Elisée Reclus, *La Chine et la Diplomatie européene* (Paris, 1900), p. 16.
11. As reported in François Bournand, *Les Juifs et Nos contemporains* (Paris, 1898), pp. 217-21. Cf. report in *La France*, 4 Mar. 1898. Cf. Karl Marx, "On the Jewish Question" in David McLellan, *Karl Marx: Early Texts* (Oxford, 1971), p. 85ff.
12. Reclus to Henri Dagan, n.d. (1898), published in *Les Droits de l'homme*, 22 Apr. 1898. See also Elisée Reclus, *Les Arabes* (Cours de M. Elisée Reclus à l'Institut des Hautes Etudes de l'Université Nouvelle de Bruxelles (année 1897-1898)—6e Conférence) (Brussels, 1898), esp. pp. 3, 14.
13. Elisée to Elie, June 1868, *Corr.* I, p. 276. Louise Michel also became involved in this society.
14. Reclus to Heath, 8 July 1882, *Corr.* II, pp. 254-55.
15. Reclus to Baud-Bovy, 19 Sept. 1894, Archives Baud-Bovy 36, BPU, Geneva.
16. Reclus to Kropotkin, 8 Jan. 1901, *Corr.* III, pp. 232-33.
17. Reclus, *L'Homme et la Terre* I, p. 239.
18. *Ibid.*, pp. 242-43.
19. *Ibid.*, p. 251.
20. Reclus to Heath, 2 Aug. 1882, *Corr.* II, p. 258.
21. Reclus to Clara Koettlitz, 12 Apr. 1895, *Corr.* III, p. 183.
22. See the address given by Elisée and Fanny at their marriage ceremony on 26 June 1870 in Papiers ER, NAF 22909 (document in Fanny's handwriting).
23. Reclus to Clara Mesnil, 25 Oct. 1904, *Corr.* III, p. 293.
24. See, for example, Reclus to Nadar, 19 Dec. 1882, *Corr.* II, pp. 263-64. Elie acted as adviser to Elisée's daughters, while Elisée remained in the background in order to avoid exerting pressure on them. After Elie's death, the editors of *La Société nouvelle* published as a brochure his address to his nieces at their wedding: Elie Reclus, *Le Mariage tel qu'il fut et tel qu'il est. Avec une allocution d'Elisée Reclus* (Mons, 1907). It appeared as *Souvenirs du 14 octobre 1882* (Paris, 1882), with foreword "Unions libres," followed by "Exposé des motifs" and "Allocution du père à ses filles et à ses gendres," and in the same form in *Les Arts de la vie*, July 1905.
25. Reclus, *L'Homme et la Terre*, Preface to Vol. 1, p. iv.
26. *Ibid.*, pp. ii-iii.
27. Elisée Reclus, "Metamorphoses du progrès" in *Almanach de la question sociale pour 1899* (Paris, 1899), p. 17.
28. Reclus, *L'Idéal anarchique*, p. 112ff. Cf. his preface to *Patriotisme, Colonisation, Bibliothèque documentaire*, No. 2 (Paris, 1903).
29. Reclus, "Metamorphoses."
30. *Ibid.*
31. *Ibid.*, p. 18.
32. *Ibid.*, pp. 18-19.
33. Reclus, "D'Histoire," p. 490.
34. *Ibid.*, pp. 490-91.
35. Cf. Reclus to Roorda van Eysinga, 16 Mar. 1891, *Corr.* III, p. 89ff.
36. See above, Chapter 6.
37. Reclus, *An Anarchist on Anarchy*, p. 7ff.
38. Reclus to his daughter Jeannie, 18 June 1889, *Corr.* II, p. 494. Cf. Elisée Reclus, "Quelques mots sur la révolution bouddhique" in *L'Humanité nouvelle*, June 1897.
39. Elisée Reclus, *La Formation des religions, Conférence à l'Ecole des Libres Etudes* (Brussels, 1894), See also his "Origines de la religion et de la morale" in *Les Temps nouveaux*, 27 Feb.-19 Mar. 1904.

40. Reclus, *La Formation*, p. 11.
41. *Ibid.*
42. Reclus's preface to Kropotkin, *Conquest of Bread*, p. 29.
43. Reclus to Grave, 25 Dec. 1899, *Corr.* III, p. 215.
44. Elisée Reclus and Georges Guyou (pseudonym of Elisée's nephew Paul), "L'Anarchie et l'Eglise" in *Les Temps nouveaux*, 8-14 Sept. 1900. See also Elisée Reclus, "Nouvelle proposition pour la suppression de l'Ere chrétienne" in *Les Temps nouveaux*, 6 May 1905.
45. Reclus, "D'Histoire," p. 492ff.
46. Elisée Reclus, "La Grande Famille" in *Le Magazine international*, Jan. 1897 (English from translation, "The Great Kinship" by Edward Carpenter, London, 1900).
47. Reclus, "Vegetarianism."
48. Reclus, "La Grand Famille."
49. *Ibid.*
50. Reclus, "Vegetarianism."
51. Reclus, "La Grand Famille."
52. *Le Travailleur*, Feb.-Mar. 1878. Cf. Reclus, *Elie Reclus*, pp. 21-22. According to Elisée, from an early age Elie had observed the motto: "And especially, my friend, especially guard yourself well against success!"
53. Reclus to Mlle. De Gérando, 1 Jan. 1882, *Corr.* II, p. 238.
54. Reclus to Louise, 21 Nov. 1887, Fonds ER, 14 AS 232, IFHS.
55. Dejongh, "The Brothers Reclus," p. 229.
56. Elisée Reclus, *Leçon d'ouverture du cours de Géographie comparée, Extrait de la Revue universitaire* (Brussels, 1894), pp. 3-4.
57. See Reclus to Nadar, 18 Apr. 1899, *Corr.* III, pp. 210-11.
58. Quoted in Albert François, *Elisée Reclus et l'Anarchie* (Ghent, 1905), pp. 23-24.
59. Alfred Russell Wallace, *My Life: A Record of Events and Opinions*, 2 vols. (London, 1905), Vol. 2, pp. 207-8.
60. Quoted in Ramus, pp. 124-25.
61. Zibelin-Wilmerding, "Elisée Reclus," p. 101.
62. L. Guérineau, "Recollections of Elisée Reclus" in Ishill, *Elisée and Elie Reclus*, p. 117.
63. Richard Heath, "Elisée Reclus" in *Humane Review*, Oct. 1905.
64. Mesnil, "Elisée Reclus," p. 189.
65. See Reclus to Paul Regnier, 2 July 1900, *Corr.* III, p. 225.
66. Mesnil, "Elisée Reclus," p. 189.
67. Dejongh, "The Brothers Reclus," p. 239; also Mesnil, "Elisée Reclus," p. 192.
68. Emile Cammaerts, quoted in Dejongh, p. 238.
69. L. Descaves, quoted in *ibid.*
70. Heath, "Elisée Reclus."
71. Zibelin-Wilmerding, "Elisée Reclus," p. 192; Mesnil, "Elisée Reclus," p. 191ff.
72. Reclus to Clara Mesnil, 25 Oct. 1904, *Corr.* III, p. 292.
73. See the discussion in Dunbar, *Elisée Reclus*, pp. 114-15.
74. Reclus to Luigi Galleani, 19 May 1905, Fonds ER, 14 AS 232, IFHS.
75. Reclus to Heath, 18 Feb. 1882, *Corr.* II, pp. 242-43.
76. Grave, *Quarante ans*, pp. 359-60.
77. Stafford, *From Anarchism to Reformism*, p. 144.
78. Reclus, "An Anarchist on Anarchy."
79. Reclus, Ferré, J.B. Clément, Audejean, Jance, and Kropotkin requested that their names be removed from the *La Bataille* list. See *Le Télégraphe*, 8 Oct. 1885, and report in P.Po. B a/1237.
80. *Le Révolté*, 11 Oct. 1885; an English version appeared in *The Anarchist*, also in 1885, and again in *Freedom*, Jan. 1910.
81. AN F7 12504.
82. Reclus, "Développement."
83. Reclus to B.P. Van der Voo, Apr. 1897, *Corr.* III, p. 201.

84. Reclus to Kropotkin, 6 Feb. 1905, *Corr.* III, p. 300.
85. For a copy of the address, see *La Terre* (Mons), 24 June-1 July 1906, and *Corr.* III, p. 302ff.
86. Zamfir C. Arbore (Ralli), "Elisée Reclus: Reminiscences" in Ishill, *Elisée and Elie Reclus*, p. 164.
87. Paul Reclus to Kropotkin, 6 July 1905, *Corr.* III, pp. 326-67.

Bibliography

Abbreviations

AEN	Archives de l'Etat, Neuchâtel
AFJ	Archives de la Fédération jurassienne
AHG	Archives historiques du Ministère de la Guerre
AN	Archives nationales
Archief ER	Archief Elisée Reclus
BFJ	Bulletin de la Fédération jurassienne
BN	Bibliothèque nationale
BPU	Bibliothèque publique et universitaire, Geneva
CIRA	Centre international de Recherches sur l'anarchisme
Dossier ER	Dossier Elisée Reclus
Fonds ER	Fonds Elisée Reclus
IFHS	Institut français d'Histoire sociale
IISG	Internationaal Instituut voor Sociale Geschiedenis
IWMA	International Working Men's Association
MEW	Marx Engels Werke
NA	Nettlau Archives
NAF	Nouvelles Acquisitions françaises, BN
Papiers ER	Papiers Elisée Reclus
P.Po.	Archives de la Préfecture de police
PV du CFJ	Procès-verbaux des séances du Comité fédéral jurassien

PRIMARY SOURCES

ARCHIVES

Archives de la Prefécture de police

B a/66 and B a/67, *Explosions* 1888-1901
B a/73, *Les activités anarchistes* 1882-1901
B a/74, *Les activités anarchistes* 1885-1886
B a/75, *Les activités anarchistes* 1887-1888
B a/76, *Les activités anarchistes* 1889-1890
B a/77, *Les activités anarchistes* 1891-1892
B a/78, *Les activités anarchistes* 1893
B a/79, *Les activités anarchistes* 1894
B a/80, *Les activités anarchistes* 1895-1896
B a/138, *Explosions* 1881-1898
B a/139, *Explosions* 1889-1892
B a/140, *Explosions* 1892
B a/141, *Explosions* 1893-1894
B a/142, *Explosions* 1894-1895
B a/143, *Explosions* 1895-1897
B a/303, a/308, a/309, *Rapports sur les anarchistes*
B a/394, *Menées des socialistes et des anarchistes révolutionnaires à Lyon*
B a/508 a/509, a/510, *Lettres de menaces* 1892
B a/928, Joseph Albert, dit: Libertad
B a/944, Michel Bakounine
B a/996, Santo Caserio
B a/1132, Ravachol
B a/1183, Louise Michel
B a/1216, Fernand Pelloutier
B a/1497, *Rapports et informations concernant les menées anarchistes* 1897-1898
B a/1498, *Rapports et informations concernant les menées anarchistes* 1899-1906
B a/1499, *Anarchistes en Provence* 1892-1894
B a/1500, *Listes et états d'anarchistes*
B a/1501, *Anarchistes étrangers*
B a/1502, *Alphabets et chiffres secrets de correspondance entre les anarchistes; Propagande anarchiste par la parole*
B a/1503, a/1504, *Surveillance des anarchistes*
B a/1505, *Procès de Trente; Groupes anarchistes du 5ème arrondissement*
B a/1506, *Rapports sur des groupes anarchistes*
B a/1507, *Groupes anarchistes du 18ème arrondissement*
B a/1508, *Anarchistes en Angleterre jusqu'en 1893; Groupes anarchistes du 20ème arrondissement*
B a/1509, *Anarchistes à l'Etranger; Anarchistes en Angleterre 1894-1896*
B a/1510, *Anarchistes en Angleterre, Allemagne, Belgique*
B a/1511, *Association internationale antimilitariste; anarchistes aux Etats-Unis; Anarchistes en Espagne*
B a/1512, *Association internationale antimilitariste*
B a/1513, *Fédération anarchiste communiste révolutionnaire*
B a/1660, *Sébastien Faure*

Archives de l'Etat, Neuchâtel

Fonds Guillaume, five boxes
Letter Reclus to Louis Jeanrenard, pièce privée

Archives générales du Royaume, Brussels

Rapports de police sur l'Internationale

Archives historiques du Ministère de la Guerre, Vincennes

Dossier Elisée Reclus, 7e Conseil de Guerre permanent, dossier no. 46
Dossier Elie Reclus, 3e Conseil de Guerre permanent, dossier no. 2084

Archives nationales, Paris

BB24 732 *Dossier Elisée Reclus*
BB24 875 *Troubles de Montceau-les-Mines 1882;* Peter Kropotkin
BB24 876 *Meeting des Invalides 9 mars 1883*
BB24 881 *Articles des journaux anarchistes*
B7 12487 *La Ligue des droits de l'homme*
F7 12488-12503 *Agissements socialistes, congrès, etc. 1876-1915*
F7 12504-12518 *Agissements anarchistes 1880-1913*
F7 12522-12525 *Congrès divers 1878-1914*
F7 12526 *Evénements de Montceau-les-Mines 1882-1883*
F7 12528-12534 *Premier mai 1898-1911*
F7 12535 *Retraites ouvrières 1901-1910*
F7 12581-12601 *Police des étrangers 1886-1906*
F7 12553 *Notes sur la situation politique 1899-1905*
F7 12554-12559 *Rapports quotidiens de la Préfecture de police 1904-1913*
F7 12560-12565 *Notes de police 1901-1909*
F7 12579-12580 *Relations avec la Suisse 1871-1899*
281 AP(1) *Fonds Edouard Charton*

Bibliothèque nationale, Salle des manuscrits, Paris

Autographes XIXème-XXème Siècles NAF 25101
Autographes Félix et Paul Nadar XXIII NAF 24282
Autographes Félix et Paul Nadar XXIV NAF 24283
Cent Lettres à Gabriel Faure 1936-1947 NAF 16421
Correspondance de Joseph Reinach NAF 13577
Correspondance de Louis Blanc NAF 11398
Correspondance Germain Bapst XIV NAF 24538
Correspondance Louis Havet NAF 24504
Lettres adressées à Ossip-Lourié II NAF 15682
Lettres à F.A. Cazals NAF 13152
Mélanges—XIXe Siècle NAF 14824
Mélanges littéraires—XIXe Siècle NAF 15892
Papiers Elisée Reclus I, Notes et Documents biographiques NAF 22909
Papiers Elisée Reclus II, Lettres 1849-1869 NAF 22910
Papiers Elisée Reclus III, Lettres 1870-1890 NAF 22911
Papiers Elisée Reclus IV, Lettres 1891-1905 NAF 22912
Papiers Elisée Reclus V, Lettres à ses trois femmes NAF 22913
Papiers Elisée Reclus VI, Correspondance A-Z NAF 22914
Papiers Elisée Reclus VII, Université Libre de Bruxelles NAF 22915
Papiers Elisée Reclus VIII, Globe terrestre pour l'Exposition de 1900 NAF 22916
Papiers Elisée Reclus XIX, Mémoires divers NAF 22917
Papiers Elisée Reclus XX, Premiers manuscrits NAF 22918
Papiers Elisée Reclus XXI, Premiers manuscrits NAF 22919
Papiers Nadar XVII, NAF 25002
Papiers Nadar XXXI, NAF 25016
Papiers Jehan Rictus, NAF 24570
Paul Martine—Mémoires I-V, NAF 12712-12716

Bibliothèque publique et universitaire, Geneva

Album domicorum de Jules Perrier, Ms. suppl. 886
Archives Baud-Bovy 23, 36, 214, 216, 237
Archives BPU, K15
Correspondance adressée au peintre Charles Giron, Ms. fr. 1825
Jacques Gross, L10
Lettres d'Elisée Reclus a Ch. Perron 1889-1904, Ms. suppl. 119
Ms. fr. 4209
Ms. fr. 4491/18
Ms. suppl. 886
Papiers Gross, Dépôt du CIRA 1964
Papiers Ph. Plan, Ms. fr. 4297
Ville de Genève, Coll. B. Reber

British Museum, London

Miscellany 1939, Brit. Mus. Add. Ms. 45,498
Miscellany 1947, Brit. Mus. Add. Ms. 46,473
Morris Papers VIII, Brit. Mus. Add. Ms. 45,345
Morris Papers IX, Brit. Mus. Add. Ms. 45,346
Morris Papers, X, Brit. Mus. Add. Ms. 45,347

Institut français d'Histoire sociale, Paris

Fonds Elisée Reclus 14 AS 232, five *dossiers*
Fonds Jean Grave 14 AS 184b

Internationaal Instituut voor Sociale Geschiedenis, Amsterdam

Nettlau Archives, which includes *Archief Elisée Reclus*; *Archives de la Fédération jurassienne*; Kropotkin-Robin correspondence
Fonds Descaves
Fonds Jacques Gross

NEWSPAPERS AND PERIODICALS

L'Association
L'Avant-garde
Bulletin de la Fédération jurassienne
Ça Ira
La Coopération
Le Cri du peuple
Le Droit social
L'Egalité (Geneva)
Freedom
L'Humanité nouvelle
L'Hydre anarchiste
L'Intransigeant
Le Libertaire
Le Monde libertaire
La République des travailleurs
La Révolte
Le Révolté
La Revue des deux mondes
La Revue socialiste
La Rive gauche
Les Temps nouveaux

Le Travailleur
Le Vengeur
La Vie naturelle

WORKS BY ELISÉE RECLUS

"De l'action humaine sur la géographie physique: L'Homme et la nature" in *La Revue des deux mondes*, 1 Dec. 1864

"Amis et Compagnons" in *La Terre de Mons*, 24 June 1906

L'Anarchie (Paris, 1896)

"L'Anarchie et l'Eglise" (with Georges Guyou) in *Les Temps nouveaux*, 1900

An Anarchist on Anarchy (Boston, 1884); as article in *Contemporary Review*, May 1884

"Aperçu géographique [sur le Mexique]" in *Le Mexique au début du XXe siècle* (Paris, 1904)

Les Arabes (Brussels, 1898)

"D'un atlas à échelle uniforme" (with Georges Guyou) in *Bulletin de la Société neuchâteloise de géographie*, T.IX, 1896-97

"Atlas de la Colombie, publié par ordre du gouvernement colombien" in *Bulletin de la Société de géographie de Paris*, 3 Aug. 1876

"Attila de Gérando" in *La Revue de géographie*, Jan. 1898

"L'Avenir de nos enfants" in *La Commune: Almanach socialiste pour 1877* (Geneva, 1877)

"Les Basques: Un peuple qui s'en va" in *La Revue des deux mondes*, 15 Mar. 1867

"Le Bosphore et la mer Noire" in *Le Globe*, 1875

"Le Brésil et la Colonisation" in *La Revue des deux mondes*, 15 June and 15 July 1862

La Chine et la Diplomatie européenne (Paris, 1900)

"Les Chinois et l'Internationale" in *Almanach du peuple*, 1874; revised version in *Le Travailleur*, Mar.-Apr. 1878

"La Cité du bon accord" in *Almanach de la question sociale (illustré) pour 1897* (Paris, 1897)

"Les Cités lacustres de la Suisse" in *La Revue des deux mondes*, 15 Feb. 1861

"De la configuration des continents sur la surface du globe" (translation of article by Carl Ritter) in *La Revue germanique*, Nov. 1859

"Les Colonies anarchistes" in *Les Temps nouveaux*, 7-13 July 1900

"Considérations sur quelques faits de géologie et d'ethnographie. Histoire du sol de l'Europe, par M. Houzeau" in *La Revue philosophique*, 1857

Correspondance, 3 vols. (Paris, 1911-25)

"Le Coton et la crise américaine" in *La Revue des deux mondes*, 1 Jan. 1862

"Deux années de la grande lutte américaine" in *La Revue des deux mondes*, 1 Oct. 1864

"Développement de la liberté dans le monde" in *Le Libertaire*, 28 Aug.-1 Dec. 1925

"East and West" in *Contemporary Review*, Oct. 1894

"Un Ecrit américain sur l'esclavage" in *La Revue des deux mondes*, 15 Mar. 1864

"L'Election présidentielle de la Plata et la guerre du Paraguay" in *La Revue des deux mondes*, 15 Aug. 1868

Elie Reclus 1827-1904 (Paris, 1905); also as "Vie d'Elie Reclus" in Paul Reclus, *Les Frères Elie et Elisée Reclus* (Paris, 1964)

L'Empire du milieu, le climat, le sol, les races, la richesse de la Chine (with Onésime Reclus) (Paris, 1902)

"De l'esclavage aux Etats-Unis" in *La Revue des deux mondes*, 15 Dec. 1860 and 1 Jan. 1861

"Etude sur les dunes" in *Bulletin de la Société de géographie de Paris*, Mar. 1865

"Etude sur les fleuves" in *Bulletin de la Société de géographie de Paris*, Aug. 1859

Evolution et Révolution (Geneva, 1880, 1884; Paris, 1891)

L'Evolution, la Révolution, et l'Idéal anarchique (Paris, 1898)
"L'Evolution légale et l'Anarchie" in *Le Travailleur*, Jan.-Feb. 1878
"The Evolution of Cities" in *Contemporary Review*, Feb. 1895
"Excursions à travers le Dauphiné" in *Le Tour du monde*, 1860
Extension universitaire de Bruxelles: Année académique 1894-1895. Cours de géographique. Amérique meridionale (Brussels, 1894)
L'Extrême-Orient, résumé d'une conférence faite, le 28 avril 1898, à la Société royale de géographie d'Anvers (Anvers, 1898)
"La Fin triomphante de la Grèce" in *L'Education sociale de Lyon*, 15 Feb. and 1 Mar. 1902
"Les Forces souterraines: Les Volcans et les tremblements de terre" in *La Revue des deux mondes*, 1 Jan. 1867
La Formation des religions (Brussels, 1894)
"Fragment d'un voyage à la Nouvelle-Orleans, 1855" in *Le Tour du monde 1er semestre*, 1860
"La Géographie" in *Almanach de l'encyclopédie generale* (Paris, 1869)
"La Grande famille" in *Le Magazine international*, Jan. 1897; translated as *The Great Kinship* by Edward Carpenter (London, 1900)
"A grande mistificaçao" in *Aurora* (Sao Paulo, Brazil), 1 Apr. 1905
"La Grève d'Amérique" in *Le Travailleur*, Sept. 1877
"La Guerre du Paraguay" in *La Revue des deux mondes*, 15 Dec. 1867
Guide du voyageur à Londres et aux environs (Paris, 1860)
Hégémonie de l'Europe (Brussels, 1894)
"Histoire des états américains" in *La Revue des deux mondes*, 1866
Histoire d'une montagne (Paris, 1880)
Histoire d'un ruisseau (Paris, 1869)
"Histoire du peuple américain, par Auguste Carlier" in *Bulletin de la Société de géographie de Paris*, Feb. 1865
L'Homme et la Terre, 6 vols. (Paris, 1905-8)
L'Idéal et la jeunesse (Brussels, 1894)
"Insurrection de Cuba" in *La Revue politique*, 1868
"John Brown" in *La Coopération*, 14 July 1867
"Sur le lac de Lugano: Extrait d'une lettre de M. Elisée Reclus au président de la Société de géographie de Paris" in *Bulletin de la Société de géographie de Paris*, Dec. 1873
Leçon d'ouverture du cours de Géographie comparée dans l'espace et dans le temps (Brussels, 1894)
"Le Littoral de la France" in *La Revue des deux mondes*, 15 Dec. 1862-1 Sept. 1864
Londres illustré: Guide spécial pour l'Exposition de 1862 (Paris, 1862)
Le mariage tel qu'il fut et tel qu'il est. Avec une allocution d'Elisée Reclus (with Elie Reclus) (Mons, 1907); also as "Unions libres" in *Les Arts de la vie*, July 1905
"Le Méditerranée caspienne et le canal des steppes" in *La Revue des deux mondes*, 1 Aug. 1861
"Metamorphoses du progrès" in *Almanach de la question sociale pour 1899* (Paris, 1899)
"Le Mississippi: Etudes et souvenirs" in *La Revue des deux mondes*, 15 July and 1 Aug. 1859
A mon Frère, le paysan (Geneva, 1893)
"Le Mont Etna et l'éruption de 1865" in *La Revue des deux mondes*, 1 July 1865
Nice, Cannes, Monaco, Menton, San Remo (Paris, 1870)
"Les Noirs américains depuis la guerre" in *La Revue des deux mondes*, 15 Mar. 1863
"Note relative à l'histoire de la mer d'Aral" in *Bulletin de la Société de géographie de Paris*, Aug. and Nov. 1873
Notice pour la carte physique de l'Amérique du Nord (Paris, n.d.)
"Notre Idéal" in *Almanach de la question sociale (illustré) pour 1898* (Paris, 1898)

Nouvelle Géographie universelle, 19 vols. (Paris, 1878-94)
"La Nouvelle-Granade: Paysages de la nature tropicale" in *La Revue des deux mondes*, 1 Dec. 1859-1 May 1860
"L'Océan: Etude de physique maritime" in *La Revue des deux mondes*, 15 Aug. 1867
"L'Origine animale dell'uomo" in *Almanaco populare socialista* (Turin, 1897)
"Origines de la religion et de la morale" in *Les Temps nouveaux*, 27 Feb.-19 Mar. 1904
"Les Oscillations de sol terrestre" in *La Revue des deux mondes*, 1 Jan. 1865
Ouvrier, prends la machine! Prends la terre, paysan! (Geneva, 1880)
"Pages de sociologie préhistorique" in *L'Humanité nouvelle*, Feb. 1898
"Le Panslavisme et l'Unité russe" in *La Revue*, 1 Nov. 1903
"La Passe du sud et le port Eads dans le delta mississipien" in *La Revue lyonnaise de géographie*, 12 Jan. 1878
"Paysages du Taurus Cilicien" in *La Revue germanique*, 15 May 1861
La Peine de mort (Geneva, 1879)
"La Perse" in *Bulletin de la Société neuchâteloise de géographie*, 1899
"La Phénicie et les Pheniciens" in *Bulletin de la Société neuchâteloise de géographie*, 1900
Les Phénomènes terrestres; Vol. 1, *Les Continents*, and Vol. 2, *Les Mers et les Météores* (Paris, 1870 and 1872)
"Les Pluies de la Suisse" in *Bulletin de la Société de géographie de Paris*, Jan. 1873
"La Poésie et les Poètes dans l'Amérique espagnole" in *La Revue des deux mondes*, 15 Feb. 1864
"Pourquoi nous sommes anarchistes!" in *La Société nouvelle*, 31 Aug. 1889
"The Progress of Mankind" in *Contemporary Review*, 1 Dec. 1896
Projet de construction d'un globe terrestre à l'échelle du Cent millième, Edition de la *Société nouvelle*, 1895
"A propos des Tuileries" in *Bulletin de la Société des amis des monuments parisiens*, 1885, No. 1
"A propos d'une carte statistique" in *Bulletin de la Société neuchâteloise de géographie*, T.V. 1889-1890
"Proposition de dresser une carte authentique des volcans" in *Bulletin de la Société belge d'astronomie*, 1903
Quelques écrits, introduction by Hem Day (Paris-Brussels, 1956)
"Quelques mots d'histoire" in *La Société nouvelle*, Nov. 1894
"Quelques mots sur la propriété" in *Almanach du peuple pour 1873* (St-Imier, 1873)
"Quelques mots sur la révolution bouddhique" in *l'Humanité nouvelle*, June 1897
"La Question d'Orient" in *La Marseillaise*, 3 Apr. 1878
"Recent Books on the United States" in *Geographical Journal*, Nov. 1895
Renouveau d'une cité (with Elie Reclus) (Brussels, 1896)
"Report on the Physics and Hydraulics of the Mississippi River" in *Bulletin de la Société de géographie de Paris*, 5 Feb. 1862
"Les Républiques de l'Amérique du Sud: Leurs guerres et leur projet de fédération" in *La Revue des deux mondes*, 15 Oct. 1866
"Russia, Mongolia and China" in *Contemporary Review*, 1895
"Du Sentiment de la nature dans les sociétés modernes" in *La Revue des deux mondes*, 15 May 1866
"La Sicile et l'Eruption de l'Etna en 1865: Récit de voyage" in *Le Tour du monde*, 1866
"The Teaching of Geography: Globes, Discs and Reliefs" in *Scottish Geographical Magazine*, Aug. 1901; also as *L'Enseignement de la géographie: Globes, Disques globulaires et Reliefs* (Brussels, 1902)
La Terre, 2 vols. (Paris 1868-69)
"A tous les démocrates" in *L'Agriculteur* (1866)
Université Nouvelle de Bruxelles: Séance solennelle de rentrée du 22 octobre 1895. Discours (Brussels, 1895)

"On Vegetarianism" in *Humane Review*, Jan. 1901; as "A propos du végétarisme" in *La Réforme alimentaire*, Mar. 1901

"Verra!" in *Cronacca Sovversiva*, 3 July 1905

Les Villes d'hiver de la Méditerranée et les Alpes maritimes (Paris, 1864)

"The Vivisection of China" in *Atlantic Monthly*, Sept. 1898

"Les Voies de communication" in *Almanach de la coopération pour 1869*

Les Volcans de la terre (Brussels, 1906-10)

Voyage à la Sierra-Nevada de Saint-Marthe: Paysages de la nature tropicale (Paris, 1861)

"Voyage aux regions minières de la Transylvanie occidentale" in *Le Tour du monde*, 1874

Introductions and Prefaces by Elisée Reclus

Bakunin, Michael, *Dieu et l'Etat* (Paris, 1882) (preface by Reclus and Carlo Cafiero)

Gaussen, Louis, *Soyons Laïques!* (Paris, 1903)

Gerlache, Adrien de, *Voyage de la "Belgica": Quinze mois dans l'Antarctique* (Paris, 1902)

Joanne, Adolphe L., *Dictionnaire des communes de la France* (Paris, 1864)

────── *Dictionnaire géographique de la France* (Paris, 1869) (introduction by Elisée and Elie Reclus)

────── *Itinéraire général de la France* (Paris, 1862)

Joanne, P.B., *Dictionnaire géographique et administratif de la France* (Paris, 1905)

Kropotkin, Peter, *La Conquête du pain* (Paris, 1892)

────── *Paroles d'un révolté* (Paris, 1885)

Levasseur, E., *Le Mexique au début du XXe siècle* (Paris, 1905)

Malato, Charles, *Religion et Patriotisme* (Rome, 1906)

Metchnikoff, Léon, *La Civilisation et les Grands Fleuves historiques* (Paris, 1889)

Myrial, Alexandra, *Pour la vie* (Paris, n.d.)

Nettlau, Max, *Bibliographie de l'anarchie* (Paris, 1897)

Nieuwenhuis, F. Domela, *Le Socialisme en danger* (Paris, 1897)

Noel, Eugène, *Fin de vie* (Notes et Souvenirs) (Rouen, 1902)

Patriotisme, Colonisation, Bibliothèque Documentaire, No. 2 (Paris, 1903)

Walker, George, *La Dette américaine et les moyens de l'acquitter* (Paris, 1865)

OTHER PRIMARY SOURCES

Amore, Henri, "La Correspondance d'Elisée Reclus" in *La Vie ouvrière*, 5 Oct.-20 Dec. 1913

Anarchism: A Bibliography of Articles 1900-1975. Political Theory, Feb. 1976

Arbore, Zamfir C. (Ralli), "Elisée Reclus: Reminiscences" in Joseph Ishill, *Elisée and Elie Reclus: In Memoriam* (Berkeley Heights, 1927)

Bakunin, Michael, *Gesammelte Werke*, 3 vols. (Berlin, 1921-24)

────── *God and the State* (New York, 1970)

────── *Oeuvres*, 6 vols. (Paris, 1907-11)

Baldelli, Giovanni, *Social Anarchism* (London, 1971)

Baldwin, Roger N. (ed.), *Kropotkin's Revolutionary Pamphlets* (New York, 1970)

Berkman, Alexander, *What is Communist Anarchism?* (New York, 1972)

Bibliographie des ouvrages de géographie et de sociologie d'Elisée Reclus (Ms. et dactylographie) (n.1, n.d.)

Bournand, François, *Les Juifs et Nos contemporains* (Paris, 1898)

Brisson, Adolphe, *Les Prophètes* (Paris, 1902)

Bulletin sténographique du deuxième Congrès de la paix et de la liberté. Stenographisches Bulletin des zweiten Friedens-und Freiheits-Kongresses (Berne, 1868)

Cattelain, P., *Mémoires inédits du chef de la Sûreté sous la Commune* (Paris, n.d. 1900)

234

Cobden-Sanderson, Anne, "Elie and Elisée Reclus" in Joseph Ishill, *Elisée and Elie Reclus: In Memoriam* (Berkeley Heights, 1927)

Coeurderoy, Ernest, *Hurrah! ou la Révolution par les Cosaques* (London, 1854)

Darnaud, E., *Notes sur le mouvement* (Foix, 1891)

Daudet, Léon, *Salons et Journaux* (Paris, 1917)

Day, Hem, *Essai de bibliographie de Elisée Reclus* (Brussels-Paris, 1956)

Dejongh, Thérèse, "The Brothers Reclus at the New University" in Joseph Ishill, *Elisée and Elie Reclus: In Memoriam* (Berkeley Heights, 1927)

Delfosse, Charles, *Elisée Reclus: Géographe* (Brussels, n.d.)

The Doctrine of Saint-Simon, translated and with an introduction by Georg G. Iggers (New York, 1972)

Dokumente aus geheimen Archiven: Übersichten der Berliner politischen Polizei über die Allgemeine Lage der sozialdemokratischen Bewegung 1878-1913, Band 1 (Weimar, 1983)

Documents of the First International, 5 vols. (Moscow)

Dubois, Félix, *Le Péril anarchiste* (Paris, 1894)

Dumartheray, François, "Elisée Reclus" in Joseph Ishill, *Elisée and Elie Reclus: In Memoriam* (Berkeley Heights, 1927)

—— *Aux travailleurs manuels: Partisans de l'action politique* (Geneva, 1876)

"Elisée Reclus, 1830-1905" in *Bulletin de la Société belge d'astronomie*, 1905

Elisée Reclus (1830-1905): Savant et Anarchiste (Paris-Brussels, 1956)

1871: Enquête sur la Commune de Paris (Paris, 1897)

Fabrequettes, P., *De la complicité intellectuelle et des délits d'opinion. De la provocation et de l'opologie criminelles. De la propagande anarchiste* (Paris, 1894-95)

François, Albert, *Elisée Reclus et l'Anarchie* (Ghent, 1905)

Freymond, Jacques, *Etudes et Documents sur la Première Internationale en Suisse* (Geneva, 1964)

—— (ed.), *La Première Internationale. Recueil de Documents*, 4 vols. (Geneva, 1962-71)

Galleani, Luigi, "A Recollection of Elisée Reclus" in Joseph Ishill, *Elisée and Elie Reclus: In Memoriam* (Berkeley Heights, 1927)

Garraud, R., *L'Anarchie et la Répression* (Paris, 1895)

Gaumont, Jean, *Histoire générale de la coopération en France*, 2 vols. (Paris, 1924)

Geddes, Patrick, "A Great Geographer: Elisée Reclus" in *Scottish Magazine*, Sept. and Oct. 1905

Ghio, Paul, *Etudes italiennes et sociales* (Paris, 1929)

—— "In Memory of Elisée Reclus" in Joseph Ishill, *Elisée and Elie Reclus: In Memoriam* (Berkeley Heights, 1927)

Giroud, G., "La Grande Erreur" in *La Regénération*, Dec. 1905

Goldman, Emma, *Anarchism and Other Essays* (London, 1911)

Grave, Jean, "Elisée Reclus" in Joseph Ishill, *Elisée and Elie Reclus: In Memoriam* (Berkeley Heights, 1927)

—— *Quarante ans de propagande anarchiste* (Paris, 1973)

Greef, Guillaume de, *Eloges d'Elisée Reclus et de De Kelles-Krauz*, Discours (Ghent, 1906)

—— *Elogie d'Elie Reclus: Discours prononcé le 31 octobre à la séance de rentrée* (Brussels, 1904)

Gross, Jacques, "Elisée Reclus" in Joseph Ishill, *Elisée and Elie Reclus: In Memoriam* (Berkeley Heights, 1927)

Gubernatis, Angelo de, *Fibre, Pagine di Ricordi* (Rome, 1900)

Guérineau, L., "Recollections of Elisée Reclus" in Joseph Ishill, *Elisée and Elie Reclus: In Memoriam* (Berkeley Heights, 1927)

Guillaume, James, *Idlées sur l'organisation sociale* (La Chaux-de-Fonds, 1876)

—— *L'Internationale: Documents et Souvenirs (1864-1878)*, 4 vols. (Paris, 1905-10)

Hamon, A., *Psychologie de l'anarchiste-socialiste* (Paris, 1895)

Heath, Richard, "Elisée Reclus" in *Humane Review*, Oct. 1905 (also in Joseph Ishill, *Elisée and Elie Reclus: In Memoriam*, Berkeley Heights, 1927)

Heim, Albert, "Recollections on Elie and Elisée Reclus" in Joseph Ishill, *Elisée and Elie Reclus: In Memoriam* (Berkeley Heights, 1927)

Hess, Moses, *Briefwechsel* (The Hague, 1959)

Horowitz, Irving (ed.), *The Anarchists* (New York, 1964)

Huxley, Thomas H., "The Struggle for Existence and Its Bearing Upon Man" in *The Nineteenth Century*, Feb. 1888

Ishill, Joseph, *Elisée and Elie Reclus: In Memoriam* (Berkeley Heights, 1927)

Jousseaume, Robert, *Etude sur les lois contre les menées anarchistes et sur les modifications que ces lois ont apportées à la legislation pénale* (Paris, 1895)

Karl Marx: Chronik seines Lebens (Frankfurt, 1971)

Krimerman, Leonard I., and Lewis Perry (eds.), *Patterns of Anarchy* (New York, 1966)

Kropotkin, Peter, *La Conquête du pain* (Paris, 1892)

—— *The Conquest of Bread* (London, 1972)

—— "Elisée Reclus" in *Les Temps nouveaux*, 15 July 1905

—— *Fields, Factories and Workshops* (London, 1898)

—— *Memoirs of a Revolutionist* (New York, 1971; new edition, Montréal, 1988)

—— *Mutual Aid* (London, 1902; new edition, Montréal, 1988)

—— *Paroles d'un révolté* (Paris, 1885)

Lazare, Bernard, "A School of Liberty" in Joseph Ishill, *Elisée and Elie Reclus: In Memoriam* (Berkeley Heights, 1927)

Lehning, Arthur, *Archives Bakounine*, 4 vols. (Leiden, 1961-71)

Leroux, Pierre, *Quelques pages de verité* (Paris, 1859)

Lissagaray, *Histoire de la Commune de 1871* (Paris, 1876)

Lombroso, Cesare, *Les Anarchistes* (Paris, 1897)

Maillard, Firmin, *Affiches, professions de foi, documents officiels, clubs et comités pendant la Commune* (Paris, 1871)

Maitron, Jean (ed.), *Dictionnaire biographique du mouvement ouvrier français* (Paris)

Marx, Karl, *Economic and Philosophic Manuscripts of 1844* (ed. Dirk J. Struik) (London, 1970)

Marx, Karl, and Friedrich Engels, *Marx Engels Werke* (Moscow)

—— *Selected Works* (London, 1970)

Marx, Karl, Friedrich Engels, and V.I. Lenin, *Anarchism and Anarcho-Syndicalism: Selected Writings* (New York, 1972)

Maximoff, G.P. (ed.), *The Political Theory of Bakunin* (New York, 1954)

Mémoire de la Fédération jurassienne (Sonvilier, 1873)

Mesnil, Jacques, "Elisée Reclus" in Joseph Ishill, *Elisee and Elie Reclus: In Memoriam* (Berkeley Heights, 1927)

Miller, Martin A. (ed.), P.A. Kropotkin, *Selected Writings on Anarchism and Revolution* (Cambridge, Mass., 1970)

Miscegenation: The Theory of the Blending of the Races, Applied to the American White Man and Negro (New York, 1864)

Les Murailles politiques françaises (Paris, 1873)

Nadar, Félix, "Elisée Reclus" in *Les Temps nouveaux*, Supplément No. 33, Dec. 1905

Nettlau, Max, *Der Anarchismus von Proudhon zu Kropotkin* (Berlin, 1927)

—— *Anarchisten und Sozialrevolutionäre* (Berlin, 1931)

—— *Bibliographie de l'anarchie* (Brussels, 1897)

—— *Elisée Reclus, Anarchist und Gelehrter* (Berlin, 1928)

—— "Elisée Reclus and Michael Bakunin" in Joseph Ishill, *Elisée and Elie Reclus: In Memoriam* (Berkeley Heights, 1927)

—— *Eliséo Reclus: La Vida de un Sabio. Justo y Rebelde* (Barcelona, 1928)

—— *Histoire de l'anarchie* (Paris, 1971)

—— *Anarchisten und Syndicalisten, Teil 1, Geschichte der Anarchie*, Band V (Vaduz, 1981)

—— *Michael Bakunin, Eine Biographie*, 3 vols. (London, 1898-1900)
—— *Der Vorfrühling der Anarchie* (Berlin, 1925)
Owen, C. Wm., "Elisée Reclus" in Joseph Ishill, *Elisée and Elie Reclus: In Memoriam* (Berkeley Heights, 1927)
Plechanoff, George, *Anarchism and Socialism* (Chicago, 1909)
Poster, Mark (ed.), *Harmonian Man: Selected Writings of Charles Fourier* (New York, 1971)
Procès des anarchistes devant la police correctionnelle et la Cour d'Appeal de Lyon (Lyons, 1883)
Les Produits de la terre (Geneva, 1885)
Les Produits de l'industrie (Paris, 1887)
Proudhon, Pierre-Joseph, *Du principe fédératif* (Paris, 1863)
—— *Qu'est-ce que la propriété?* (Paris, 1873)
Putnam, Ruth (ed.), *Life and Letters of Mary Putnam Jacobi* (New York, 1925)
Read, Herbert, *The Philosophy of Anarchism* (London, 1940)
Reclus, Elie, *La Commune de Paris au jour le jour 1871 (19 mars-28 mai)* (Paris, 1908)
—— *Le Mariage tel qu'il fut et tel qu'il est. Avec une allocution d'Elisée Reclus* (Mons, 1907)
Reclus, Paul, "Biographie d'Elisée Reclus" in Paul Reclus, *Les Frères Elie et Elisée Reclus* (Paris, 1964)
—— "A Few Recollections on the Brothers Elie and Elisée Reclus" in Joseph Ishill, *Elisée and Elie Reclus: In Memoriam* (Berkeley Heights, 1927)
—— *Les Frères Elie et Elisée Reclus* (Paris, 1964)
La Richesse et la Misère (Paris, 1888)
Roubakine, N., "Elisée Reclus and the Russian Readers" in Joseph Ishill, *Elisée and Elie Reclus: In Memoriam* (Berkeley Heights, 1927)
Salt, Henry, S., "The Many-sided Man of Genius" in Joseph Ishill, *Elisée and Elie Reclus: In Memoriam* (Berkeley Heights, 1927)
Schurz, Carl, *Lebenserinnerungen* (Berlin, 1952)
Tchernoff, I., *Le Parti Républicain au coup d'état et sous le Second Empire* (Paris, 1906)
Wertheim, W.F., *Evolution and Revolution: The Rising Waves of Emancipation* (London, 1974)
Vandervelde, Emile, *Souvenirs d'un militant socialiste* (Paris, 1939)
Vaughan, E., "The Criminal Record of Elisée Reclus" in Elisée Reclus, *An Anarchist on Anarchy* (Boston, 1884)
Zibelin-Wilmerding, Lilly, "Elisée Reclus" in Joseph Ishill, *Elisée and Elie Reclus: In Memoriam* (Berkeley Heights, 1927)

SECONDARY SOURCES

Abramsky, Chimen, and Henry Collins, *Karl Marx and the British Labour Movement* (London, 1965)
Ansart, Pierre, *Marx et l'Anarchie* (Paris, 1969)
Apter, David E., "The Old Anarchism and the New: Some Comments" in David E. Apter and James Joll (eds.), *Anarchism Today* (London, 1971)
Arvon, Henri, *L'Anarchie* (Paris, 1951)
Bartsch, Günter, *Anarchismus in Deutschland*, 2 vols. (Hanover, 1972-73)
Becker, Carl J., *The Heavenly City of the Eighteenth-Century Philosophers* (New Haven, 1932)
Bergère, Marie-Claire, "La Chine: Du mythe de référence au modèle d'action" in *International Review of Social History*, Vol. 17, 1972, Parts 1 & 2
Berstein, Samuel, *Auguste Blanqui and the Art of Insurrection* (London, 1971)
Bestor, A.E., *Backwoods Utopias* (Philadelphia-London, 1950)
Bookchin, Murray, *Post-Scarcity Anarchism* (Montréal, 1986)
Bossu, Jean, *Elisée Reclus* (S. et O. Herblay, n.d.)

Bourgin, Georges, *La Commune* (Paris, 1953)

Braunthal, Julius, *History of the International 1864-1914* (London, 1966)

Brenan, Gerald, *The Spanish Labyrinth* (Cambridge, 1962)

Campion, Léo, *Les Anarchistes dans la F.M.* (Marseilles, 1969)

Carr, E.H., *Michael Bakunin* (New York, 1961)

—— *The Romantic Exiles* (Boston, 1961)

—— *Studies in Revolution* (New York, 1964)

Carr, Reg, *Anarchism in France: The Case of Octave Mirbeau* (Montréal, 1977)

Carter, April, *Direct Action and Liberal Democracy* (London, 1973)

—— *The Political Theory of Anarchism* (London, 1971)

Cole, G.D.H., *A History of Socialist Thought*, 5 vols. (London, 1958ff.)

Caute, David, *The Left in Europe Since 1789* (London, 1966)

Cohen, G.A., *Karl Marx's Theory of History* (Princeton, 1978)

Dautry, L., and L. Scheler, *Le Comité central républicain des vingt arrondissements de Paris* (Paris, 1960)

Day, Hem, *Deux frères de bonne volonté: Elisée Reclus et Han Ryner* (Paris-Brussels, 1956)

—— *Elisée Reclus en Belgique* (Paris-Brussels, 1956)

Dolléans, E., *Proudhon* (Paris, 1948)

—— *Histoire du mouvement ouvrier*, 3 vols. (Paris, 1957)

Dommanget, Maurice, "La Premiere Internationale à son declin" in *La Revue d'histoire économique et sociale*, Vol. 43, No. 3, 1964

Drachkovitch, Milorad M. (ed.), *The Revolutionary Internationals 1864-1943* (Stanford, 1966)

Dunbar, Gary S., *Elisée Reclus: Historian of Nature* (Hamden, Conn., 1978)

Durkheim, Emile, *Socialism* (New York, 1962)

Eltzbacher, Paul, *Anarchism* (London, 1960)

Escher, Hans, *Ravachol, Ein Zyklus* (Vienna-Munich, 1969)

Fleming, Marie, *The Anarchist Way to Socialism: Elisée Reclus and Nineteenth-Century European Anarchism* (London, 1979)

—— "Life, Liberty and the Pursuit of a Natural Order: The Anarchism of Elisée Reclus" in *Social Anarchism*, Vol. 2, No. 1, 1981

—— "Propaganda by the Deed: Terrorism and Anarchist Theory in Late Nineteenth-Century Europe" in *Terrorism: An International Journal*, Vol. 4, Nos. 1-4, 1980

Fowler, R.B., "The Anarchist Tradition of Political Thought" in *Western Political Quarterly*, Dec. 1972

Freymond, Jacques, *Etudes et Documents sur la Première Internationale en Suisse* (Geneva, 1964)

Freymond, Jacques, and Miklós Molnár, "The Rise and Fall of the First International" in Milorad M. Drachkovitch (ed.), *The Revolutionary Internationals 1864-1943* (Stanford, 1966)

Gross, Feliks, *European Ideologies* (New York, 1948)

Gysens, Guy, "Elisée Reclus: Un Cœur d'or," stencilled brochure, 1974

Harrison, Frank, *The Modern State: An Anarchist Analysis* (Montréal, 1983)

Horne, Alistair, *The Fall of Paris* (London, 1965)

Howard, Michael, *The Franco-Prussian War* (London, 1967)

Joll, James, "Anarchism Between Communism and Individualism" in *Anarchici e Anarchia nel Mondo Contemporaneo, Atti del Convegno promosso dalla Fondazione Luigi Einaudi (Torino 5, 6, e 7 décembre 1969)* (Turin, 1971)

—— *The Anarchists* (London, 1964)

—— *The Second International* (London, 1955)

Kolakowski, Leszek, and Stuart Hampshire (eds.), *The Socialist Idea* (London, 1974)

Laidler, Harry W., *History of Socialism* (New York, 1934)

Landauer, Carl, *European Socialism*, 2 vols. (Berkeley, 1959)

Langhard, J., *Die Anarchistische Bewegung in der Schweiz* (Berlin, 1903)

Lefranc, Georges, *Le Mouvement socialiste sous la Troisième République, 1875-1940* (Paris, 1963)
Lichtheim, George, *Marxism in Modern France* (New York, 1966)
────── *A Short History of Socialism* (New York, 1970)
Lida, Clara E., *Anarquismo y Revolución en la Espana del XIX* (Madrid, 1972)
Ligou, Daniel, *Histoire du socialisme en France* (Paris, 1962)
Longoni, J.C., *Four Patients of Dr. Deibler* (London, 1970)
Louis, Paul, *L'Avenir du socialisme* (Paris, 1905)
────── *Histoire du socialisme en France* (Paris, 1901)
Maitron, Jean, "L'Anarchisme français 1945-1965" in *Le Mouvement social*, Jan.-Mar. 1965
────── *Le Mouvement anarchiste en France*, 2 vols. (Paris, 1975)
────── "Das Leben Ravachols" in Hans Escher, *Ravachol, Ein Zyklus* (Vienna-Munich, 1969)
Malia, Martin, *Alexander Herzen and the Birth of Russian Socialism* (Cambridge, Mass., 1965)
Manuel, Frank E., *The Prophets of Paris* (New York, 1962)
Masters, Anthony, *Bakunin: The Father of Anarchism* (London, 1974)
McKercher, William R., *Libertarian Thought in Nineteenth Century Britain* (New York, 1987)
McLellan, David, *Karl Marx: His Life and Thought* (London, 1973)
────── *Karl Marx: Early Texts* (Oxford, 1971)
Miller, Martin A., *Kropotkin* (Chicago, 1976)
Nicolaevsky, Boris, "Secret Societies and the First International" in Milorad M. Drachkovitch (ed.), *The Revolutionary Internationals 1864-1943* (Stanford, 1966)
Nicolaevsky, Boris, and Otto Maenchen-Helfen, *Karl Marx: Man and Fighter* (London, 1973)
Nomad, Max, "The Anarchist Tradition" in Milorad M. Drachkovitch (ed.), *The Revolutionary Internationals 1864-1943* (Stanford, 1966)
────── *Apostles of Revolution* (New York, 1961)
Nye, Robert A., *The Origins of Crowd Psychology: Gustave LeBon and the Crisis of Mass Democracy in the Third Republic* (London, 1974)
Paterson, R.W.K., *The Nihilistic Egoist: Max Stirner* (London, 1971)
Prolo, Jacques, *Les Anarchistes* (Paris, 1912)
Richards, Vernon (ed.), *Errico Malatesta: His Life and Ideas* (London, 1965)
Rihs, Charles, *La Commune de Paris: Sa structure et ses doctrines* (Geneva, 1955)
Rocker, Rudolf, *Johann Most: Das Leben eines Rebellen* (Berlin, 1924)
Rougerie, Jacques, "L'A.I.T. et le Mouvement ouvrier à Paris pendant les événements de 1870-1871" in *International Review of Social History*, 1972, Parts 1 & 2
────── *Procès des Communards* (Paris, 1964)
Rubel, Maximilien, *Karl Marx: Essai de biographie intellectuelle* (Paris, 1957)
Ruggiero, Guido de, *The History of European Liberalism* (Boston, 1966)
Ryner, Han, *Crespuscolo di Eliseo Reclus* (Florence, 1954)
────── *Elisée Reclus (1830-1905)* (Paris, 1928)
Schraepler, Ernst, *Quellen zur Geschichte der sozialen Frage in Deutschland 1800-1870* (Göttingen, 1955)
Schulkind, Eugene (ed.), *The Paris Commune of 1871* (London, 1972)
Segall, Marcelo, "En Amérique" in *International Review of Social History*, 1972, Parts 1 & 2
Sergent, Alain, and Claude Harmel, *Histoire de l'anarchie*, Vol. 1 (Paris, 1949)
Stafford, David, *From Anarchism to Reformism: A Study of the Political Activities of Paul Brousse 1870-1890* (London, 1971)
Stekloff, Y., *History of the First International* (London, 1928)
Taylor, Michael, *Anarchy and Cooperation* (London, 1976)
Varennes, Henri de, *De Ravachol à Caserio* (Paris, n.d.)
Venturi, Franco, *Roots of Revolution* (New York, 1966)

Vizetelly, Ernest Alfred, *The Anarchists* (New York, 1972)

Vuilleumier, Marc, "Les Archives de James Guillaume" in *Le Mouvement social*, July-Sept. 1964

—— "Elisée Reclus et Genève" in *Musées du Genève*, Apr. 1971

—— "La Première Internationale en Suisse" in *La Revue syndical suisse*, Vol. 9, 1964

—— "Les Sources de l'histoire sociale: Max Nettlau et ses Collections" in *Cahiers Vilfredo Pareto*, No. 3, 1964

Wilson, Nelly, *Bernard-Lazare* (Cambridge, 1978)

Wolff, Robert Paul, *In Defence of Anarchism* (New York, 1970)

Wood, Allen, *Karl Marx* (London, 1981)

Woodcock, George, *Anarchism* (London, 1963)

—— *Pierre-Joseph Proudhon: A Biography* (Montréal, 1987)

Woodcock, George, and Ivan Avakumović, *The Anarchist Prince: Peter Kropotkin* (New York, 1971)

Zenker, E.V., *Anarchism* (London, 1898)

Zévaes, A.L., *Socialisme en France depuis 1871* (Paris, 1908)

Index

Alexander II, Czar of Russia, 157
Alfonso XII, King of Spain, 157
Alliance of Social Democracy, 61
Alsace, 64, 75, 115
American Civil War, 43, 55,
anarchism and socialism, 21, 24, 94-
96, 98-101, 107-8, 111, 125,
171-73
anarchist "colonies," 39, 47-49, 131,
174-75
anarcho-syndicalism, 170-71, 173,
179
see also trade unionism
anarchy, 20, 36, 98, 101-2, 104, 107,
113, 122, 124, 127, 149, 158-
59, 165, 179
animals, 191-92
anti-Semitism, 184-85
L'Association, 58
L'Association générale d'approvisionnement et de consommation, 58

attentats, 94, 156-65, 167, 169, 175-
76
see also terrorism, violence
L'Avant-garde, 106, 108, 156-57

Bakunin, Michael, 11-12, 22-24, 54,
58, 61, 100, 109, 118, 120,
122, 124, 129, 143, 148, 167,
173
and League of Peace and Freedom, 62-65
and Marx, 13, 21-22, 66, 99
differences with Reclus, 66-70,
96, 104, 107
Barrot, Odillon, 31
Bastiat, Frédéric, 59
Bellegarrigue, Anselme, 36
Béluze, J.P., 58
Benevento, 131
Bertoia, Oscar, 143, 147
Beslay, Charles, 149
Bismarck, Otto von, 72, 76, 79, 117,
119, 124

Blanc, Louis, 35, 40, 58-60
Blanqui, Auguste, 55, 71, 75-76
Blum, Léon, 99
Bradlaugh, Charles, 60
Brouckère, Florence de, 198
Brousse, Paul, 101, 104-9, 127, 129, 132, 136, 138, 153, 157, 195
Brunel, Jacques, 159
Brussels, 166-68
    Free University of, 165-66, 168
    New University of, 166, 174, 179
Bulletin de la Fédération jurassienne, 101, 106, 108, 110, 116, 127, 128, 132
Butler, Josephine, 186
Buurmans, Victor, 84, 96, 117

Cabet, Etienne, 58-59
Cafiero, Carlo, 100, 109-10, 124, 131
capitalism, 119, 142-50, 175, 177, 184
Carnot, Sadi, 159, 165
Caserio, Santo, 159
Casse, Germain, 89
Casse, Julie Reclus, 89
Champseix, Madame (André-Léo), 67, 75, 107, 145, 185
Charton, Edouard, 81
Chaves, Louis, 158
China, 183
Christianity, 13-15, 25, 27-31, 34-38, 113, 189-90, 192
    see also religion
class, 148, 187
Clemenceau, Georges, 61, 79-80
Coeurderoy, Ernest, 40
collectivism, 101, 109-10, 170
Colombia, 45-47, 55
communards, 88-90, 92-93, 105-6
commune, 65
    Flemish communes, 117
    see also Alsace, Lorraine, Paris Commune
communism, 34-35, 41, 142-44, 146, 148, 150, 155, 181
    anarchist communism, 109-11, 149, 171, 187
    utopian communism, 34-36
communitarianism: see anarchist "colonies"

Comte, Auguste, 31, 59, 177
conscience, 34, 121, 152
consciousness, 102, 136, 143, 163, 176, 180, 187
cooperation, 119-20, 148-49
    see also mutual aid, solidarity
La Coopération, 58
cooperativism, 58-59, 66, 94, 103-4, 130
Costa, Andreas, 108, 110, 129, 137, 195
Crédit mobilier, 55, 59
Curien, Paul-Marie, 158
Cuisinier, Jeannie Reclus, 55, 67, 96, 152, 178, 194

Darwin, Charles, 119
    theory of evolution, 118
decentralisation, 102, 115
    see also federalism
Defaure law (1872), 168
Delescluze, Charles, 71, 74, 75
division of labour, 143-45, 177
Dreyfus Affair, 184, 188
Dumartheray, François, 109, 110, 137
Dumesnil, Alfred, 72, 81, 83
Dumesnil, Louise Reclus, 28, 34, 167
Dunbar, Gary S., 19-20
Duval, Clément, 150
Duval, Emile Victor, 81
Duveyrier, Henri, 167

Eastern Question, 116
    see also Russia
L'Egalité, 66-67
education, 105, 125, 127-30, 185
    see also science
electoral abstentionism, 108-9, 195-97
    see also franchise
Eltzbacher, Paul, 24
Emmanuel II, Victor, 56, 116
Engels, Friedrich, 58, 61, 186
England, 117, 125

Fanelli, Giuseppe, 65-66
Fanquiez, 109
Faure, Félix, 170
Faure, Pierre, 69-70

Faure, Sébastien, 175
Favre, Joseph, 97
Favre, Jules, 69, 74, 76-77, 91
federalism, 63-65
    see also decentralisation
Ferry, Jules, 158
Florian, Emile, 158
Foucault, Michel, 20
Fourens, Pierre, 75, 76, 81
Fourier, Charles, 31, 35, 41, 59
Fourierists, 55, 58, 66, 69
Fournier, 133
franchise, 69-70, 88, 99, 195-97
    see also electoral abstentionism
Franco-Prussian War, 71-80, 115-16, 123
Frankel, Léo, 73, 80
Freedom, 138
Freemasonry, 59-61, 166
Freethinkers, 61
Fribourg, E.E., 56

Gallifet, Marquis de, 81
Gallo, Charles, 158
Gambetta, Léon, 158
Gambon, 106
Gambuzzi, Carlo, 64
Garibaldi, Giuseppe, 68
Garraud, R., 160, 165
Garrido, Fernando, 66
Gauthier, Emile, 111, 134
geography, 82-83, 96-97, 112-15, 128, 136-37, 147, 165-68, 177-78, 191, 193, 195
    and anarchism, 12, 15, 20, 27
    early interest in, 39, 41-42, 55
Germany, 75-76, 116-17, 121-22
Gobineau, Count Joseph-Arthur, 43, 181
Godwin, William, 23
government, 90-91, 102-5, 135, 149, 162
    revolutionary government, 98-99
    see also state
Grave, Jean, 137-39, 167, 173-74, 195-96
    and terrorism, 160
    and theft, 94, 150-54
    and religion, 189-90
Grimard, Edouard, 33
Gross, Jacques, 122-23, 138, 167

Guérineau, L., 177-78
Guesde, Jules, 137, 195
Guillaume, James, 62, 101, 105, 107-8, 127, 171

Hardie, Keir, 172
Harrison, Frank, 22-23
Henry, Emile, 159, 164
Herzen, Alexander, 40, 61
Herzig, 178
Hess, Moses, 57
Huxley, Aldous, 15

Individual autonomy, 130, 155, 156, 162-63
International Alliance of Socialist Democracy, 65-68
International Brotherhood, 61, 66, 69
International Working Men's Association (IWMA), 56-57, 61-66, 69, 73, 75, 77, 80-81, 95, 98-101, 111, 145, 172, 198
    federalist International, 13, 95-111, 116, 143
Italian Alliance of Social Democracy, 61

Jaurès, Jean, 99
Joukowsky, Nicholas, 101, 106, 109, 116, 132
Jura Federation, 95-97, 105, 110-11, 116, 127, 129, 133, 143, 171

Kahn, Rodolphe, 106
Das Kapital, 57-58, 145
Klementz, 132
Kossuth, Louis, 32
Kropotkin, Peter, 20, 23-24, 91-92, 101-2, 104, 120, 125, 132, 134, 136, 157, 167-68, 195-96
    and federalist International, 106-8
    and Reclus, 11-13, 15-16, 20-22, 105-10, 112, 118-19, 123, 127-29, 133, 136-39, 148-49, 153, 167, 175, 179, 182, 197
    and terrorism, 160-61, 164
    and theft, 94, 150, 153-54

243

Kropotkin, Sophie, 137-38

Lamennais, Félicité de, 31
Landsberg, Natalie, 108
League of Peace and Freedom, 62-
    65, 68, 88, 148,
Léauthier, Léon-Jules, 159
Leblanc, F.D., 80
LeBon, Gustave, 181
Lefort, Henri, 57
Lefrançais, Gustave, 101, 106, 109
Lemmonier, Charles, 62
Leroux, Pierre, 40, 59
Liberalism, 35, 149, 157
Liebknecht, Wilhelm, 58, 76
Limousin, Charles, 56
Lissagaray, 196
Lodge of Philadelphians (London),
    60
Loge des Philadelphes, 60
lois scélérates, 164-65
London (Black) International Con-
    gress, 111, 132, 157
Lorraine, 75, 115

Malatesta, Errico, 12-13, 109-10,
    131
Malon, Benoît, 57, 73, 75, 107, 195
Mann, Tom, 172
Martin, Pierre, 132
Marx, Karl, 32, 54, 57-58, 61-62,
    74, 95, 98, 100, 125, 145, 148,
    182, 186
    and Bakunin, 13, 21-22, 66, 99,
    173
Marxism, 20, 98, 105, 112
Mazzini, Guiseppe, 67
Metchnikoff, Léon, 181
Metternich, 32
Morris, William, 137, 178
Most, Johann, 20, 120, 193
mutual aid, 118-20
mutualism, 149

Nadar, Félix, 73, 78, 93, 107, 167,
    169
Napoleon, Louis, 36-37, 41, 54-56,
    59, 69, 72-73, 76, 143
Naquet, Alfred, 62
Narodnaya Volya (People's Will),
    132, 157

Narodniks (Populists), 132
nationalism, 32, 41, 75, 115-17, 181
neo-Malthusianism, 175
Nettlau, Max, 19-20, 66, 110, 179
Nieuwenhuis, Ferdinand Domela,
    20

Odger, George, 56
Ollivier, Emile, 72
Owen, Robert, 35

pacifism, 122-23, 162
Paepe, Caesar de, 100, 107
Paris Commune, 12, 21, 70, 79-85,
    96, 98-99, 105-6, 113, 122-24,
    127
    response to Commune, 87-94,
    132, 167, 176, 195-97
parliamentary politics, 104, 130,
    171, 195
parliamentary socialism, 129, 172-
    74, 189
peasants, 103, 144-48, 167, 176,
    197
Pelloutier, Fernand, 170
Péreire, Isaac and Emile, 55
Périer, Casimir, 83
Perovskaya, Sophie, 153, 157
Perron, Charles, 97, 106
Philippe, Louis, 31-32, 74, 167
Pini, 151-52
Pratt, Hodgson, 88
Procès des Trente (Trial of the
    Thirty), 169
progress, 35, 44, 118, 121-22, 124,
    147, 154, 176, 180, 187-88,
    191, 197
propaganda, 104, 107, 126-27, 145,
    151, 154, 157, 163, 165, 174,
    180
Propaganda by the Deed, 94, 104,
    131-34, 156
property, 103-4, 123, 129, 134, 142-
    46, 149-51, 186, 190
Proudhon, Pierre-Joseph, 12-13, 20,
    23-24, 36, 55, 57, 148-51, 185
Putnam, Mary, 81

race, 42-44, 181-85
Ralli (Zamfir C. Arbore), 106, 132
Ravachol (François Koenigstein),
    158-61, 163-64, 191

Read, Herbert, 15
Reclus, Armand, 84
Reclus, Clarisse Brian, 54-55, 67
Reclus, Elie, 88, 132, 185, 197-98
  childhood friend, 29-33, 37
  New University, 178
  1870-71 period, 75, 80-81
  Second Empire, 39-47, 54-63, 66-68
Reclus, Ermance Beaumont-Trigant, 97, 194
Reclus, Fanny L'Herminez, 72, 96-97
Reclus, Pastor Jacques, 27-34, 38
Reclus, Marie, 67
Reclus, Noémi, 45, 54-55, 185
Reclus, Paul (brother), 80
Reclus, Paul (nephew), 55, 142, 152-54, 165, 178, 198
Reclus, Susi, 30
Reclus, Marguerite Zéline Trigant, 29, 37, 42, 67
Régnier, Megali Reclus, 55, 67, 96
religion, 143, 151, 188-89
  see also Christianity
reprise individuelle, la (individual recovery of products of labour), 94, 139, 142-55
La Republique des travailleurs, 75
La Révolte, 138, 151-52, 154, 158, 160, 162, 164-65, 157, 173
Le Révolté, 109, 133, 137-38, 150, 156, 196
revolution, 21, 124-25, 127-28, 130, 135, 139, 142, 145, 148, 151-53, 155, 157, 167, 172-76, 180, 187, 192-93, 197-98
  Evolution and Revolution, 69-70, 123-25, 127, 135-36
Rey, Aristide, 57, 61, 63, 65
Ricard, Xavier de, 195
Richard, Albert, 65
Ritter, Carl, 33, 113, 115
Robin, Paul, 105-8, 127, 175
Rochefort, Henri, 68-70
Rossier, Samuel, 97
Royal Geographical Society of London, 166
Russia, 116-17, 121, 132, 134, 146, 157, 197-98
  see also Eastern Question

Saint-Simon, Henri de, 31, 55, 59, 148
Say, Léon, 59
science, 15, 22-23, 54, 61, 65, 112-24, 127-29, 134, 142, 144, 147-48, 157, 163, 169, 176-79, 181-83, 188-89, 191
Second International, 13, 21, 170-71, 173
Simon, Jules, 59, 84
socialism, 95, 98, 100-1, 104, 113, 131, 139, 146, 149-50, 171, 186-87, 189
La Société de Géographie de Paris (Geography Society of Paris), 83, 166-67
La Société du crédit au travail, 58-59
solidarity, 89, 108-11, 118, 130, 132, 135, 138-39, 142, 146, 151, 153, 175-76, 184, 189
Spain, 66-68
state, 90-91, 99, 101-2, 104-5, 122, 125-26, 130, 134, 151, 155, 165, 187, 196
  public service theory of, 100-1
  see also government
Stirner, Max, 23
students, 174, 177, 179, 193

Talandier, Alfred, 61
Templier, Emile, 83
Les Temps nouveaux, 162, 174, 190, 195
terrorism, 94, 131-32, 134, 139, 164, 166, 175-76, 178, 180
  see also attentats, violence
theft: see la reprise individuelle
Thiers, Adolphe, 32, 69, 71, 74, 80
Tolain, Henri, 56-57, 73
Tolstoy, Leo, 23, 162
trade associations, 130-31
trade unionism, 94, 120, 171
  see also anarcho-syndicalism
Le Travailleur, 87, 101, 105-9, 116, 124, 156
Trochu, General, 76, 89, 91
Tucker, Benjamin, 23, 120

Umberto I, King of Italy, 157
United States, 42-48, 120, 144

Vaillant, Auguste, 159, 164
Varlin, Eugène, 57, 73
vegetarianism, 35, 191-92
Verhaeren, 178
Viñas, Garcia, 108
violence, 94, 125, 134, 156, 163-64
 see also attentats, terrorism

Wallace, Alfred Russell, 193

Walras, Léon, 59
Washburne, American Ambassador,
 81
women, 185-87
Woodcock, George, 24
Woodward, Henry, 82

Zasúlitch, Vera, 132, 157

Black Rose Books
3981, boul. St. Laurent
Montréal, Québec
H2W 1Y5

Printed by
the workers of
Ateliers Graphiques Marc Veilleux Inc.
Cap-Saint-Ignace, Qué.
for
Black Rose Books Ltd.